Indigenous Cultures and Sustainable Development in Latin America

Timothy MacNeill

Indigenous Cultures and Sustainable Development in Latin America

palgrave
macmillan

Timothy MacNeill
Faculty of Social Science and Humanities
Ontario Tech University
Oshawa, ON, Canada

ISBN 978-3-030-37022-0 ISBN 978-3-030-37023-7 (eBook)
https://doi.org/10.1007/978-3-030-37023-7

This Palgrave Macmillan imprint is published by the registered company Springer Nature Switzerland AG.
The registered company address is: Gewerbestrasse 11, 6330 Cham, Switzerland

Acknowledgement

Thanks to my beautiful family for their continued support and patience during an unending process of research, and to experts, indigenous communities, and organizations across Latin America and Canada who have advised me, trusted me, and inspired me. Thanks to the Social Sciences Research Council of Canada for their ongoing support.

This research was supported by the Social Sciences and Humanities Research Council of Canada.

Social Sciences and Humanities Research Council of Canada
Conseil de recherches en sciences humaines du Canada
Canada

Contents

CHAPTER 1

Introduction

Where does indigenous culture fit into the twenty-first-century challenge of creating a sustainable, and equitable, global society on a habitable planet? At first blush, there seems to be little place for indigenous culture in this immense project. In the 2030 Agenda for Sustainable Development, where the United Nations Sustainable Development Goals (SDGs) are meticulously displayed, there is little mention of indigenous people other than an appearance in longish lists of vulnerable populations that should be targeted and consulted during sustainable development planning. The 17 SDGs and 169 associated targets make no mention of indigenous culture. If we look at the SDGs in isolation, we may feel that indigenous peoples feature only as targets of modernist, managerial, technocratic development. The SDGs certainly do not evoke a sense that sustainable development will be guided in any way by indigenous cosmovisions and holistic understandings of nature–human relationships.

Away from the strict delineations of the SDGs, however, we do see many instances where indigenous culture is described as integral to environmental sustainability. In places, indigenous culture has been evoked as a discursive corridor through which we may access another, amodern, and perhaps premodern form of development to challenge extractivist, modernist development teleologies (Blaser et al. 2004). It has also been framed as a political–economic resource with which equity and environmental protection may be produced (Yúdice 2003). The United Nations Education, Science, and Cultural Organization (UNESCO 2019)

T. MacNeill, *Indigenous Cultures and Sustainable Development in Latin America*, https://doi.org/10.1007/978-3-030-37023-7_1

recognizes culturally embedded indigenous knowledge of ecosystems as essential "for developing meaningful action worldwide" in the interest of sustainable development. Similarly, the UN Department of Economic and Social Affairs (UNDESA) website claims that "[i]ndigenous communities play a vital role as custodians of our planet, possessing vital knowledge that will support global efforts to achieve the Sustainable Development Goals." In a *National Geographic* magazine article, Raygorodetsky (2019) has echoed these refrains, suggesting that modern society must learn the holistic relational viewpoints integral to indigenous culture in order to solve the challenging environmental problems of the Anthropocene.

But what does the indigenous contribution to the economics and politics of sustainable development look like from the ground up? What has been, is, and may be, the contribution of indigenous culture to the reimagining of human progress? This book explores indigenous cultures and movements in Latin America, as well as the history of culture in development thinking, to answer these questions. Far from being an antithesis of development in general, the argument will be presented that indigenous culture has always been present, if greatly marginalized, in the intellectual movements that frame progress, environment, and development. Similarly, it will be argued that although indigenous culture continues to be marginalized in very violent and systematic ways, it inhabits a creative and increasingly important place in the economic, ecological, social, and cultural reimagining of global human and non-human society. To make this case, it will be necessary to wrestle with some famously ambiguous concepts.

It is difficult to imagine a triumvirate of words that could be more ambiguous than *culture*, *sustainability*, and *development*. The first of these words has been noted by Raymond Williams (1977) as being "one of the two or three most complicated words in the English language" (p. 76); the next has been criticized for being an empty notion that changes meaning depending on the user (Redclift 2005); and the third is an embattled concept that continues to have multiple definitions (Cowen 2003). Despite the semantic ambiguity of these terms, however, engagement with them cannot be avoided if we care about making life more livable for the majority of people on the planet.

There are good reasons for believing this. In contrast to the stale economism of the twentieth century, the twenty-first century has seen a rise in awareness that culture, politics, and economy are inseparable. A steadily accumulating mountain of literature contains arguments to this effect from many perspectives. Particular cultures, it has been argued, can act as the rich soil in which economies and political systems flourish. Others have been cast as barren dustbowls in which these systems perish (Harrison and Huntington 2002). From a different perspective still, it has been argued that competitive consumer culture in the West may have precipitated the multiple, and continuing, series of economic bubbles and corresponding crashes that have tormented the globe in recent years and that this same culture may have pushed global ecosystems beyond their capacity to sustain us (Heinberg 2011; Schor 2004). More substantively still, it has been argued that it is culture that shapes our values—determining what counts as progress and development in the first place (Sen 2004).

All of these cultural considerations complicate both the everyday practice of development and the theoretical underpinnings of this practice. Before conceiving of development projects, for example, practitioners must decide whose cultural idea of development ought to be the goal—that of the funding agency, or its home country; that of the practitioner, or that of the target population. Similarly, questions must be addressed regarding the value of culture. Should traditional culture be shed as an impediment to development? Should traditional societies be protected from the cultural change that development seems to carry with it? Is there such a thing as traditional culture at all? Can traditional or indigenous culture be retained while still achieving something that might be called development? Finally, can development be reimagined from the non-Eurocentric starting point of indigenous culture?

Understanding the interaction of culture and development is not only important for development practitioners working in the Global South, however. We live in a time of global ecological, political, and economic crisis. Many have wondered if it is not modern culture itself that is at the root of such upheaval (Hamilton et al. 2015). As we face ecological and political barriers to the expansion of the current global economic system, it is culture that will allow us to imagine the social and economic innovations that will help us transcend the global turmoil of the early twentieth century. This may involve a re-evaluation of our personal goals, desires, values, and aspirations. It may also include a reimagination of what we call progress, development, economic growth, and *the good life*, on a global level. Such moves would require a reformulation of the social, political, and economic policies that we use to achieve these lofty goals. It may be the case that traditional or indigenous culture has something to teach modern culture in this regard.

Exploring the folds, fissures, and fuzzy edges of culture is not an easy task, however. Culture, of course, is the very thing we use to order and understand our social world. Policymakers, practitioners, consumers, voters, and intellectuals alike can only think through their own culture. It frames our thoughts—determining what is imaginable and comprehensible to us. Ideas such as *progress*, *development*, and *gross domestic product* are entrenched in the culture of modernity and are ubiquitous in our globalized world. There is no escape, or outside vantage-point from which to gaze on these complex perceptions. One cannot escape their cultural logic by going to the remote beaches of the Corn Islands, the mysterious oxbows of the Amazon basin, or the lush highlands of Guatemala. We will not meet an indigenous tribe on an excursion to the interior of Sumatra that will impart on us the lost and pristine wisdom of an ancient culture—helping us to see clearly an alternative to corrosive Western practices, or the secret of culturally appropriate development. How, then, do we begin to rethink some of our most dearly held beliefs and associated social and economic policies?

In the absence of a clear "outside-looking-in" position, there is no easy way to rethink our world. Given this reality, what is required is a careful and open-minded look at the history of policy related to the idea of development. We must understand the ways in which we have thought of the economy and its relation to culture in the past before we can open new territory for the future. In other words, we must understand culture of development the way it *is* before pushing it in new directions. This is the only way we can avoid falling into past habits of thought.

That is the first step in imagining new directions in social and economic policy. The second step is to try and understand instances where modern culture is already being pushed in new directions. All culture is varied, constantly changing, but also connected. This is certainly the case in our often contested and diverse global culture. From this, we can realize that although there is no outside to the culture of global modernity, it constantly mutates and it does have edges. Amongst these edge-areas we may include things such as tribal wisdom from the Amazon, the colonially suppressed knowledge of Maya cosmovision, or anarchist strains of North American and European intellectualism. These ephemeral and constantly changing edges of modernity can be explored in order to imagine alternative futures. By doing such exploration, new ideas can be folded into mainstream society from its innovative edges, and more effective development projects can be devised.

Transmodernity and Neoliberal Multiculturalism

The purpose of this book is to begin the work of reimagining development by taking two important first steps. First, there will be a detailed look at the way in which culture relates to the long history of thought on development and progress. Second will be an investigation of three examples of indigenous-driven sustainable development projects from Latin America. These edge-ideas occur on multiple scales within three countries—Guatemala, Honduras, and Ecuador—and have international linkages between each other, as well as with broader indigenous rights and environmental movements.

Through the relation of Latin American indigenous movements and the history of Western thought on culture and development, the argument will be made that indigenous sustainable development is not an amodern or postmodern idea. It is better framed as *transmodern*. When discussing indigenous ideas of development, it is easy to fall into two conceptual traps. The theoretical construct of transmodernity helps us to avoid these errors. The first, the essentialist trap, results from the reification of indigenous cultures as eternal, pre-historical, and unchanging. The second, the strategic essentialist trap, positions indigenous movements, politics, and identity solely as calculated tactical reactions to current legal institutions and discourses (Paradies 2006).

The theory of transmodernity is part of a research paradigm that is emerging largely from Latin America, but is applicable throughout the globe (Dussel 2012; Herrera Guillén 2016; Arias 2017; Escobar 2007). The theory begins with the assertion that non-modern cultures were not erased by colonialism or neocolonialism, but remained hidden, subverted, and marginalized. As Dussel (2012) argues, they were pushed to the edges, or the borders of modernity, where they continued to interact creatively with it. In fact, these cultures contributed to the creation of modernity through their labour, cultural traditions, and struggles for rights, freedoms, and nations. Modernity, this implies, was not fully established before colonization, but evolved with substantial contributions from the premodern cultures at its edges. As such, transmodern cultures do not reject all elements of modernity (Escobar 2007). These points differentiate transmodern movements from anti-modern and postmodern ones according to Dussel (2012). As he explains, transmodernity "assumes the positive moments of Modernity" as cultures that have been pushed to its edges to deconstruct their own traditions, while they challenge European cultural hegemony using "critical elements" adopted from their own traditions and also "others adopted from Modernity itself" (18–21).

Dussel's argument suggests that transmodern cultures cannot be accurately described as postmodern, since the bulk of their cultural elements have never been entirely modern, and draw substantively on the premodern. Importantly, the movements associated with transmodernity seek decolonization through self-valorization as they combine their own premodern cultural elements with the most progressive tools of modernity, and discursive exchange with other transmodern elements across the globe. In this way, subsistence practices, nature-relatedness, and diverse cosmovisions are combined discursively with appeals to rights, democracy, sovereignty, and equality, while local, national, and transnational identities are reformed and reworked (Escobar 2007).

Another important concept related to current articulations of culturally sustainable development is *neoliberal multiculturalism*. This concept, which has been most notably explored by Charles Hale (2006), forefronts a rarely acknowledged tension within the current manifestation of neoliberalism. In our current post-Washington Consensus global policy climate, collective government political power has been diminished, while the economic power of markets has become dominant. As property rights have been sanctified and individualistic ideology has been reinforced, non-governmental organizations, community groups, and indigenous movements have asserted rights through claims to collective cultural rights. As Hale (2006) put it:

> Neoliberalism encompasses economic doctrine but also promotes a reorganization of "political society" along the lines of decentralization, trimming down of the state, affirming basic human rights, and calling for minimally functional democracies. …[N]eoliberalism brings forth a new direction in social policy, emphasizing the development of civil society and social capital, and an approach to cultural rights that at first glance appears highly counter-intuitive. (p. 12)

As we will explore in this book, the neoliberal period has also seen the rise of movements for cultural protection and indigenous rights. In many Latin American countries, indigenous culture has moved in status away from that of a remnant of pre-Columbian backwardness and towards a national resource to be embraced. Accordingly, states such as Ecuador, Honduras, and Guatemala have come to support the resuscitation of indigenous dress, language, tradition, and culture. This process is helped along by an international development funding system that has come to recognize indigenous culture as a form of social capital. Along with this, national commitments to indigenous rights instruments such as the *International Labour Organization Convention 169 Convention on Indigenous and Tribal Peoples* have also helped.

The elevation of indigenous rights and culture goes only so far, however. Where indigenous rights and community organizations threaten transnational capital investments, neoliberal multiculturalism reaches its limit. Repression of indigenous groups and communities becomes common in such instances. Neoliberal multiculturalism has no difficulty respecting the rights of individuals to not be discriminated against due to their ethnicity or any other reason. It protects private capital with legal instruments, and often repressive power, however, when ethnic minorities make claims to material resources such as land, wage shares, or personal wealth. This is the tension faced by transmodern Latin American indigenous groups as they seek to rewrite the concept of development from their perspective.

Outline of the Book

Tensions around transmodernity and neoliberal multiculturalism will be apparent in the explorations of this book. We will see that indigenous ideas of development are at once old and new, modern and amodern—properly transmodern. We will explore the way in which indigenous cultural understandings can inform, and are informed by, new global ideas of development that are respectful of cultural differences and ecological limits. We will also see how transmodern indigenous development draws from and continues to contribute to centuries-old political–economic thinking about the meaning of progress, development, and culture. It is hoped that understanding indigenous redefinitions of these concepts will aid development thinkers, policymakers, practitioners as well as citizens in reimagining social, political, and economic policy in a time of multiple global crises.

As argued earlier, *culture* is a central term in this discussion. Understanding the place of this term vis-à-vis ideas of development and progress is key to developing the understanding we need in order to take the first step in reimagining development thinking. This work will begin in Chaps. 2 and 3 by tracing the strands of culture in ideas of development and progress that began in the late eighteenth century. Allusions (or lack thereof) to the concept of culture and to culture-like ideas will be located in the works of Adam Smith, Karl Marx, Alfred Marshall, and others. These works are keystones to the large edifice of modern thought on progress and development. To examine them is to examine the intellectual history of our culture and the cultural history of our intellect as it relates to progress, development, politics, and economy.

This analysis will continue in Chaps. 4 and 5, but the focus will be shifted to post-WWII development thought. This is a time in which discourses around the topics of economy, politics, development, and progress were extraordinarily diverse and contested. Different policy frameworks were imagined, and the politics around these had immense human and environmental consequences. Works produced by W.W. Rostow, Andre Gunter Frank, Amartya Sen, Arturo Escobar, and many others will be mapped according to their treatment of culture. They will be also historically contextualized as key features of discourses that spin around the central concept of development.

In Chap. 6, attention will be turned to Guatemala, *El Centro Pluricultural para la Democracia,* and the Maya idea of *culturally sustainable development* (CSD). An attempt will be made to understand the historical forces out of which *El Centro* and CSD have emerged. The hope is that such historical understanding will help in the proper conceptualization of the work and the ideas of the organization. This is a story of marginalization, global economics, and civil war, mixed with allusions to Maya cosmovision and aspirations to a better future—that is, to progress and development. It is a story of continuing struggle to develop and implement a new kind of development amidst racial and economic marginalization, genocide, and war.

The historical and spatial situation of *El Centro* from Chap. 6 will serve as the contextual basis for a description of the organization, its ideas, and its work that will be expounded in Chap. 7. This account is based on textual interpretation of the organization's publications, participant observation, qualitative interviews, and focus groups undertaken with members of *El Centro* between 2006 and 2015.

It is in this chapter where the idea of culturally sustainable development will be described and explored in full. This chapter represents and attempts to answer the question "what is CSD and how does it work?" Central to the topic is the concept of *cosmovision*—the component of culture that orders the way in which one understands the functioning of the cosmos, the relation of human to human, and human to nature. Members of *El*

Centro argue that to make development culturally sustainable in Guatemala's Western Highlands requires that the entire process be guided by Maya cosmovision. To understand CSD, one must have at least a clumsy understanding of Maya cosmovision, among other important elements. All of these are explored in Chap. 7.

Chapter 8 results from ongoing field research I have undertaken since 2011 with Afro-indigenous Garifuna communities in Honduras. To understand the Honduran Afro-indigenous movement, and locally sourced sustainable development ideas that are associated, it is necessary to grasp important elements of Garifuna history and current political economy. The chapter shows how hybrid Garifuna culture formed via colonialism and anti-colonialism, how the repressive Honduran state and predatory international capital constrain current development possibilities, and how the Garifuna use international solidarities to form a resistance, and development alternative, around the idea of indigenous food sovereignty.

Chapter 9 looks at a national-level project in Ecuador, where I have been involved in research since 2007. Indigenous sustainable development in that context revolves around the idea of *Sumak Kawsay* (living well), which has been incorporated, somewhat problematically, into the national constitution. This particular cosmovision will be discussed, as will events around the formation of the national constitution. Following this, I will describe the life and death of an innovative national programme to acquire international funding to "keep the oil in the ground" in biologically sensitive indigenous territories. This description of the Ecuadorian case provides a nuanced understanding of the key multiscale issues facing indigenous sustainable development.

In Chap. 10, these indigenous alternative ideas of development will be compared and contrasted with the discourse of international development literature that was set out in Chaps. 2, 3, 4, and 5. This will be done by attempting to understand where indigenous sustainable development can easily be incorporated into the more well-known theories, when it cannot, and when such incorporation threatens to mutate powerful theories of development into something very new. This last consideration becomes particularly interesting when the relationship between development economics and indigenous development is considered. The work of this chapter helps us to begin to think outside of our culturally prescribed intellectual boxes in tackling the most important issues of our time.

All of the ideas of the book are synthesized and reflected on in Chap. 11, the final chapter. More importantly, this chapter specifically engages the idea of sustainable development. Mainstream ideas, encapsulated in the SDGs, are compared with indigenous ideas of sustainable development. Important tensions between the two are located, and ways in which indigenous thought can guide mainstream development policy are suggested.

The book in total seeks less to find easy answers than to begin a long intellectual journey. This journey may well end in the transformation of society, but this book only begins to address that great challenge. Both the journey and the book start with an attempt to understand how the concept of culture has been intertwined with our ideas about development, progress, economy, and policy. That work needs to be followed by the examination of multiple indigenous transmodern edge-ideas in our globalized neoliberal society.

Interpreting Indigenous Culture

As we have discussed already, the second part of this book is an interpretation of the most prominent Latin American examples of such ideas. An attempt is made to understand the complex historical terrain that has produced these indigenous movements, their members, and their ideas. The ideas themselves are interpreted and elucidated, and finally—in an attempt to make them more intelligible to Western-trained academics and policymakers—they are explored in relation to the more globally powerful discourses on development that were delineated in the beginning of the journey. It is hoped that others may take this framework to study other edge-ideas—perhaps eventually helping us to think our way out of our current global conundrum of economic instability, inequality, and environmental catastrophe, and perhaps helping us to devise better development projects.

For me personally, this intellectual journey was accompanied necessarily by a continuing ethical introspection. At its core, this project is an attempt to create a representation of members of historically marginalized groups. Such work must be done with a strong sense of ethical responsibility to both the politics of the represented "Other" and to the validity of the research. Nowhere has this type of self-reflection proven more important than in discussions of indigeneity in Guatemala. Even the most careful of sympathetic ethnographies, for example, have been criticized by their subjects as undermining their political objectives (Warren 1998). Accounts of Guatemalan history, which arose from the mouths of indigenous Maya leaders through their Western anthropological intermediaries, have been criticized as misrepresentations (Menchú and Burgos-Debray 1984; Stoll 2008). These criticizers have then been critiqued themselves for undermining the political and social justice objectives of marginalized peoples all in the name of the Western ideal of objective truth (Arias 2017).

All of this implies that a representation such as that which appears in this study is necessarily undertaken through dense tangles of political and ethical underbrush. Throughout the process, the need to create a critical and accurate description will be acknowledged. But this will constantly be balanced with a necessity to avoid undermining Latin American indigenous political movements, of which even the most integrated investigator can only hope to attain a partial understanding.

To the extent to which such a balance is achieved, it will not be accomplished by avoiding criticism of indigenous movements and their ideas. The "hard" questions must be asked of movements for indigenous development, but they are asked while members are both literally and figuratively "in the room." Such open criticism was built into the research process for this book. Tricky questions were posed to indigenous leaders. In this context, for example, members were asked questions about the possibility that the largely university-educated members of *El Centro* are disconnected from the often illiterate members of the communities with which they work. In other words, are the people who work at *El Centro* really members of the communities with which they work, or part of an educated indigenous elite class that has separate interests and understandings from the most impoverished Maya citizens?

Another difficult question involved claims of culturally rooted proclivities to environmental stewardship that are the centrepiece of many indigenous organizations' programmes. Are these little more than politically motivated fictions? Similarly, is gender equality really a central feature of Maya, Garifuna, and Kechwa culture as advocates seem to assume, or would a revitalization of indigenous belief systems simply work to reinforce culturally rooted inequalities? Such questions were asked openly, and the responses generated understandings that were integrated into my interpretation of indigenous movements and their ideas. This interpretation was then presented to community members themselves, in a focus-group setting, for their consideration and discussion. Often, follow-up contact was made in order to validate the accuracy of my interpretations.

Conclusion

Holding these interpretive and representational issues aside, this work does have a central focus. It seeks to describe indigenous sustainable development and compare it with other ideas of development to the end of developing new policy and new perceptions of the possibilities of human society. In the end, it is found that the inclusion of edge-ideas and indigenous cosmologies in conversations about development necessitates a major rethink of traditional Western frames of analysis. This is a good thing since now, more than ever, we are in need of modifying the central ideas of our global civilization and of devising more effective development programmes.

Constantly circling this central question, however, are issues related to representation, essentialism, and politics. Just as important as the conclusions attained regarding the central question, were the necessary conclusions reached on these encircling issues. What were these conclusions? First, ideas of development are political. There is no avoiding the politics in the name of some imaginary "truth." Second, representations that foreigners create of their often romanticized "Others" will always be imperfect. The trick is to be aware of this throughout the project and to integrate participatory safeguards into the research or development project.

Finally, questions regarding the historical factuality of indigenous essentialist cultural claims will always miss the point. Cultures move, and they are always projects of construction and reconstruction. Claims to cultural essences that are made by indigenous organizations are part of this process. They are part of a global-scale imagining of indigeneity that is not just set on the work of defining indigenous culture, but perhaps of redefining all cultures as they interact with one another and engage with issues of poverty, development, democracy, and environment. In the case of the indigenous ideas presented in this book, the best, most democratic and environmentally sound aspects of a diverse cultural heritage are being centralized in this process. This is part of a cultural project to create a sustainable and democratic future, not to glorify an imaginary past.

Before joining indigenous movements in the re-evaluation of the political and economic structures of our world and the reimagination of development practice, however, we must understand where these ideas came from. That requires us to explore the murky ambiguities, stark disjunctures, and not-so-subtle politics of the intellectual and cultural history of the idea of development. This will be the work of the text two chapters.

References

Arias, A. (2017). Indigenous Knowledges and Sites of Indigenous Memory. *TRANSMODERNITY: Journal of Peripheral Cultural Production of the Luso-Hispanic World, 7*(1).

Blaser, M., Feit, H. A., & McRae, G. (Eds.). (2004). *In the way of development: Indigenous peoples, life projects, and globalization*. IDRC.

Cowen, M. P. (2003). *Doctrines of Development*. Routledge.

Dussel, E. D. (2012). Transmodernity and Interculturality: An Interpretation from the Perspective of Philosophy of Liberation. *Transmodernity, 1*(3), 28–59.

Escobar, A. (2007). Worlds and Knowledges Otherwise: The Latin American Modernity/Coloniality Research Program. *Cultural studies, 21*(2–3), 179–210.

Hale, C. (2006). Neoliberal Multiculturalism: The Remaking of Cultural Rights and Racial Dominance in Central America. *Political and Legal Anthropology Review, 28*(1), 10–28.

Hamilton, C., Gemenne, F., & Bonneuil, C. (Eds.). (2015). *The Anthropocene and the Global Environmental Crisis: Rethinking Modernity in a New Epoch*. Routledge.

Harrison, L. E., & Huntington, S. (2002). *Culture Matters: How Values Shape Human Progress*. Basic Books.

Heinberg, R. (2011). *The End of Growth: Adapting to Our New Economic Reality*. New Society Publishers.

Herrera Guillén, R. (2016). The Lost Modernity: 1436–1439 (Alfonso de Cartagena and Leonardo Bruni). *TRANSMODERNITY: Journal of Peripheral Cultural Production of the Luso-Hispanic World, 6*(2).

Menchú, R., & Burgos-Debray, E. (1984). *I, Rigoberta Menchú: An Indian Woman in Guatemala* (A. Wright, Trans.). London: Verso.

Paradies, Y. (2006). Beyond Black and White: Essentialism, Hybridity and Indigeneity. *Journal of Sociology, 42*(4), 355–367.

Raygorodetsky, G. (2019). Indigenous Peoples Defend Earth's Biodiversity – But They're in Danger. *National Geographic*, June, 2019.

Redclift, M. (2005). Sustainable Development (1987–2005): An Oxymoron Comes of Age. *Sustainable Development, 13*(4), 212–227.

Schor, J. (2004). *Born to Buy: The Commercialized Child and the New Consumer Culture*. New York: Scribner.

Sen, A. (2004). How Does Culture Matter? In *Culture and Public Action* (p. 38). Stanford, CA: Stanford University Press.

Stoll, D. (2008). *Rigoberta Menchú and the Story of All Poor Guatemalans*. Boulder: Westview Press.

UNESCO. (2019). Indigenous Peoples. Retrieved June 21, 2019, from https://en.unesco.org/indigenous-peoples.

Warren, K. (1998). *Indigenous Movements and Their Critics: Pan-Maya Activism in Guatemala*. New Jersey: Princeton University Press.
Williams, R. (1977). *Marxism and Literature*. Oxford and New York: Oxford University Press.
Yúdice, G. (2003). *The Expediency of Culture: Uses of Culture in the Global Era*. Durham: Duke.

CHAPTER 2

Classic Ideas of Modernity, Culture, and Progress

My first assignment as a graduate student in development economics in 2003 was to write a critique of an econometric study on land tenure and productivity in Burkina Faso. Having just graduated from an undergraduate programme in international development studies, I was eager to display my ability to undertake the most thorough and cutting critique possible—that, for me, implied an analysis from a post-development perspective. With a level of diligence and care only achievable by an insecure first-year graduate student, I prepared what was essentially a culture-based critique of the study. The gist: due to the author's hopeless immersion in an enlightenment-based, Western worldview, the variables used in the study were incorrectly chosen, and, furthermore, assumptions made about human "nature" were Eurocentric and not applicable to the African context. This, I argued, caused the author to generate misleading, irrelevant, and potentially harmful conclusions.

The head of the development economics programme at my university was a brilliant neoclassical economist who was clearly dedicated to improving the lot of the world's poor. He was trained in one of the highest ranked and liberal economics departments in the United States, and he had a reputation for pushing the limits of that discipline by writing about things like culture, arts, and social cohesion. The papers he would be grading from other students, I was sure, would be critiquing only the superficial parameters of the econometric analysis. But I was utilizing a theoretical perspective that had, arguably, emerged from marginalized

T. MacNeill, *Indigenous Cultures and Sustainable Development in Latin America*, https://doi.org/10.1007/978-3-030-37023-7_2

peoples themselves—one that challenged the authority of Western technocratic experts, questioned the discourse of development itself, and was inspiring radical new grass-roots revisualizations of the problems of development all over the "Third World." I was certain that my ability to slice into deeper issues and to understand the substantive critiques of development that were erupting forcefully from non-Western academics and social movement leaders would impress this cutting-edge economist as he graded my paper—securing for me his immediate respect, and a correspondingly high grade. I was wrong. As he handed back my work, he explained to me that he didn't grade it, that he didn't know how to grade it, that he had never seen anything like it, and that, frankly, he didn't understand it. There was an uncomfortable silence.

In this chapter and the next, I will try to locate the source of this uncomfortable silence. This will require a thorough review of the history of culture in development thinking. I will begin this review with a consideration of the historical roots of development theory in general in the current chapter. This will be followed by a taxonomy of postwar schools of thought on culture and development in the next chapter. I will argue that an intellectual break exists at theoretical and methodological levels between neoclassical economics and the other social sciences—one which precludes any meaningful discussion of culture. Further, I hope to explain that this uncomfortable silence is also represented in a fissure in understanding between Western enlightenment thinking and understandings that emanate from, or are at least embraced and transformed by, other traditions. The small pause in conversation that occurred between my professor and I was just one of many similar silences which pervade development theory, policy, and planning. These, I will argue, are symptoms of an ontological barricade that can and must be overcome if we are to have meaningful transdisciplinary discussions regarding development.

As Escobar (1999) has reminded us, the idea of development emerged in force in the immediate postwar period of the twentieth century. With the advent of the statistic of "annual per capita income," he explained, "almost by fiat, nearly 70 percent of the world's population were transformed into poor subjects" (p. 382). Resultantly, needs for economic growth and development "became self-evident, necessary, and universal truths" to the Western technocratic mind (ibid.). It was within this climate that, as Escobar (2005) would continue to argue,

> full of hopes and aspirations, scouting the landscape with fruition and eager to apply the best of his knowledge to a complex but exciting task, after having just left behind the cataclysm of the War and perhaps with the smile of somebody who is new to the world, there arrived in the Third World, dressed in full regalia, the Development Economist. (171)

This development economist was not, however, to remain a cohesive subject, nor was he alone. As I will argue later in this chapter, postwar development economics was split into two enduring schools: *Neoclassical Development Economics* and *Critical Political Economy of Development*. Furthermore, the technocratic and often materially reductionist experts of these two schools were joined quickly in the debate by postcolonial theorists who articulated the earliest of the *Cultural Approaches to Development*. It is around these three schools of thought that the story of the next chapter will pivot, but it will not do to start abruptly here. Despite the apparent suddenness with which he appears in Escobar's account, the liberal development economist was the product of a tangible history of thought—as were the critical political economist and the cultural theorist. It is to these histories that we must first turn if we are to understand development theory, and the place of culture within it.

It is the work of the current chapter to explore the important thinking that existed before the "invention" of the ideas of "development" and "underdevelopment" that occurred in the mid-twentieth century (Escobar 1999). It was this *pre-development* thinking that would make post-WWII ideas of culture and development possible. In this exploration, I will be looking to outline the main tenets of the various theories presented, and also to focus on the ideas of culture and development that appear, explicitly or tacitly, in each. Both the concepts of "development" and "culture" will be accorded a very wide definitional range in this review, since the goal is to tease-out the ways in which the theorists discussed tended to define these concepts themselves. Accordingly, any allusion to, or assumption of, what constitutes positive social change or progress will be considered a discussion of "development." "Culture" will be considered to be at issue when a theorist discusses any extra-individual social force that is presumed to impact the preferences, habits, motives, values, and valuations of actors, or their understanding of the way the world works. These concepts will be tracked through literature in *classical political economy*, early *neoclassical economics*, *Marxian political economy*, and *sociology*.

Classical Political Economy

Adam Smith

The bulk of mid-twentieth-century thinking on development stems from the same origin. Many claim that what I am calling both the neoclassical economic and the critical political economy traditions of development theory began with the publication of Adam Smith's foundational work of classical political economy *An Enquiry into the Nature and Causes of the Wealth of Nations* in 1776 (Deane 1978). Polanyi (1944/2001) goes further in suggesting that it was our very market-capitalist "civilization which started approximately with the publication of *The Wealth of Nations*" (47). These two opinions regarding the social role of Smith's text are telling and yield two key principles that will be assumed during the extent of this review of literature. First, texts such as *The Wealth* are *descriptive* let us understand the varying ways in which social phenomena have been understood in varying times and places. Second, they may be thought of as *productive* or *performative*. This, following Foucault (1969/2002), is meant to imply that such texts are embedded in larger discourses which tend to produce the very social forms that they mean to describe. In this sense we can examine *The Wealth* as an artefact that exhibits a particular way of thinking about economy and development, but we can also place the text within the context of historical social change in which ideas and discourses play an active part. That is, we can remember Polanyi's assertion regarding Smith's Opus that "no misreading of the past ever proved more prophetic of the future" (45).

In *The Wealth*, Smith embraced the enlightenment thinking of his time. It is no secret that he was an admirer of Sir Isaac Newton. In fact, Newton's depiction of the universe as a great machine in which particles were acted upon by a limited number of inalienable natural laws to produce a stable system was lauded by Smith as being "the greatest discovery that has ever been made by man" (1759: 3). It is evident that Smith followed Newton's lead in his own work. In the economic system that he described, human particles were propelled by a lust for individualistic personal gain—having a natural "propensity to truck, barter, and exchange on thing for another" in an attempt to satisfy their own self-interest (22–23). An anarchic and cruel Hobbesian jungle does not result for Smith, however, since two other laws—those of supply and demand—guide human interaction, through price signals, towards a stable, mutually beneficial equilibrium. In this way, the raw power of self-love inspires profits to be sought via division of labour, which allows economic man to take advantage of economies of scale and the benefits of trade. Smith argued that "although he intends only his own gain," this economic man—or *homo economicus*—is "led by an invisible hand to promote an end which was no part of his intention" (572). This end is greater economic output—the wealth of nations, or what it would later be called: development.

This simple depiction of the market as an efficient self-adjusting system that synthesizes self-interest with aggregate economic betterment is often all that is taken from *The Wealth*. To do so, however, is to forget much of what Smith wrote. First, he seems to have had a keen sense of the cultural construction of his seemingly "natural" economic man. Of the propensity to engage in market exchange in atomistic self-interest, Smith offers that,

> whether this propensity be one of those original principals of human nature, of which no further account can be given; or whether, as seems more probable, it can be the necessary consequence of the facilities of reason and speech, it belongs not to our present subject to inquire. (22)

Later, he argues that "the difference between the most dissimilar characters, between a philosopher and a common street porter, for example, seems to arise not so much from nature, as from habit, custom, and education" (25). This admission of the culturally situated character of homo economicus is not central to the thesis of *The Wealth*, however, since the topic is strictly related to economic action of humans within a market structure. Culture and non-price communication are almost exclusively assumed to exist a priori to and outside of the economy.

Smith's scepticism regarding the ability of markets to function in the real world, as his model suggests, is also often overlooked. For Smith, relation to the three essential means of production—land, labour, and capital—corresponded to three classes: "those who live by rent, those who live by wages, and those who live by profit" (336). The latter should not be trusted since "the rate of profit does not, like rent and wages, rise with the prosperity, and fall with the declination of society. On the contrary, it is naturally low in rich, and high in poor countries" (338). This is the case since high wages or rents necessarily erode profits. "The interest of this third order," Smith argued, "has not the same connection with the general interest of the society as that of the other two" (338). Government, according to Smith, must be wary of the strong political influence of this class and seek to protect competition in the face of their propensity to collude to create monopoly power. Furthermore, he believed that government should intervene in the economy to provide schooling, which he hoped would allow workers an opportunity to escape the routine and degrading work which resulted from the division of labour. He also saw an active government role regarding defence, protective tariffs, rule of law, quality control, banking regulation, public goods provision, postal service, administering copyrights and patents, according temporary monopoly rights to corporations in order to direct commerce towards socially beneficial ends, public health measures, maintenance of infrastructure, taxation to discourage improper or overly luxurious behaviour, and establishing ceilings on interest rates (Heilbroner 1996: 104).

The Wealth, for Smith, was meant to be contextualized within the larger philosophical theory that he outlined earlier (1759) with his *Theory of Moral Sentiments*. In that text, Smith insists that there are natural needs that humans are compelled to fulfil, such as needs for nutrients and shelter, but that these needs have an upper-bound—that homo *economicus* is not insatiable. What makes man seem insatiable, for Smith, is the need to communicate social belonging and status to others. As he explains, "the rich man glories in his riches, because he feels that they naturally draw upon him the attention of the world" (I.III.16). As a result, the compulsion to amass wealth is driven by "that emulation which runs through all the different ranks of men" (I.III.16). Furthermore, humans, Smith argues, are fundamentally creatures of empathy and sympathy, and these sentiments, in the end, trump any tendency to emulative self-interest. Markets, where humans compete and communicate only through prices, are well and good to the extent that they efficiently create wealth. In moments of crisis, however, humans adhere to higher sentiments of morality, ethics, and empathy. There is a "stronger power," he argues, that is "capable of counteracting the strongest impulses of self-love":

> It is reason, principle, conscience, the inhabitant of the breast, the man within, the great judge and arbiter of our conduct. It is he who, whenever we are about to act so as to affect the happiness of others, calls to us, with a voice capable of astonishing the most presumptuous of our passions, that we are but one of the multitude, in no respect better than any other in it; and that when we prefer ourselves so shamefully and so blindly to others, we become the proper objects of resentment, abhorrence, and execration." (III.I.46)

In summarizing Smith's thinking, it is evident that the "natural" propensity to barter in maximizing self-interest is, in fact, a result of human social and communicative activity—a cultural activity. Further, the drive to self-interested behaviour that results from this social activity, according to Smith, is easily subdued by a higher propensity to engage in other-regarding behaviour. Markets, for Smith, may be capable of generating great wealth, but must be monitored and regulated not only by government, but also by the higher order of ethics and morality.

It should be no surprise that Smith gave ethics a central role in his conception of society. To do so was in keeping with much the rich tradition of Western economic thought that had preceded him. As Heilbroner (1996) insists, in economic thought in the Bible, by Aristotle, the Physiocrats, and by St. Thomas Aquinas, for example, the economy was not a separate system, but rather the economic was a type of action that must be morally judged as are all other forms of human conduct. Even with the "commercial revolution" in economic thought, beginning approximately with Mendeville in the seventeenth century, and continuing through with the mercantilists, economic action needed ethical justification. With Smith, and Cantillon before him, Heilbroner argues, focus shifted from the study of economics as an action, to the study of a *system* called the economy. But still, as we have seen, the discussion was morally, culturally, and politically situated.

David Ricardo

This tendency in political economy towards holistic analysis began to change with Ricardo, as the laws that Smith had referred to were taken out of cultural and ethical context (Deane 1978). The insatiability of homo economicus was assumed instead of historically or philosophically situated. The economic system was studied as just that—a system—not as a type of behaviour that should be morally judged (Heilbroner 1996). Importantly, as Deane (1978) explains, Ricardo's methodology "was mathematical rather than historical or philosophical," and his "technique of abstracting reasoning from a priori postulates … had important implications for the methodology of orthodox economic theory," in that "it helped to draw theoretical economics away from the real world" and "permitted economic theory to develop independently of other social sciences" (82–84). With Ricardo, classical political economy began to undertake a momentous shift that would eventually result in the dropping of the adjective "political" from the moniker, the pushing aside of ethics, and the expulsion of any concept of culture from its purview.

John Stuart Mill

This was not to happen immediately, however. J.S. Mill, widely regarded as the last of the great classical political economists, actually straddled thinking in the style of the classical school while prefiguring the coming marginalist revolution in economic thought—a revolution which would mark the end of the classical era. In keeping with the classical school, Mill importantly retained the labour theory of value from Smith and Ricardo, admitted political factors into his analysis, incorporated ethics (importantly, of a particular kind) into his analysis, and even left a bit of room for culture to seep in.

For Mill (1909), political economy was the study of "the nature of Wealth, and the laws of its production and distribution" (PR.2). One of the most important of these laws was encapsulated in the labour theory of value. For Mill, like Smith and Ricardo, the value of a good is ultimately "determined by the amount of labour needed to produce the good," and this, in turn, determines the "natural price" towards which market valuation will tend (III.15.11). The incorporation of the labour theory of value had consistently led earlier economists to insert a notion of conflict in their thinking of market—as the labouring class as makers of value were confronted by capitalists who, due to their negligible contribution to value, would need to take from the labouring class for their own material benefit (Hunt 2002, pp. 189–191). This inherent class conflict was downplayed by Mill, however, through his insistence that the provision of capital was a service provided by the capitalist and that this service contributed to the value of a good as well—an assertion he imported from Say (1863). Action in a market system, then, became a more cooperative affair, with both great classes contributing to the value of the goods created, but not one of assured social harmony. There existed a danger of class-based conflict within a capitalist system, but this tendency was eased by a need for cooperation between classes (Mill 1909, III.III–III.V).

Culture was admitted into Mills' (1909) analysis in some ways, and excluded in others. In order for a good to be ascribed a value in a market, for example, Mill argues that, "the thing must not only have some utility, there must also be some difficulty in its attainment" (III.2.1). The bulk of the text in Mills' *Principles*, is dedicated to the supply side of this equation. Of the origin of the utility values that are placed on goods—a topic that might well require a cultural analysis—Mill has nothing to say, choosing like Smith and Ricardo before him to limit the purview of political economy so as not to have to question the origin of desires. On the other hand, in his preliminary remarks to *Principles*, Mill suggests that culture and economy are linked together in a dialectic fashion as, "the creed and laws of a people act powerfully upon their economical condition; and this again, by its influence on their mental development and social relations, reacts upon their creed and laws" (pr.3). Other aspects of the institutional structure of a society, it seems, can also impact the internal constitution of its members. For example, when,

> all real initiative and direction resides in the government, and individuals habitually feel and act as under its perpetual tutelage, popular institutions develop in them not the desire of freedom, but an unmeasured appetite for place and power: diverting the intelligence and activity of the country from its principal business to a wretched competition for the selfish prizes and the petty vanities of office. (V.11.15)

Further, as Hunt (2002) explains,

> Mill … did not believe that all actions were motivated by self-interest. He believed only that most people whose personalities were moulded by a competitive capitalist culture acted out of self-interest in their economic behaviour. He looked forward, however, to a future, when, in a socialist or communist society, people would act from "higher" or "nobler" motives. (188)

Indeed, Mill suggested that although there are natural laws of production, no such laws exist relating to exchange or distribution of wealth. These things, such as markets and the institution of private property, result from "the existing state of knowledge and experience, and the existing condition of social institutions and intellectual and moral culture" (II.1.3). So, although culture is excluded from his theory of value, a fairly sophisticated dialectical and institutional version of the concept enters into his analysis in other places.

Mill, like Smith, incorporated a wider discussion of ethics within his economic analysis. It is this, along with his use of the labour theory of value, and his scattered cultural musings that make it fitting to call him a classical political economist. Mill incorporated and then expanded upon Bentham's (1781/2000) utilitarianism in his treatment of ethics. Bentham had argued that mankind acts under the impulse "of two sovereign masters, *pain* and *pleasure*," which "govern us in all we do, in all we say, in all we think" (p. 14). For Bentham, the use or *utility* of any object or action is determined by the extent to which "it tends to produce benefit, advantage, pleasure, good, or happiness, ... or ... to prevent the happening of mischief, pain, evil, or unhappiness to the party whose interest is considered" (14–15). Bentham argued that the impulse to maximize utility takes the form of an indisputable natural law, as it is dictated "by the natural constitution of the human frame" (16). He also thought of it as an ethically correct impulse. Since action that is "comfortable to the principle of utility" is by definition one that intends the increase of pleasure (or the decrease of pain), it is an action that "ought to be done" (15).

Unlike Say (1821/1863), Bastiat (1850/1964), Senior (1836/1928), and the many neoclassical economists that would come, Mill augmented Bentham's utilitarianism substantially. He asserted that although natural laws are present in production, in the sphere of distribution, humans obey the laws and customs of society. This implied that utilitarianism need only apply in one limited sphere and may be transcended as humans move further from the necessities of production. Principles of private property and even of utility maximization were denied the status of inevitable, natural, or even just by Mill in the socially mediated sphere of distribution. For Mill, human behaviour was tempered by human social institutions, and some acts could be judged as more ethical than others in the sphere of distribution (Hunt 2002, pp. 187–188).

Mill's use of the labour theory of value, his modification of Benthamite ethics, and his musings about culture-like phenomena could only confound those who wished to make a Newtonian-style science of political economy. A formal linear scientific model of economy required a particle (homo economicus) with clear natural propensities which, in the acting out of these propensities, would interact with a few natural laws in the production of a predictable equilibrium condition. The labour theory of value seemed always to inspire a sense of conflict—or disequilibrium—in models. His musings about culture and separation of production and distribution implied that homo economicus did not behave according to any immutable rules, but would change according to circumstance, and, in turn, would change those very circumstances—a very nonlinear concept that could never yield equilibrium in the Newtonian sense.

Mill was an ardent libertarian, however. The "business of life," he insisted, "is better performed when those who have an immediate interest in it are left to take their own course, uncontrolled either by the mandate of the law or by the meddling of any public functionary" (V.11.22). He held that the liberty of the individual "ought to include all that part which concerns only the life, whether inward or outward, of the individual, and does not affect the interests of others" (V.11.4). "In sum," he argued, "*laisser-faire* ... should be the general practice: every departure from it, unless required by some great good, is a certain evil" (V.11.16). This libertarianism, mixed with positivist scientism and use of the concept of utility, prefigured much of the neoclassical economics that would emerge shortly after Mill's death. But, as we will see, for classical political economy to be transformed into the pseudo-science of neoclassical economics, ethics, history, culture, and the labour theory of value would all need to be ejected from the core of economic theory.

Neoclassical Economics

The Marginalists

The tension between the libertarian elegance of the self-regulating market and the conflict implied by the postulate that all value is produced by human labour would not do for those who would wish to make a Newtonian science of economics. The natural laws of the physical sciences at the time had no such conflict—only equilibria. No historical inquiry was required to predict the trajectory that an apple might choose in falling from a tree. The tendency of classical political economists to historically and socially situate their analyses and to shroud talk of the efficacy of the invisible hand with discussions of its failures could only distance economics from the status of pure science. Near the end of the nineteenth century, however, the marginalist movement managed to change the study of economics substantially. To Jevons, Walras, and later Marshall, this accomplishment represented a substantial move towards the perfection of the science of economics. It involved the permanent transformation of the historically situated social science that was classical political economy into the ahistorical mathematical pure science of neoclassical economics. In this transition, however, as much was lost as was gained. Among the gains were parsimony, elegance, and stature within the (social)scientific community. Among the losses were any engagement with the ideas of politics, culture, or development.

An important change that marked this revolution was made to the theory of value. Jevons (1871/1882) adamantly opposed the "prevailing opinions" that "make labour rather than utility the origin of value" and asserted instead that "value depends entirely on utility" (I.2). For marginalists, there must exist, a priori, a human want, or there can be no value. Humans would engage in exchange in order to maximize their utility by satisfying pre-existing wants and, in doing so, would establish, through the laws of supply and demand, the market price for all goods (Walras 1892/1996). The trick here is that it is not the total utility gained through consumption that is important in determining whether an exchange will take place at a particular price—it is the utility gained from the consumption of the last amount of commodity exchanged (the "marginal" utility). Furthermore, the utility gained through consumption decreases as the same commodity is consumed successive times (the marginal utility is diminishing). I may be willing to pay $5 for a glass of milk if I am really thirsty, for example, but not so much for my second glass, and I may refuse to purchase the tenth glass even if it is offered for free. Notice that the value of the milk does not depend on how much labour was used in its production here—it changes depending on the utility the consumer can expect to gain.

There is a lower bound to this price, of course, and it is determined by the marginal cost of production—the cost of producing the last unit. The price of labour would be included in this, as would the price of capital and land, but it is not the process of production that is thought to be the determinant of value—rather, it is the price for which labourers, capitalists, and landowners are willing to exchange their services in a competitive market. Given that the marginalists assumed that exchanges were entered into by free individuals who simply calculated utility gained minus utility lost for any given action, it seemed fair to Marshall (1890) to claim that "by far the greater number of events with which economics deals affect in about equal proportions all the different classes of society" (I.II.15). In a state of equilibrium (which is presumed to hold), all inputs are paid their proper price, and the proper price is presumed to be the equilibrium price. In this tautology, economics moved from being concerned with the study of the spheres of production and distribution with the aim of increasing national wealth, to being concerned only with the act of exchange which Walras (1892/1996) claimed, "constitutes the very foundation of the whole edifice of economics" (p. 44). Economics, as a result, was depoliticized—since value was presumed not to be the result of labour exerted but the act of free exchange, tensions between labouring and capitalist classes over the product of labour were removed from economic theory. This move from intrinsic conflict to harmonious exchange precipitated the change in moniker from "classical political economy" to "neo-classical economics."

Besides the depoliticization that resulted from the marginalist revolution, ideas related to culture were dropped as well. For either general (Walras 1892) or partial (Marshall 1890) equilibrium to hold, it was necessary to presume economic actors to have stable, unchanging preferences. As Jevons (1871/1882) asserted, "anything which an individual is found to desire … must be assumed to possess for him utility," and the impulse that drives the action of this individual is "to satisfy … wants to the utmost with the least effort" (III.2). The "utility" that each actor derives from his or her action, Walras (1892/1996) claims, "remains *fixed* for each party" (p. 117). This assumption of stable preferences precluded any idea of socially organized beliefs and values, unless these were presumed to be pre-formed and immutable. Thus, culture either did not exist, or existed outside of the purview of exchange, and therefore outside of the purview of economics.

Inquiries into wealth, development, or progress were set aside as well. At least since the publication of *The Wealth of Nations*, political economy had been given the central goal examining the mysteries of national economic development. This goal became secondary after the neoclassical turn. Economics became the science of exchange, and equilibrium models presumed that free exchange in competitive markets was, by definition, efficient in that it would only occur if the end result increased the utilities of all involved. The efficiency of markets implied that the maximum possible utility would be attained in the aggregate, given the current state of technology. Questions regarding the causes of technological change were set aside. Wealth, then, was assumed to be maximized as the result of free exchange, and economists, as a result, had no need to be worried directly about the laws of its production (Heilbroner 1999, pp. 197–228; Hunt 2002, pp. 372–395).

The ejection of politics, culture, and development from the purview of economics was part of the neoclassical turn from a *methodological holism* to *methodological individualism*. The former had looked at the actions, motives, positions, incentives, and beliefs of groups of people in its analysis. Methodological individualism mixed with marginalism tended to deny the significance of groups and conflict between them and focus analysis on individuals who engaged in free and harmonious trade. Importantly, humans are assumed in this model not to communicate directly with other humans. Homo economicus can communicate only through prices. The type of non-price communication that might lead to the social development of understandings and values cannot exist in a neoclassical world, since it would imply changeable, negotiable utility functions. This would introduce a nonlinearity into equations, which would make it impossible to claim that markets function efficiently, and would make the application of linear calculus impossible as well.

Basing analysis on the marginal unit, and combining this with the assumption that economic action was conducted by rational, atomistic individuals with stable preferences, was methodologically expedient in that it allowed "the application of differential calculus" to the concepts of "utility, value, demand, supply, capital, interest, labour, and all of the other quantitative notions belonging to the daily operations of industry" (Jevons 1871/1882, I.4). This mathematization finally gave economics the look of Newtonian physics, as "the pure theory of economics or the theory of exchange and value in exchange" became, as Walras (1892/1996) emphatically claims, "a physico-mathmatical science like mechanics or hydrodynamics" (p. 224). Such mathematical theory-building was to be the basis of a deductive, apolitical science of economics that focussed on the idea of efficiency at the expense of virtually all other concepts.

Despite the claims of the marginalists that theirs was an objective science rooted in laws of nature, neoclassical economics was endowed from the beginning with an ethical bias. Theory and mathematical exposition, as Walrus explained, was to come first in neoclassical methodology, followed by empirical observation which economists should use "not to confirm but to apply their conclusions" (qtd in Heilbroner 1999, p. 225). The assumption that economic life was rooted in the action of free individuals, then, was not to be questioned, but assumed, and historical or social data would not be permitted to show otherwise in analysis. This tended to lend itself to the scientific fortification of liberal ideals. Following in the libertarian tradition of Say and Mill, for example, Menger (1871/1950) used neoclassical assumptions regarding human nature to make a case for the sanctity of private property:

> Human economy and property have a joint economic origin since both have, as the ultimate reason for their existence, the fact that goods exist whose available quantities are smaller than the requirements of men. Property, therefore, like human economy, is not an arbitrary invention but rather the only practically possible solution of the problem that is, in the nature of things, imposed upon us by the disparity between requirements for, and the available quantities of, all economic goods. (p. 97)

Similarly, Walras (1892/1996) touted the inevitability, naturalness, and optimality of equilibria established in free-market transaction, arguing that "any value in exchange, once established, partakes of the character of a natural phenomenon, natural in its origins, natural in its manifestations and natural in essence" (p. 69), and that "the equations we have developed do show freedom of production to the superior general rule" (p. 256). More precisely, Walras believed that his equations showed that "exchange of several commodities for one another in a market ruled by free competition is an operation by which all holders of one, several or all of the commodities exchanged can obtain the greatest possible satisfaction of their wants" (p. 173).[1]

By depicting the economy as nothing more than a simple aggregate of rational, egoistic, autonomous individuals, by restricting the study of economics to the study of exchange, by jettisoning the labour theory of value for one based entirely on utility, and by formalizing their claims in mathematics (other than Menger), early neoclassical economists were able to add a strong discursive force to the argument for *liaises faire*—one that did not have to be validated by, or situated in, a study of history. In fact, to do the latter would, according to the proponents of the new science, be purely inductive and therefore ascientific. As a result, pure neoclassical economics is ultimately conservative and avoids any questioning of this ethic, as Hunt (2002) explains:

> Neoclassical welfare economics accepts as the ultimate ethical criteria of social value the existing personal desires, generated by the institutions, values, and social processes of existing society, and weighted by the existing distributions of income, wealth and power. Thus the theory becomes incapable of asking questions about the nature of an ethically good society and the ethically good person that would be its product. (p. 396)

The Keynesian Challenge

A major revision of neoclassical economics did not occur until the mid-twentieth century, in the writings of John Maynard Keynes. Although the

[1] Walras was never, in fact, able to show this to hold true even mathematically. Later Vilfredo Pareto would improve on Walras' exposition, and this work would be formalized by Arrow and Debreu (1954) but with similarly incomplete results.

extent to which Keynes' work represents a substantive challenge to neoclassical economics, as opposed to a mild revision, is debatable, Keynes did, at least in rhetoric, take issue with much of the core of neoclassicalism. For Keynes (1936/2006), economics was a human science—a social science—and it followed that attempts to mimic the physical sciences were misguided:

> The classical [and neoclassical] theorists resemble Euclidean geometers in a non-Euclidean world who, discovering that in experience straight lines apparently parallel often meet, rebuke the lines for not keeping straight—as the only remedy for the unfortunate collisions which were occurring. (p. 15)

This was a direct reproach of the neoclassical insistence on deductive methodology. Contrary to this, Keynes chose to build his theory from empirical observation first—inductively. He set out primarily to explain the existence of the violent economic waves of high economic output and low that were business cycles—those which seemed arbitrarily to either call on the great populations of the Western countries to employ their industriousness nearly completely, or to cast them in the thousands on the streets as vagabonds (Deane 1978).

His methodological break with mainstream neoclassical economics, however, did not represent a substantial break with neoclassical technique. In his *General Theory* (1936/2006), Keynes maintained the important neoclassical convention that wages were equal to the marginal productivity of labour. This generally led to the assertion that there was no such thing as involuntary unemployment—just that there were many workers who would not agree to work unless they were paid at a rate higher than the value of the extra output their labour created. He explained the obvious existence of intra-war involuntary unemployment as the result, ironically, of affluence combined with diminishing propensity to consume relative to wealth. The wealthy, Keynes argued, simply did not consume enough output to justify the employment of the entire labour force—this would produce both a glut of goods and high unemployment. The remainder of wealth in the hands of the more affluent was generally saved since, in absence of effective demand, there was little opportunity to undertake in employment-inducing investment.

Other than this assertion, and his accompanying insistence that monetary policy can have an impact on the general output of an economy, Keynes adopted virtually every neoclassical principal in his *General Theory*.

Importantly, this included the maintenance of the theoretical construct of homo economicus. He took, for example, "the tastes and habits of the consumer [and] the disutility of different intensities of labour" as "given" (p. 221). He also assumed that this creature was involved in calculations regarding how best to maximize his or her utility function—although restricted by an inability to accurately predict the future or know completely the nature of the current economic universe.

Changing the postulates that he did, however, yielded some important revisions in economic thought. The most important implication of Keynes' work was that the economy was not self-correcting. The problem of unemployment and stagnation amidst glut could not work itself out, and would instead result in a permanent downward spiral in absence of substantial countervailing external shock or government intervention. Keynes, therefore, called for the extensive use of monetary policy coupled with substantial government spending that would be designed to replace the lost consumption that affluence had created. Abhorring communism and highly disrespectful of Marxism, Keynes believed this to be the only way of saving the capitalist system from self-induced collapse.

The need for intervention made it necessary for an evaluation of ends and means by policy analysts. This, for Keynes, meant that ethics were a necessary part of economic thought. He wrote in a letter to Harrod in 1938 that economics "is essentially a moral science and not a natural science." He continued,

> I mentioned before that it deals with introspection and with values. I might have added that it deals with motives, expectations, psychological uncertainties.... It is as though the fall of the apple to the ground depended on the apple's motives on whether it is worthwhile falling to the ground, and whether the ground wanted the apple to fall, and on the mistaken calculations on the part of the apple as to how far it was from the centre of the earth. (Keynes 1994, pp. 297–300)

Whether this quotation represents an allusion to something resembling the idea of culture, is unclear. This is the case with the bulk of Keynes' writing. In his earlier work (1920), he alluded to the idea that propensities to save could be impacted by public policy, for example, but his *General Theory* (1936/2006) treats humans very much like neoclassical automatons. Humans do interact and communicate in Keynes' depiction, but only with the inclination to guess the intentions of others in conditions of uncertainty based on incomplete information—the underlying tastes of economic actors remain stable, and they are therefore expected to react in more or less expected manner when government policy is exerted.

Although Keynes was emphatically not a Marxist, he did touch on the idea of ideology, which, as we will discuss, is central to the Marxian concept of culture. For Keynes, however, ideas, it seems, had impact by changing people's conception of the way in which the world and economy work. This does not necessarily imply an ideological influence on the tastes, propensities, and attitudes of human actors, rather the power of ideas to influence perceptions (in conditions of imperfect information) regarding the complexities of economic life. Furthermore, Keynes (1936) comes to different conclusions regarding the independence of these ideas from vested material interests compared with the Marxian conception:

> The Ideas of economists and political philosophers, both when they are right and when they are wrong, are more powerful than is commonly understood. Indeed the world is ruled by little else. Practical men, who believe themselves to be quite exempt from any intellectual influences, are usually the slaves of some defunct economist. Madmen in authority, who hear voices in the air, are distilling their frenzy from some academic scribbler of a few years back. I am sure that the power of vested interests is vastly exaggerated compared with the gradual encroachment of ideas. (p. 351)

The idea of *development* exists only in seed form in Keynes' work. Developmentalism—the idea that "less developed countries" could be reformed in the image of capitalist Europe via government intervention—would be strongly influenced by Keynes' General Theory. He was instrumental in the founding of the Bretton Woods Institutions, including the World Bank—whose role it would become to oversee development projects in the Western-influenced post-WWII world (Martinussen 1997, p. 25). His General Theory, however, was more concerned with problems of unemployment and instability inherent in a capitalist system than with development per se. Nonetheless, he did realize that these phenomena impacted the "growth of wealth" in economies and the general well-being of populations (1936, p. 342).

The Austrian School

Another stream of economic though that is closely related to the neoclassical school should be discussed here, as it will influence post-WWII development theory substantially. This is the Austrian school of marginalist economics. It is not clear if this school should properly be thought of as a stream of marginalist economics that is to be distinguished from the neoclassical school of Walras, Jevons, Marshall, and Keynes, for example (de Soto 2008, pp. 2–4), or if Austrian economics is, in fact, neoclassical itself, and should be differentiated from the latter in terms of mainstream versus Austrian streams (Hunt 2002, pp. 264–276). If neoclassical economics is to be defined simply as a mode of analysis that uses marginal theory, assumes an actor with stable preferences, and tends towards the *laissez faire,* then the Austrian school is neoclassical. If it insisted that neoclassical economics must engage in mathematical exposition based on static equilibrium models, then Austrian economics is not neoclassical.

From its inception with the early marginalist work of Menger (1871/1950), the Austrian school has shunned mathematical exposition, since the latter is presumed to unsatisfactorily restrict the descriptive capabilities of the discipline. Other than this aversion to mathematics, three distinguishing features emerged through the evolution of Austrian thinking, via notable contributions from von Mises (1949/1996), von Böhm-Bawerk (1895), von Weiser (1911/1994), Hayek (1945), and Schumpeter (1942/1976).[2] These three distinguishing features are based around the idea of the entrepreneur, the way in which information is understood, and the treatment of time. Unlike mainstream neoclassical economics, the human actor in the Austrian conception is not just a docile calculator who tends to choose the easiest of a number of choices in maximizing his or her utility. According to Austrian theorists, the economic actor is motivated by an innate desire to create and discover his or her own world—of which there is always imperfect information—in the pursuit of increased utility. As opposed to the reacting atom of homo economicus, then, the Austrians have conceived an active, adventurous economic agent: the entrepreneur.

Austrian economists depict this entrepreneur as an engine that propels the ever-changing, ever-advancing economic system through time. This characterization of human nature allows the Austrians, unlike mainstream neoclassical theorists, to explain technological change. Through his or her

[2] Although a student of Weiser and Böhm-Bawerk at the University of Vienna, Schumpeter is only loosely affiliated with the Austrian school. This may be due to his lack of complete aversion to communism, his inconsistent methodology, his reluctance to credit his own teachers, or simply his arrogance. He did, however, maintain the centrality of the entrepreneur in driving a dynamic economy, which, despite his own accolades to Walras, positions him closer to the Austrians than to any other school.

creativity and inquisitiveness, the Austrians argue, the entrepreneur discovers and creates new information in an economy where information about the world is dispersed and subjective. Discovered or created information is then transmitted through price signals which ripple through the economy as the action taken by an entrepreneur with new information impacts his or her valuation of particular goods, thus provoking price changes. The progressive change this inspires in the pricing scheme of an economy in effect reorders the economic system—changing the economic landscape for all entrepreneurs. This inspires others to change their actions and create or discover new information—inciting further change. This, unlike the static depiction of mainstream neoclassicism, is a story of an economy that is constantly changing, and never quite in equilibrium, as it advances through time.

This is also a story of development. And development has a clear hero: the entrepreneur—whose action should not be interfered with. Menger (1871/1950) had insisted that the process of "development" begins with the entrepreneurial discovery of the division of labour, which "signifies a considerable step forward in economy and comfort" (p. 238). Schumpeter (1942/1976) lauded the gales of "creative destruction" unleashed by the capitalist businesses, as new opportunities and information are continually discovered by entrepreneurs which provided temporary advantage—yielding profits—and continual change and improvement. Entrepreneurs, for the Austrians, can create such innovation because they are masters of knowledge regarding their particular situation. Much of this knowledge is tacit and virtually unknowable to others. The portion of his or her knowledge that is pertinent to others, however, is transmitted through market prices. Austrian economists claim that it would be ludicrous for any individual, government, or other agency to presume to be able to apprehend all information, since information is nearly infinite, is constantly being invented or changing, is subjective, and is dispersed. No agent, then, should be allowed to constrain the action of the entrepreneur or the functioning of the price system. To do so would be to stifle efficiency, suppress entrepreneurial energy, distort price information, and consequently retard progress—perhaps precipitating economic crises. This, combined with an entrenched fear of overly powerful government, led Hayek (1944) to conclude that the strict economic controls and public works projects advocated by Keynes would lead countries down "the road to serfdom." "Development," for the Austrians, needs the entrepreneur, and regulation inhibits his or her heroic creativity, and misdirects his or her energy.

Culture is not a prevalent theme in Austrian thought. We are all entrepreneurs in this thinking. Some of us simply prefer current consumption to future discovery, or may not have the talent necessary to be successful. People have set interests, they,

> tend to discover that which interests them and, hence, if they are free to accomplish their ends and promote their interests both of these [ends and interests] will act as incentives to motivate them in the exercise of entrepreneurship. (de Soto 2008, p. 24)

Culture has not crept in here to impact these interests. Insufficient information about the world has, as Menger (1871/1950) argues, caused traditional peoples to misinterpret the "causal connection with the satisfaction of human needs" connected with certain objects and therefore to falsely value things such as "charms," "divining rods," and "love potions" (p. 53). But these are informational problems, not differences in cultural value systems. Traditional societies consist of individuals with specific interests just as do modern capitalistic ones. People's preferences, it seems, remain stable for Austrian economists—it is the constellation of prices, information, and institutions that changes, resulting in different behaviours (Menger 1871/1950).

Conclusion

As this chapter has hopefully revealed, classic liberal political economy is a more diverse and sometimes critical field than has been often admitted. Adam Smith's work stands as the most obvious example of this complexity of thought. Although his defining work abstracted from this, Smith repeatedly held space for both culture and ethics to enter political economic analysis. Similarly, Smith was concerned with the tendency of market-based economies to generate extremities of inequality, which would ultimately corrupt democratic systems if left unchecked.

These substantive complexities within liberal economic thought were slowly replaced by simplified mathematics as the discipline continued following Smith's death. The idea of development moved away from human flourishing and towards economic growth. Markets were increasingly viewed as ideal forms, and humans were increasingly viewed as insatiable units of consumption whose only important communication was performed through price-based market interactions. Eventually, instead of being the communicative act that continually re-formed desires and proclivities, culture became thought of as unimportant at best. At worst, culture was viewed as a traditionalist trap that locked primordial, change-resistant groups into enduring states of poverty. As the next chapter will show, many of these enduring assumptions would be challenged by critical political economists and sociologists, who would introduce concepts such as ideology while returning to Smith's concerns with inequality.

References

Arrow, K. J., & Debreu, G. (1954). Existence of an Equilibrium for a Competitive Economy. *Econometrica, 22*(3), 265.

Bastiat, F. (1850/1964). *Economic Harmonies*. Princeton, NJ: D. Van Nostrand.

Bentham, J. (1781/2000). *An Introduction to the Principles of Morals and Legislation*. Kitchener: Batoche Books.

von Böhm-Bawerk, E. (1895). Professor Clarke's Views on the Genesis of Capital. *Quarterly Journal of Economics, 9*, 113–131.

De Soto, J. H. (2008). *The Theory of Dynamic Efficiency*. Routledge.

Deane, P. (1978). *Evolution of Economic Ideas*. London and New York: Cambridge University Press.

Escobar, A. (1999, November). The Invention of Development. *Current History*, 382–386.

Escobar, A. (2005). Economics and the Space of Modernity: Tales of Market, Production and Labour. *Cultural Studies, 19*(2), 139–175.

Foucault, M. (1969/2002). *The Archeology of Knowledge*. London and New York: Routledge.

Hayek, F. A. (1944). *The Road to Serfdom*. London: Routledge & Kegan Paul.

Hayek, F. A. (1945). The Use of Knowledge in Society. *American Economic Review, 35*(4), 525.

Heilbroner, R. (1996). The Embarrassment of Economics. *Challenge, 39*(6), 46–49.

Heilbroner, R. (1999). *Teachings from the Worldly Philosophy*. New York and London: W.W. Norton and Company.

Hunt, E. K. (2002). *History of Economic Thought: A Critical Perspective*. New York: ME Sharpe.

Jevons, W. S. (1871/1882). *The Theory of Political Economy*. London: Macmillan & Co.

Keynes, J. M. (1920). *The Economic Consequences of Peace*. London: Harcourt Brace and Howe.

Keynes, J. M. (1936/2006). *The General Theory of Employment, Interest and Money*. New Delhi: Atlantic.

Keynes, J. M. (1994). Economic Model Construction and Econometrics. In *The Philosophy of Economics: An Anthology* (2nd ed., pp. 286–288). Cambridge: Cambridge University Press.

Marshall, A. (1890/1920). *Principles of Economics*. London: Macmillan & Co.

Martinussen, J. (1997). *Society, State & Market A guide to competing theories of development*. London & New York: Zed Books.

Menger, C. (1871/1950). *Principles of Economics*. New York: Free Press.

Mill, J. S. (1909). *Principles of Political Economy … Edited with an Introduction by WJ Ashley*. Longmans & Company.

von Mises, L. (1949/1996). *Human Action: A Treatise on Economics*. New York: Foundation for Economic Education.

Polanyi, K. (1944/2001). *The Great Transformation: The Political and Economic Origins of Our Time*. Boston: Beacon Press.

Say, J. B. (1821/1863). *A Treatise on Political Economy*. Philadelphia: Lippincott.

Schumpeter, J. A. (1942/1976). *Capitalism, Socialism, and Democracy*. New York: Harper Collins.

Senior, N. (1836/1928). *Industrial Efficiency and Social Economy*. New York: Holt.

Smith, A. (1759/1790). *The Theory of Moral Sentiments*. London: A. Millar.

Smith, A. (1776). *The Wealth of Nations*. New York: Bantam Dell.

Walras, L. (1892/1996). Geometrical Theory of the Determination of Prices. In R. Heilbroner (Ed.), *Teachings from the Worldly Philosophy* (pp. 221–227). NY: WW Norton.

von Weiser, F. (1911/1994). The Nature and Substance of Theoretical Economics. In I. M. Kirzner (Ed.), *Classics in Austrian Economics: A Sampling in the History of a Tradition*. London: William Pickering.

CHAPTER 3

Culture in Critical and Sociological Thought

Marxian Political Economy

Marx was a contemporary of Mill, but it is not clear that the latter had ever heard of the former or read his work (Hunt 2002, p. 204). Marx, on the other hand, thought of himself as a rival of Mill in that he was offering a radical revision of classical political economy to counterpoise Mill's bourgeois liberalism (Deane 1978). The men did have much in common intellectually, however. From classical political economy, both Marx and Mill imported the labour theory of value, belief in the falling rate of profit in capitalist industry, ideas about technologically induced unemployment, and the tendency to begin the analysis of economy with the assumption of three groups: landlords, capitalists (bourgeoisie), and labourers (proletariat). Marx, like all the classical political economists, was a holistic social scientist of the economy, as explained by Deane (1978),

> The salient characteristic that Marx shared with Adam Smith, Jeremy Bentham, and JS Mill and which distinguished him from Ricardo … was that he was a philosopher first and an economist second—a social scientist rather than a 'pure' economist. For Marx, political economy was merely one branch … in the study of human social behaviour. (p. 126)

Perhaps, then, it is more useful to note the strong division between Marx and the neoclassical economists that would appear after his death, than to overly emphasize a schism between him and the classical political

T. MacNeill, *Indigenous Cultures and Sustainable Development in Latin America*, https://doi.org/10.1007/978-3-030-37023-7_3

economists. The ahistorical, reductionist, methodological individualism of the neoclassical economists seems much more at odds with Marxian method than is the historically, politically, and ethically infused method of the political economists.

Despite his aversion to Ricardian economic reductionism, the theoretical cornerstone of Marx's work—the labour theory of value—was imported from Ricardo. He then mixed this theory of value with the Hegelian concept that history is propelled by conflict. The result was a materialist concept of history. Whereas Hegel's dialectic posited that social change stemmed from a conflict over ideas as the world was apprehended in different ways, Marx created a dialectic method that assumed the opposite—that history is driven by inherent conflict within the mode of material production, and that ideas emerge essentially as reflections of this material arrangement.

For Marx, "development" in Europe had been a process of historical change that was rooted in the social mode of production. In *The German Ideology* (2001), he argued that history passed through a number of phases. The first was a tribal phase—where production and consumption were based on kinship relationships and "the natural division of labour existing in the family" (p. 44). Population growth, however, intensified the aggregate "growth of wants," providing an impulse for increased trade and the establishment of a system of slavery (p. 44). Complexity, class divisions, conquest, slavery, and serfdom were intensified as European societies passed through periods of "primitive communism" and feudalism (pp. 44–46). The seeds for the transition to capitalism were planted in the feudal period—and this transition was largely made possible by the exploitation of colonial territories and the people that inhabited them. As Marx expressed in *Das Kapital*:

> The discovery of gold and silver in America, the extirpation, enslavement and entombment in mines of the aboriginal population, the beginning of the conquest and looting of the East Indies, the turning of Africa into a warren for the commercial hunting of black-skins, signalled the rosy dawn of the era of capitalist production. (Marx 1867/1961, p. 751)

The bulk of the wealth expropriated through colonization was amassed by a merchant class. This process of amassing private wealth, along with the creation of a class of landless labourers, was called by Marx, the process of "primitive accumulation" (Marx 1867/1961, Part VIII). The warlike feudal aristocracy became increasingly indebted to the merchant class, and, as a result, the latter experienced increased political power. This, according to Marx, culminated in multiple revolutions that sought to replace the feudal system with one based on private property during the seventeenth and eighteenth centuries. The resultant privatization of feudal lands required the displacement of serfs who had no means left for survival beyond the sale of their own labour power—serfs, then, were transformed into a class of landless labourers:

> The spoliation of the Church's property, the fraudulent alienation of the state domains, the robbery of common lands, the usurpation of feudal and clan property, and its transformation into private property under the circumstance of reckless terrorism, were just so many idyllic methods of primitive accumulation. They conquered the field for capitalist agriculture, made the soil part and parcel of capital, and created for the town industries the necessary supply of a "free" ... proletariat. (Marx 1867/1961, pp. 732–733)

For Marx, the existence of this landless labour force, the sanctification of private property, the accumulation of wealth from colonial pillage, and the productive technological innovations of the industrial revolution were the necessary preconditions for the existence of a capitalist society. Due largely to his adoption of the labour theory of value, however, Marx predicted that this system would end in a culmination of repeated crises that were rooted in its own internal contradictions. The culmination of these crises would see the marginalized, impoverished, and numerous proletariat expropriate capitalist industry, thus ushering in an era of socialism which would eventually transform itself into communism (Marx 1867/1961, Part VIII).

Starkly brandishing the enlightenment positivism that he, along with his contemporaries, was immersed in, Marx explained of his major contribution, *Das Kapital*, "it is the ultimate aim of this work to lay bare the economic law of motion of modern society" (p. 10). This method is evident in the teleology presented earlier. Marx's positivism did not, however, begin with an unqualified assumption about human nature similar to that which is embodied in homo economicus. Quite the reverse, he assumed that human activity was conditioned extensively by the material environment in which he existed, and that this material environment resulted from the technological method with which society produced the goods that it consumed. Deane (1978) explains regarding the seeming veracious greed of the capitalist; in the Marxian model, "accumulation is stimulated not by an innate psychological propensity on part of entrepreneurs, but by the social pressures of competitive society" (139). As Marx argued, the capitalist "shares with the miser the passion for wealth. But that which in the miser is a mere idiosyncrasy, is in the capitalist the effect of the social mechanism of which he is but one of the wheels" (1867/1961, pp. 236). Furthermore, regarding both the working class and the capitalist class, Marx and Engels assert in *The Communist Manifesto* (1848/1965) that the capitalist system made possible,

> no other nexus between man and man than naked self-interest, than callous "cash payment." It has drowned the most heavenly ecstasies of religious fervour, of chivalrous enthusiasm, of philistine sentimentalism, in the icy water of egotistical calculation. (p. 15)

For Marx, then, self-interested behaviour was a cultural expression of capitalist relations of production.

Culture entered Marx's theory in two additional but interrelated ways—through the concept of ideology and the concept of fetishism. For Marx (1846/1968), ideology represented,

> ideas which increasingly take on the form of universality. For each new class which puts itself on the place of the ruling class before it is compelled, merely in order to carry through its aim, to present its interest as the common interest of all the members of society, that is, expressed in ideal form: it has to give its ideas the form of universality, and present them as the only rational, universally valid ones. (chpt 1A, para. 21)

Which ideas would become dominant in such a way depended entirely on the social structure of production in a given society. Since, "the class which has the means of mental production at its disposal, consequently also controls the means of mental production," it follows that "the ideas of the ruling class are in every epoch the ruling ideas" (ibid., para. 1). In such a way, Marx argued, the sanctity of private property, and liberal values in general, became part of the "hegemony of the spirit" that existed in capitalist society. These ideas were naturalized—rendered unquestionable—even though they so obviously (for Marx) benefitted only one class at the expense of another (ibid., para. 25). Ideology, then, was an image of society that was produced by the powerful and internalized by all (except for critical thinkers such as Marx himself apparently). It presented a mythical conception of reality that obscured to the proletariat the true nature of the exploitation that it was suffering, and called upon the working class to act voluntarily in the interest of the bourgeoisie and therefore against its own interest. Escape from this mystical snare was not possible through thought, due to Marx's assumption that it was the economic base that dictated through itself. The end of this delusion would be assured, however, as the contradiction in the material relations of production yielded the system's inevitable collapse (Marx 1867/1961).

Marx's concept of fetishism is also important if we are to explore the nature of culture in development theory. The period of high capitalist development that is to precede socialism, as we have noted, is typified in Marxian thought by an unprecedented capacity for the industrial production of commodities. These commodities, however, take on a mystical form, according to Marx, when they enter the sphere of exchange. Regarding the commodity:

> So far as it is a value in use, there is nothing mysterious about it ... It is clear as noon-day that, that man, by his industry, changes the forms of the materials furnished by nature, in such a way as to make them useful to him ... But, so soon as it steps forth as a commodity, it is changed into something transcendent. It no longer stands with its feet on the ground, but, in relation to all other commodities. (Qtd in Heilbroner 1999, p. 165)

Upon encountering a commodity, a consumer is estranged from any knowledge of the nature of its production, and importantly, from the labour involved in its creation. Since Marx assumes all use value to be the measure of the labour used up in a commodity's production, it follows that the consumer has no means with which to judge the true value of the good. The commodity, then, has no obvious relation to the materiality of its production and becomes suspended in a relative system in which its value becomes arbitrarily designated. The exchange value which emerges is a "fetish"—a phantasm that is disconnected from the tangible reality of use value. Furthermore, since humans in a capitalist society come to relate to one another more and more solely through the purchase of commodities, they increasingly live life in relation to the sphere of exchange, with little understanding of the realm of production. As a result, they come to see their existence falsely as a competition with others for a limited supply of goods (Marx 1867/1961, Chpt. 1, Sct. 4).

To summarize Marx's ideas as they relate to our present topic, he sees development as a unidirectional ascent from tribal society through feudal and capitalist epochs, finally to socialism and then to communism. All this movement is propelled by contradiction inherent in each stage. This transition is typified, at least until the socialist period, with the expansion of industrial output, but the change to capitalism that made this possible in Europe was predicated on the exploitation of colonized territories and peoples. Culture appears in Marx's thought as a form of "false consciousness," to use Engels' term (qtd in Eagleton 1991, p. 89). It is a naturalized worldview that supports the maintenance of a system of exploitation, it is a natural-seeming selfish form of action that is in fact the result of the conditioning of a system of production, and finally it is an imaginary relation to commodities which serves to obscure their true values of commodities. Culture, in Marx's thought, appears to us either as a mere reflection of an underlying power relation which compels humans to act against their own interests, or as a fanciful cloak which obscures from us a view of the hard reality of material production.

Marxian Theories of Imperialism

In *The Communist Manifesto*, *Gundrisse*, and *Capital*, Marx noted the tendency for capitalist nations to expand colonial territories in search of cheaper resources and to relieve negative pressures related to overproduction of commodities, through the establishment of new markets. This thesis was expanded upon later by Marxist scholars—most notably Hobson, Luxemburg, and Lenin. Marx had described the vital role that early colonialism played in providing the means of "primitive accumulation" that made European capitalism possible in the sixteenth, seventeenth, and early 8eighteenth centuries. Hunt (2002) explains, however, that this period was followed with a cooling of the drive to conquest as capitalist systems became entrenched and increasingly concentrated in the colonial centres themselves. In the final third of the nineteenth century, however, all of that changed as Great Britain, France, Germany, Belgium, Russia, Italy, and the United States embarked on intense and violent colonial expansion throughout Africa and Asia, and the Americas.

It was within this context that perhaps the three most notable Marxian thinkers of the late nineteenth and early twentieth century published their work on imperialism. The theories of Hobson, Luxemburg, and Lenin are remarkably similar in most respects.[1] All claimed that the pressure for colonial expansion was a symptom of the contradictions inherent in the capitalism system. Hobson (1965), like Keynes, argued that the extreme concentration of wealth that had occurred in capitalist Europe and North America created an unstable economic situation. He argued that poor workers did not have enough wealth to purchase the commodities that were produced, and, since the wealthy could not possibly spend all of their huge earnings, there was at once a glut of consumer goods on European markets and excess capital available for investment. Hobson argued that this pressure led directly to colonialism:

> Everywhere appear excessive powers of production, excessive capital in search of investment. It is admitted by all businessmen that growth of the powers of production in their country exceeds the growth in consumption, that more goods can be produced than can be sold for profit, and that more capital exists than can find remunerative investment. (p. 81)

As a result, Luxemburg (1972) adds, "capitalism needs … a market for its surplus value, a source of supply for its means of production and … a reservoir of labour power for its wage system" (pp. 368–369). Colonial expansion serves this purpose, but it is necessarily a culturally and materially destructive action as Luxemburg explains:

> Capital is faced with difficulties because vast tracts of the globe's surface are in the possession of social organizations that have no desire for commodity exchange or cannot, because of the entire social structure and the forms of ownership, offer for sale the productive forces in which capital is primarily interested.… Since the primitive associations of the natives are the strongest protection for their social organizations and for their material bases for existence, capital must begin by planning for the systematic destruction and annihilation of all non-capitalist social units which obstruct its development. (pp. 370–371)

Wealthy capitalists, argues Hobson (1965), whose economic power and political influence put them "in a unique position to manipulate the policy of nations" (p. 53), pressure imperial governments to "create new public debts, float new companies, and to cause constant considerable

[1] They differ in their opinions on whether capitalism can be tamed through reform, or must be dismantled though revolution.

fluctuations of values" (p. 53), and, finally, to generate "an enthusiasm for expansion" (p. 59). Lenin (1967), demonizing the banking industry primarily in this respect, agrees, writing that,

> As long as capitalism remains what it is, surplus capital will be utilized not for the purpose of raising the standard of living of the masses in a given country, for this would mean a decline in profits for the capitalists, but for the purpose of increasing profits by exporting capital abroad to the backward countries. In these backward countries profits are usually high, for capital is scarce, the price of land is relatively low, wages are low, raw materials are cheap. (p. 724)

Thus, according to Hobson, Luxemburg, and Lenin, capitalism breeds violent colonial expansion, and this, in turn, incites cultural destruction.

Gramsci

Another important expansion on Marxian thought was introduced by Gramsci (1957). As we discussed earlier, Marx had assumed that the cultural beliefs, ideas, and moors in a society were more or less a mere reflection of the power structures in its economic base. Ideology, in this perception, served only the dominant class in the maintenance of its power. Gramsci certainly agreed that this ideological hegemony tended to serve the maintenance of existing structural inequalities, but accorded a degree of autonomy to the world of ideas vis-à-vis the economic base. Ideological dominance, according to Gramsci, was often necessary for a dominant class to maintain its power. The ideological realm could, then, become a field in which the subaltern could resist its own marginalization. Despite the immense power the "dominant class" has in "maintaining, defending and developing the theoretical or ideological 'front'," Gramsci (1985) argued, an innovative subaltern group could counteract this with its own ideological production via the creation of,

> The spirit of scission, in other words the progressive acquisition of the consciousness of its own historical personality, a spirit of scission that must aim to spread itself from the protagonist class to the classes that are its potential allies—all this requires a complex ideological labour. (p. 389)

Gramsci's formulation is important because it introduces for us the space of "civil society"—a third sector that is interwoven with the state and the economy. Ideology and culture are the same things for Gramsci; these exist in this third sector, and so do ideological or cultural resistance. Resistance in the third sector would become central to many conflict-conscious concepts of development that would emerge later in the twentieth century.

Sociological Approaches

With Compte's (1856) attempt to establish the discipline of sociology as a form of "social physics," an alternative way of viewing the relationship between progress and culture became available. The early sociological approaches turned the economistic depiction of human society and economy on his head. Sociologists tended to refuse the depiction of economy as a sphere that was separable from society. They also rejected the idea that economy or society was little more than the resultant of the actions of individuals or groups which acted to satisfy their own pre-ordained interests. Ideas of progress remained deep-rooted in these arguments, but culture was given a leading role in its actualization. The most important amongst these early sociological thinkers were Emile Durkheim and Max Weber.

Emile Durkheim

Durkheim speaks of culture in terms of the "moral" or "social" forces which actively shape each member of society. As a result, the existence of an asocial individual such as the homo economicus of neoclassical thought is considered to be a misnomer. "Our tendencies," writes Durkheim (1895/2003), "are not developed by ourselves but come to us from without" (p. 128). The set of needs, tastes, and wants that would be interpreted by economists as a stable utility function of the individual is, for Durkheim, "a group condition repeated in the individual because imposed on him. It is found in each part because it exists in the whole, rather than in the whole because it exists in the parts" (p. 130). Durkheim (1893/2000) holds that, if there is a dominant tendency in human nature, it is a predisposition to build solidarity between members of a society—a solidarity which gives form and meaning to the world. Individuals, their values, tastes, beliefs, and habits are the product of this solidarity (p. 43).

Durkheim (1893/2000) discusses two important types of solidarity which link the idea of culture directly to the idea of progress. "Mechanical solidarity" exists in "traditional" or primitive" societies. This solidarity is based on sameness, as each member carries out more or less the same social roles as all others. As "population is continually becoming more concentrated," resulting from the "the formation and development of towns" and an increase in "the number and speed of the means of communication," a new, more intense type of solidarity becomes possible (ibid., pp. 48–49). With this newly emergent "organic solidarity," a division of labour occurs. This division does not, however, imply a diminishment of solidarity in general—rather the opposite. The division of labour, Durkheim argues, has as its main purpose a deepening of social solidarity, for it allows individuals and groups of individuals to act as separate specialized organs within a greater social organism. This organic form of solidarity, which is established most completely in modern Europe and North America, is, for Durkheim, the evolutionary end to which human societies progress. He argued that "to struggle against nature," as human density increases, "we need to possess more vigorous faculties, deploy more productive energies" (p. 38). The division of labour, therefore, becomes unavoidable as human societies progress. With all biological life forms, "an organism occupies the more exalted place in the animal hierarchy the more specialized its functions are" (p. 38). "The division of labour in society" then,

> appears no more than a specialized form of this general development. In conforming to this law societies apparently yield to a movement that arose long before they existed and which sweeps in the same direction the whole of the living world. (Ibid.)

Social progress as depicted by Durkheim (1893/2000), then, is a natural evolutionary move from simple (traditional) to complex (modern) society. Spurred by demographic growth, society advances into a kind of superorganism with an increasing number of specialized organs, and deepening interdependence. Economic growth and increased industrialization result from this change, but are not the goal of it. These things are secondary effects—positive symptoms of the social need to increase solidarity. Since needs and wants, for Durkheim, are set by society, an innate drive to acquire more material goods cannot possibly drive or define social progress. This, for Durkheim, is the point on which the political economists tended to err. Their resultant analyses have been misconstrued as a result. The discipline of sociology must, therefore, be established as the preeminent social science in providing the policy prescriptions that will guide social progress according to Durkheim.

Max Weber

In the work of Weber, one does not find mention of a natural and inevitable historical progression from a less desirable state to a more desirable one. The word "progress," in fact, usually appears in quotation marks in his work (1919, p. 78). One does, however, find a detailed historical interpretation of the way in which modern capitalist bureaucratic society came to exist. Certainly, in *The Protestant Ethic and the Spirit of Capitalism*, Weber (1905) concedes that the appropriation of material means of production, free markets, mechanization, and a particular legal regime all contributed causally to the rise of capitalist society, but he holds that these were necessary, but not sufficient, conditions. Many civilizations had existed before with these traits, he argued, and yet they did not develop into modern capitalist states. The key input into the rise of capitalism, for Weber, was a particular cultural manifestation—a capitalistic spirit.

This spirit was rooted originally in religion. In the Old Testament, Weber (1905) reminds us that "wealth" in itself was considered "morally suspect" (p. 68). With the rise of Protestantism which preceded the industrial revolution, however, this association was subtly changed. With Protestantism it was believed that a man was assigned a calling by God—labour in His service. It was believed, specifically for the Calvinists and Puritans, that individual ascendance into heaven was preordained. Success in a calling came to stand as proof of predestination. "Wealth," Weber suggested, came to be understood as "bad ethically only in so far as it is a temptation to idleness and sinful enjoyment of life, and its acquisition is bad only when it is the purpose of later living merrily without care" (p. 70). "But as a performance of duty in a calling," Weber continues, "it is not only morally permissible, but actually enjoined" (ibid.). "Favour in the sight of God" became demonstrable in "private profitableness," for if God "shows one of His elect a chance of profit, he must do it with a purpose. Hence the faithful Christian must follow the calling by taking advantage of the opportunity" (ibid.).

At the same time, however, frugality was religiously encouraged. "Protestant asceticism," Weber (1905) continued, "acted powerfully against the spontaneous enjoyment of possession; it restricted consumption, especially of luxuries" (p. 72). This religiously initiated frugality mixed with industriousness, Weber argues, provided the conditions for the inception of the capitalist order:

> When the limitation of consumption is combined with this release of acquisitive activity, the inevitable practical result is obvious: accumulation of capital through ascetic compulsion to save. The restraints which were imposed upon the consumption of wealth naturally served to increase it by making possible the productive investment of capital. (Ibid.)

Modern rationalistic-secular capitalist society proceeded from the cultural prerequisite of Protestantism. "The Puritan outlook," Weber argued, "stood at the cradle of economic man" (ibid.). "Today the spirit of religious asceticism," he continued, "has escaped from the cage. But victorious capitalism, since it rests on mechanical foundations, needs its support no longer" (p. 73). This secular capitalism was a snare, according to Weber (1919). The human creature, usually fantastically engaged with mutable culture, became subdued by a capitalist bureaucratic system. Weber lamented that mankind had become trapped in a bureaucratic rationalized intellectualism which,

> means that principally there are no mysterious incalculable forces that come into play, but rather that one can, in principle, master all things by calculation. This means that the world is disenchanted. One need no longer have recourse to magical means in order to master or implore the spirits, as did the savage, for whom such mysterious powers existed. Technical means and calculations perform the service. (p. 78)

As we will see, this sudden disappearance of culture in the magical hands of capitalist scientific modernity, although lamented by Weber, would become central to early forms of developmentalist theory in the mid-twentieth century.

Veblen and the Institutional Economists

It may count to some as somewhat of a heresy to list the institutional economists here under the heading of "sociological approaches to development." Indeed, the institutionalists, from the school's founder Thorstein

Veblen to later proponents of "old" institutionalism such as Robert Frank, were and are all trained as economists who worked/work in economics departments. It is their theoretical assumptions, however, that set them apart from orthodox economists and placed them within the realm of sociology. All economic action, for institutionalists, is conditioned, even determined, by the place of the actor within institutions. An institution, according to Commons (1931),

> ranges all the way from unorganized custom to the many organized going concerns, such as the family, the corporation, the trade association, the trade union, the reserve system, the state. (p. 649)

As a result of this thinking, the institutionalists condone a shift in economic thinking. As Commons explains,

> It is this shift from commodities and individuals to transactions and working rules of collective action that marks the transition from the classical and hedonic schools to the institutional schools of economic thinking. The shift is a change in the ultimate unit of economic investigation. The classic and hedonic economists, with their communistic and anarchistic offshoots, founded their theories on the relation of man to nature, but institutionalism is a relation of man to man. (p. 652)

The problem for many is that to formulate economic theories as social relations between human beings is to do sociology. It is for this reason that Talcot Parsons (1937) would denounce institutional economics as a field. In fact, most institutional economists, when pressed, have had difficulty differentiating their field from the economic sociology that was initiated by Weber and Durkheim, and vice versa. The fields remain quite insulated from one another, regardless (Velthuis, 1999). Perhaps the placement of this entry will go some small way towards the erosion of this unnecessary divide.

Culture is the fundamental institution for institutional economists. This is evident in Veblen's (1899/1994) foundational work on modern consumer society. Such a society, argued Veblen (not unlike Adam Smith), is based on emulative action in which the object of the economic actor is to demonstrate success in life through the consumption of goods and services of a quality and quantity equal to or greater than other members of the social group. Quality of such good is socially defined, or "canonized" as often as it is an objective feature. Human action, for Veblen, was propelled not by an insatiable set of stable wants as the neoclassical economists insisted, but by a positional game whose goal was status and belonging in a particular type of society.

The particular society that Veblen was concerned with emerged from a "predatory," competitive, "barbarian" culture, as it achieved technology that allowed for the production of goods in excess of the amount required for survival (pp. 1–6). Veblen argued that to display status, it was necessary to show the absence of a need to work in order to acquire the means of subsistence. Occupations, such as lawyer or professor, correspondingly gained prestige, and those such as farmer or factory worker lost it. In fact, the former were not so much occupations for Veblen, as shows of "conspicuous leisure" (p. 23). Similarly, the famous phrase "conspicuous consumption" was coined by Veblen in order to describe the use of goods and services with the intent of displaying their non-necessary nature (for subsistence) and, in so doing, to display one's place in a social structure (p. 43).

Development, defined as an increase in material production, is constant, yet largely unexplained in the account—its advance is accorded to technological change (which is unexplained). Because of emulative effects, however, development that has the aim to satisfy human needs through increased production has little use for Veblen. "Evidently" he argues,

> a satiation of the average or general desire for wealth is out of the question.... [N]o general increase of the community's wealth can make any approach to satiating this need, the ground of which is the desire of everyone to excel everyone else in the accumulation of goods. (p. 39)

Later, Dusenberry (1949) would argue that an egalitarian redistribution of income would quell competitive consumption, decrease waste, and increase contentment. This would reduce what he called the "demonstration effect" that caused unhappiness as one individual witnessed and wished to emulate the consumption practices of others. Later, Nurkse (1957) would relate this directly to the development of formerly colonized nations by introducing the "international demonstration effect," arguing that,

> when people come into contact with superior goods or superior patterns of consumption, with new articles or new ways of meeting old wants they are

> apt to feel after a while a certain restlessness and dissatisfaction. Their knowledge is extended, their imagination stimulated; new desires are aroused. (p. 112)

Nurkse's thesis was presented as an analysis of a phenomenon he believed to be blocking capital accumulation, and therefore material production. It should be noted however that Nurkse's, Duesenberry's, and Veblen's work introduced an uncertainty in economic theory regarding the meaning of progress. This was perhaps an unavoidable result of the insistence that human wants are culturally conditioned, since it begs the question: is it more prudent to increase production to increase well-being, or to change wants? This kind of critical questioning of the use of material production was not present in Marxism, nor neoclassicalism, nor even in the sociology of Weber or Durkheim.

The institutionalist critique would lose force quickly, however. Although it was actually the most prominent school in the field of economics in the early twentieth century, institutionalism would virtually disappear until the end of that century.[2] This fall from grace was likely initiated by both the rise of neoclassicalism in economics departments and by Parson's chastising of the institutionalists for overstepping the bounds of economics and wandering into the sociological realm (Velthuis 1999).

Conclusion

It was the purpose of Chaps. 2 and 3 to explore the rich intellectual traditions that underlie the post-WWII development thinking, which will be discussed in the next two chapters. Particular attention was paid to the ways in which the concepts of culture and development appeared in these traditions. This pre-WWII thought was divided into four major groups for the purpose of this exposition: classical political economy, neoclassical economics, (the topic of Chap. 2), critical political economy, and sociological approaches (the topic of the current chapter). For the classical political economists, development clearly implied an increase in material wealth, but this was a quest that was to be tempered with ethics, and the

[2] This is thought to generally be true as economics departments became satiated with neoclassicalism. But the very notable prevalence of institutional economists such as John Kenneth Galbraith and Robert Heilbroner, throughout the twentieth century, must be noted as exceptions to this rule.

knowledge that social conflict may emerge from divergent class interests. Human behaviour was depicted as atomistic and self-interested in the economic realm, but this was realized to be an abstraction from the cultural situation of human values, and this cultural situation was actively explored by the classical political economists themselves.

The marginal revolution, Marx's critique, and the inception of the science of sociology emerged at approximately the same time. This may be viewed as the splitting of the older holistic study of political economy into three different traditions. To the neoclassical economists went the classical political economist's appreciation for the market and the tendency to sever economic action from culture and ethics. To the Marxists went the labour theory of value and the social conflict that was implied. To the sociologists went the larger questions of the ways in which social interaction and cultural situation formed human values and economic action. All inherited the concept that human societies progress as they gain material wealth through technological innovation (although this was qualified substantially by the institutionalists). Not to do so was, for all, to be stuck in a "barbarian," "primal," or "traditional" form of existence. In this form of society, it was assumed humans were subject to the whims of nature instead of dominating it to their own ends. Such a life had been described to all of these thinkers by one of their most notable intellectual forbearers, Thomas Hobbes (1651), as being "nasty, brutish and short" (p. 52). There is little wonder, then, that each if the theorists discussed in Chaps. 2 and 3 tacitly or explicitly defined progress as any movement away from this condition. As we will see in the next chapter, this definition will be refined substantially by the post-WWII development theorists.

References

Commons, J. R. (1931). Institutional Economics. *American Economic Review, 21*, 648–657.

Compte, A. (1856). *Cours de Philosophie Positive.* London: Bell.

Deane, P. (1978). *Evolution of Economic Ideas.* London and New York: Cambridge University Press.

Durkheim, E. (1893/2000). "Sociological Method" from The Rules of Sociological Method. In G. Bailey & N. Gayle (Eds.), *Social Theory: Essential Readings.* New York: Oxford.

Durkheim, E. (1895/2003). The Division of Labour in Society. In J. T. Roberts & A. Hite (Eds.), *From Modernization to Globalization: Perspectives on Development and Social Change*. Malden, MA: Blackwell.
Dusenberry, J. S. (1949). *Income, Saving and the Theory of Consumer Behavior*. Cambridge, MA: Harvard University Press.
Eagleton, T. (1991). *Ideology: An Introduction*. London: Verso.
Gramsci, A. (1957/1971). *Selections from the Prison Notebooks*. New York: International Publishers.
Gramsci, A. (1985). *Selections from the Cultural Writings* (D. Forgacs & G. Nowell, Eds.). London: Lawrence and Wishart.
Heilbroner, R. (1999). *Teachings from the Worldly Philosophy*. New York and London: W.W. Norton and Company.
Hobbes, T. (1651). *Leviathan*. Glasgow 1974.
Hobson, J. A. (1965). *Imperialism: A Study* (Vol. 103). University of Michigan Press.
Hunt, E. K. (2002). *History of Economic Thought: A Critical Perspective*. New York: ME Sharpe.
Lenin, V. I. (1967). *Lenin on the National and Colonial Questions: Three Articles*. Foreign Languages Press.
Luxemburg, R. (1972). The Accumulation of Capital: An Anti-critique. Imperialism and the Accumulation of Capital. *Monthly Review Press*.
Marx, K. (1846/1968). *The German Ideology*. Delhi: Progress Publishers.
Marx, K. (1867/1961). *Capital* (Vol. 1). Moscow: Foreign Languages.
Marx, K. (2001). *The German Ideology Part One, with Selections from Parts Two and Three, Together with Marx's "Introduction to a Critique of Political Economy"*. New York: International Publishers.
Marx, K., & Engels, F. (1848/1965). The Communist Manifesto. In A. P. Mendel (Ed.), *Essential Works of Marxism*. New York: Bantam.
Nurkse, R. (1957). *Problems of Capital Formation in Underdeveloped Countries*. Oxford: Blackwell.
Parsons, T. (1937). *The Structure of Social Action*. New York: McGraw-Hill.
Veblen, T. (1899/1994). *The Theory of the Leisure Class*. New York: Dover Publications.
Velthuis, O. (1999). The Changing Relationship Between Economic Sociology and Institutional Economics. *American Journal of Economics and Sociology, 58*(4), 629–649.
Weber, M. (1905/2000). The Protestant Ethic and the Spirit of Capitalism. In J. Roberts & A. Hite (Eds.), *From Modernization to Globalization: Perspectives on Development and Social Change*. Oxford: Blackwell.
Weber, M. (1919/2000). Science as a Vocation. In R. Roberts & A. Hite (Eds.), *From Modernization to Globalization: Perspectives on Development and Social Change*. Oxford: Blackwell.

CHAPTER 4

Culture in Development Theory

During the early- and mid-twentieth century, strong nationalist struggles in the colonial territories of the European powers gained increasing strength. By the 1960s, as a result, most former colonies of Africa and Asia had gained official independence (Chamberlain 1999). Amidst the hopeful energy of the postcolonial world, intellectuals, primarily in the former colonial powers, took on the task of designing plans which would assist the newly emergent nations to achieve the levels of affluence that had been attained in Europe and the United States. A worldview that consisted of colonies and colonizers was replaced by a worldview that was based on the premise that there existed "developed" nations and correspondingly "underdeveloped" ones. In the mid-twentieth century, it became increasingly the task of the great technocratic minds in the governments and universities of the former colonial powers to help the "underdeveloped" to become "developed" (Escobar 1994; Tucker 1999). The purpose of this chapter is to locate the idea of culture in the development theory that emerged in this period, and that which followed it into the twenty-first century.

The overall purpose of this undertaking, you will remember, was to search for the source of the uncomfortable silence I experienced when trying to communicate with a professor of neoclassical development economics about the idea of culture. I suggested that this silence was but a singular example of the many such silences that pervade, and impede, development thinking in general. Proposing that this silence had something to do with

T. MacNeill, *Indigenous Cultures and Sustainable Development in Latin America*, https://doi.org/10.1007/978-3-030-37023-7_4

the evolution of disciplinary thinking regarding development and its relation to culture, I set out to explore this thought as it evolved in from the late eighteenth to early twentieth centuries. The story began with classical political economy and its holistic treatment of questions regarding wealth creation in national economies. We then saw what I suggested to be a splitting of this great discipline into three schools—neoclassical economics, critical political economy, and sociology. This taxonomic classification will be retained in the work of the current chapter with the exception of the last school of thought in the list.

The category of sociology will no longer be useful in creating the distinctions necessary for discussing post-WWII development theory. There are two reasons for this. First, the field of sociology had changed so much by the postwar period that any general characterization would be futile. Some sociologists, instead of being sceptical of neoclassical economic methods, conspired with neoclassical economists in the postwar period in the creation of modernization theory (Parsons 1937, 1935a, b), or, later, through the adoption of rational action theory (Coleman 1973). Furthermore, after the fall of classical political economy, Marxian theory was incorporated into sociological thought to the extent that Marx is now considered one of the three classical sociologists along with Durkheim and Weber.

Although postwar development thinking, as we will see, fluctuated from being interdisciplinary to disciplinary, it did move roughly around three axes. *Neoclassical Economics* would prove to be the most powerful of these (in the hegemonic sense). *Critical Political Economy* would maintain a Marxian scepticism of the liberal view. Finally, *Cultural Approaches* arose from multiple disciplines, asserting the importance, if not the primacy, of culture in human existence. I will use these headings as classificatory tools throughout the following two chapters. It should be noted, however, that due to the range, complexity, and quantity of work in the field of development studies in the latter half of the twentieth and early twenty-first centuries, no classification could be perfect. Nonetheless, these categories are useful in emphasizing the place of culture in development theory, and therefore serve the present undertaking particularly well.

That undertaking, of course, is to pinpoint the source of the uncomfortable silence that arose between myself and my neoclassically trained professor, as I attempted to hand him a culture-based critique of an economic study. Part of the answer is apparent if we consider the work of the previous chapter. The splitting of the holistic study of classical political economy into the three relatively insulated fields of *Neoclassical Economics*, *Critical Political Economy*, and *Sociology* could have curtailed conversation. But it is also possible that such a division of labour could have yielded a Durkheimian organic solidarity amongst the social sciences—one in which economies of scale, due to specialization, were made accessible via cross-disciplinary communication and cooperation. I will suggest that the latter did not occur, and that the gap in conversation between myself and my professor stands as a symptom of the inability of these Durkheimian disciplinary organs to speak effectively to one another.

What I hope to show in this chapter is that although a great deal of communication and interaction has been possible—especially of late—between Cultural Theory and Critical Political Economy approaches to development, the neoclassical school remains relatively insular. Critical Marxian approaches tend to bleed into cultural approaches, for example, making any clear distinction between the two somewhat arbitrary. Ontological, epistemological, and methodological differences between neoclassical economics and the other two fields, on the other hand, have pre-empted meaningful conversation. These differences stem from the rigidity of the enduring Newtonian method in neoclassical economics on one side, and the inability of the other approaches to accept such a simplistic depiction of human life on the other. In conversation with other social scientists, the methodological individualism of the neoclassical economist meets a "big intangible something" that does not optimize properly. The "big intangible something" meets, in the methodological individualism of the neoclassical economist, a straightjacket that it just can't quite fit into. Conversation stops.

Neoclassical Approaches

Modernization Theory

Economists, of course, have not always had such a difficult time conversing with other social scientists. As we saw in the first chapter, the classical political economists combined cultural, ethical, and political insights with their economic analyses while retaining a linear Newtonian-Cartesian method. They did this, however, by holding the social apart from the economic. Smith, for example, allowed his *Theory of Moral Sentiments* to sneak into his *Wealth of Nations* only in a vague footnote. A similar uneasy interaction of methods occurred in the postwar period in development thinking, within the surprisingly interdisciplinary approach of *modernization theory*. This stream of thought—the most prominent in the postwar era—combined skillfully the sociological approaches of Durkheim and Weber with Keynesian and Austrian economics.

The thinking behind modernization theory is fairly straightforward: Keynesian neoclassical economists had shown that markets inhabited by rational individuals can achieve allocative optimality when these markets are guided properly by governments. Durkheimian and Weberian sociologists, on the other hand, had discovered the sociological secrets by which humans had shed their traditional ways and become rational and entrepreneurial. Effective development policy would therefore seek to install market systems in developing countries while helping their citizens to become rational and business-like, that is, to become a mixture of the homo economicus of the mainstream neoclassicalists and the entrepreneur of the Austrian school. In this concept, we see cooperation between neoclassical and sociological approaches. It was as if the Weberian and Durkheimian sociologists were embarking on the task of creating rational economic actors out of traditional peoples in the former colonies so that they could deliver them, fully formed, to the neoclassical economists. The latter would then submit these properly behaving actors to the invisible hand of the market, intervening from time-to-time with the benevolent hand of the state. The result would be development—defined as increased economic output. The only thing missing in this mixture was critical thought (in the Marxian sense).

One of the prominent features of modernization theory was a claim that human societies tend to pass through a number of stages as they evolve historically. Parsons (1964) had suggested, for example, that this involved a passage from the traditional, to the archaic, to the modern—the latter representing the apex of human social achievement. Following Durkheim's lead, Parsons implied that the modernization of human society was an extension of evolutionary tendencies in the biological world. The physiological innovations of the human brain and human hands, Parsons argued, endowed the species with a "biological potential for social and cultural evolution" (p. 84). This capacity, he continues, improves the "mastery, or the ability to change the environment to meet the needs of the [social] system" (p. 85).

Once endowed with the physical ability to make culture and to manipulate its own environment, Parsons (1964) argues, societies pass through a number of "evolutionary universals" on their road to modernity. The first of these is "social stratification" which "tends to exert a pressure to generalized hierarchization" (pp. 89–90). This propensity, combined with its "cultural legitimation," stimulates the existence of "prestige" positions which are the "prerequisite for responsible concentration of leadership" (ibid.). These advents, for Parsons, "are closely related to the "breaking out" of what might be called the "primitive" stage of societal evolution (p. 87). Next, the evolutionary universal of "bureaucratic organization" is developed "in societies that have moved considerably past the primitive stage" (p. 92). This "authority of office" is found primarily in government, but also "within money and markets" (ibid.). The "system of money and markets," another evolutionary universal, provides a similar organizational function as a bureaucratic system, but is more adaptable. It follows for Parsons that "those who restrict [the market] too drastically are likely to suffer from severe adaptive disadvantages in the long run" (p. 95). Excessive state control of economies, then, will impede evolution.

The next evolutionary universal that Parsons (1964) proposes is a ubiquity of "generalized universalistic norms"—the erasure of cultural difference, which was a "distinctive" step that "more than the industrial revolution itself, ushered in the modern era of social evolution" in Europe (p. 95). Parsons argues that such cultural homogeneity allows a legal order to be established on universally held principles and clears the ways for the institution of the final evolutionary universal of "democratic association" (p. 96). This generalized universality and democratic association, along with the advent of markets and bureaucracies, exerts a social pressure on the human actor that stimulates a "formal rationality" (ibid.). That is, a type of rationality in which human actors are endowed with more or less homogenous beliefs and tastes, and go about pursuing the satisfaction of these within a "general type of legal order" typified by bureaucratic governments, markets, and democratic association (pp. 96–97). In this stage, homo economicus is at long last fully evolved and may present himself to the neoclassical economist—perfectly amenable to his calculus.

The most commonly noted articulation of modernization theory, following Parsons' general framework, is to be found in economic historian W.W. Rostow's (1960/2000) *The Stages of Growth: A Non-Communist Manifesto*. Rostow suggested that societies pass through five stages on their journey to maturity. First, "traditional society" develops "within limited production functions, based on pre-Newtonian science and technology, and on pre-Newtonian attitudes towards the physical world" (p. 100). Rostow uses Newton "as a symbol for that watershed in history when men came widely to believe that the external world was subject to a few knowable laws, and was systematically capable of productive manipulation" (ibid.). In the traditional period, productivity was greatly limited due to technology and the "value system ... was generally geared to what might be called a long-run fatalism," typified by the belief that "the range of possibilities open to one's grandchildren would be just about what it had been for one's grandparents" (p. 101).

In the second phase, "the Preconditions for Take-Off," Rostow (1960/2000) argues that "the insights of modern science began to be translated into new production functions both in agriculture and industry" and that these processes are "given dynamism by the lateral expansion of world markets" (p. 102). In this environment, "the idea spreads not merely that economic progress is possible, but that economic progress is a necessary condition" (ibid.). We see the emergence of the entrepreneur as "new types of enterprising men come forward ... willing to mobilize savings and to take risks in the pursuit of profit" (ibid.). Quite often, the emergence of this epoch was motivated externally, "from some external intrusion by more advanced societies," such as colonial intrusions, which "shocked the traditional society [and] set in motion ideas and sentiments which initiated the process" (ibid.). Even so, Rostow argues that this period is often finalized by "the building of an effective centralized nation state" and sentiments of nationalism in opposition to colonial powers (p. 103).

According to Rostow's argument, the seeds for the transformations in the last three phases were planted in the first two. It is in the period of "Take-Off" that,

> the old blocks and resistances of steady growth are finally overcome. The forces making for economic progress, which yielded limited bursts and enclaves of modern activity, expand and come to dominate the society. Growth becomes its normal condition. (p. 103)

Following this period, the "Drive to Maturity" is epitomized by "a long interval of sustained if fluctuating progress" (p. 104). Finally, in the "Age of High Mass Consumption," the "leading sectors shift towards durable consumers' goods and services" (p. 105). This is the age that Rostow believed the American people were at his time emerging into. The consumerist ethic of this period, Rostow argued further, was accompanied by the emergence of the welfare state—a symbiosis of modern democratic state and capitalist market.

Rostow's model and the work of Parsons stand as typical examples of modernization theory. There also have been more economistic versions of the theory, based on neoclassical theory—focusing on moves from traditional agriculture to modern manufacturing as a source of growth (Lewis 1955). Some studies have focused more on political aspects, regarding the formation of modern institutions and cultures of political participation (Huntington 1968). Some have stressed the importance of the dissemination of knowledge, creation of new imaginations, and consequently entrepreneurial and politically active subjects via the increased communication and understanding that come first with urbanization, then with literacy, then with mass media (Lerner 1958). There have also been attempts to designate exact behavioural traits that are typical of modernity, and therefore conducive to development (Inkeles and Smith 1974).

There are important commonalities in these works. Each tends to define underdevelopment as a lack of productive capacity. Each of these works represents an attempt to locate the source of underdevelopment in a set of "primitive" institutions, cultural, economic, or social practices. Each of these tends to cast the solution to the problem of underdevelopment as the adoption of European or North American-style norms, institutions, and technologies. Consequently, each of these various modernization theories tends to blame the poor for their own poverty and prescribe more contact with, and diffusion of, the culture and technical knowledge of Western civilization as the remedy. Rational homo economicus looms in the background of each theory as the ideal type of human actor towards the creation of which policy should be directed—perhaps with a bit of the entrepreneur sprinkled in for good measure.

Modernization theory undergirded the development policy that emanated from the United Nations institutions—especially UNESCO and the World Bank—as well as all the official aid agencies of the Western powers in the postwar period. Policies encouraged the proliferation of global markets under the Bretton Woods system—presided over by the IMF, World Bank, and GATT. National democratic governments based on a Western-style state, active political participation, and strong national identities were encouraged in the former colonies (Martinelli 2005; Thussu 2000). Large infrastructure projects were initiated, typically funded through international loans and encouraged by the World Bank (McMichael 1996, p. 31).

Finally, the diffusion of Western ideas, culture, and technologies was encouraged via the expansion of open markets, the imposition of development projects that were designed by the Western powers, and the insertion of organizations such as the US Peace Corp into the former colonies (Webster 1984, pp. 53–56; Dube 1988, p. 4; Thussu 2000). This was a deliberate homogenizing process which was bolstered greatly by the international expansion of American and European mass media conglomerates. This mass communication system was to be used, as Thussu (2000) explains, "to spread the message of modernity and transfer the economic and political models of the West to the newly independent countries of the South" (p. 56). The largely American-produced content of these mass media networks "championed the Western way of life and its values of capitalism and individualism," in an attempt not only to incite cultural change for development, but also to create foreign consumers for Western-made goods and services. All of this—the building of markets, dissemination of knowledge, and creation of national identities—would be guided nationally by states, and internationally by the Bretton Woods system. All of this was accompanied by Keynes' general theory which advocated state intervention in market-based societies towards the universal institution of modern welfare states (ibid.).

New Classical Economics and the Washington Consensus

In 1947, Friedrich von Hayek organized a meeting of thirty-six of the top free-market scholars in the world—mostly economists—at Mont Pélerin, Switzerland. Hayek and the other attendees had great misgivings about the Keynesian turn towards the state-led economic development that accompanied modernization theory. They also lamented the persistence of planned economies in the Soviet Union and elsewhere. The purpose of the Mont Pélerin meeting was to begin work on an intellectual counter to these ideas, as participant Milton Friedman (2000) explains:

> The point of the meeting was very clear. It was Hayek's belief, and the belief of other people who joined him there, that freedom was in serious danger. During the war, every country had relied heavily on government to organize the economy, to shift all production toward armaments and military purposes. And you came out of the war with the widespread belief that the war had demonstrated that central planning would work.... Hayek and others felt that freedom was very much imperilled, that the world was turning

> toward planning and that somehow we had to develop an intellectual current that would offset that movement. … Essentially, the Mont Pelerin Society was an attempt … to start a movement, a road to freedom as it were. (para. #3)

This project more or less involved a cooperation of neoclassical economists from the Austrian tradition and those, such as Friedman, George Stigler, and Frank Knight, from the Chicago school of economics to forward the cause of a free-market-based opposition to the state-led model (ibid.). Hayek ended this meeting with a plea for all those involved to work towards this end, warning that it may take twenty years or more, but that the ideal would eventually prevail (Harris 2000). Hayek and his work would remain greatly involved in this process until his death—his (1944) *Road to Serfdom* served as a great inspiration to both Margret Thatcher and Ronald Reagan in their push for market deregulation in the 1980s (Harris 2000). The bulk of the heavy-lifting in this project, however, would be carried out by Chicago school economists—primarily by Milton Friedman.

"Friedman," writes Van Overtveldt (2007), was "probably one of the most enthusiastic and articulate supporters of a free-market economy that has ever lived" (p. 91). One could only imagine, then, that he was more than willing to take up the challenge posed by Hayek. Keynes' *General Theory*, as Hazlitt (1977) explains, "constitutes the most subtle and mischievous assault on orthodox capitalism and free enterprise that has appeared in the English language" (345). To dismantle the prevailing ideology of state-led economy, then, Friedman would have to directly attack Keynes' ideas. Since Keynes' *General Theory* was an integral part of modernization theory, this meant as substantial attack on mainstream development theory as well.

Friedman chose first to challenge the core Keynesian (and Marxian) idea that the propensity to save increased with income. This, we should remember, was used by Keynes to predict crises of underconsumption that would occur in the event that free markets produced high degrees of income inequality. Keynes had used this assertion to justify government intervention both to redistribute income and to undertake spending to offset the lack of private expenditure. Marxian theorists, as was discussed in Chap. 2, used a similar assumption in their theories of imperialism. Friedman forcefully dislodged the Keynesian claim regarding the propensity to consume by arguing that it did not fit historical data. He then presented his own *permanent income hypothesis* that entrenched in mainstream economics the idea that savings rates remain constant regardless of income levels, and therefore that there is simply no such thing as a crisis of overproduction. Friedman's seemingly small technical refutation about savings rates, in effect, denied the Keynesian claim that fiscal policy could be used by governments to any positive effect—and, he believed, showed that this market interference could in fact harm economic performance.

Key to the Keynesian advocacy for fiscal policy was a claim that the other economic policy choice available to governments—monetary policy—was not effective. Basing their argument on empirical data, Friedman and Schwartz (1963) showed that monetary policy can have a devastating impact. In fact, they claimed their data to show that monetary mismanagement in the early twentieth century, leading to a monetary contraction, had caused the Great Depression. This would lead Friedman (1998) to comment later that, "far from the great depression being a failure of the free-enterprise system, it was a tragic failure of government" (p. 233). Expansionary monetary policy was similarly dissuaded by Friedman (1968), as he insisted that an increase in the money supply would cause inflation, which would, in turn, cause unemployment and recession. As a result of these insights, Friedman (1962/1982) proposed the *Monetarist Rule*—that the money supply should be expanded only at a rate equal to long-run growth. Through his arguments, then, Friedman made the case for a severe curtailment of government activity in both monetary policy and fiscal policy.

Other Chicago school economists attacked interventionist policy just as vehemently. Stigler (1988) used empirical testing to show that competition existed amongst large companies, and that prices were flexible to market conditions. Implying that markets function competitively even under oligopolistic conditions, he maintained that "competition is a tough weed, not a delicate flower" (p. 104). Lucas (1997) used the idea of rational expectations to argue that government policy is often ineffective anyway, and that tax cuts are the best way to induce economic growth. The effort of both these economists worked to dissuade the government intervention in markets, the restriction of monopoly power, and progressive taxation.

Finally, in Friedman's (1962/1982) *Capitalism and Freedom*, these economic theorems were linked with an ideal of political freedom. In the text, Friedman argued that economic freedom is important in its own right—regardless of impact on economic growth. He also argued, however, that economic freedom is a necessary condition for the existence of political freedom. Economic control, he insisted, is always accompanied by political repression, and free markets are more difficult to coerce than are government production and distribution systems.

These neoclassical economic arguments had an incredibly strong impact on economic development policy. The first experiment in extreme free-market economics was orchestrated by Chicago-trained economists in Chile in the early 1970s, then other Latin American countries, and later former Soviet Bloc nations. In all instances, these policies were instituted with the help of severe political repression (Klein 2007). The height of Chicago School's impact on development policy would be achieved later, in the 1980s and 1990s, with the reformulation of development policy as enacted by the World Bank, IMF, and bilateral agencies. During this period, policy measures in these institutions were changed from modernization-theory inspired state-mediated-market-based strategies to state-minimizing market-centric ones. The institution of these policies was forced through conditionalities that were attached to World Bank and IMF loans. These structural adjustment programs (SAPs), as they were called, contained measures to reduce budget deficits and government subsidies, cut marginal tax rates, deregulate interest rates, devalue currencies, reduce tariffs, encourage foreign direct investment through the deregulation of the national economy, privatize state-owned enterprises, and establish and reinforce private property rights (Van Waeyenberge 2006). Resultantly, by the end of the 1990s, most of the world was arguably embedded in a neoliberal world system that relied on Chicago School's neoclassical economics for scientific justification.

Culture has little place in neoliberal economic analysis. Since, as with all neoclassical method, stable preferences are prefigured, there is no room for social action to have an impact on these preferences. Tyler Cowen (2002) has presented what is probably the most complete new classical treatment of culture available. Cowen argues that a diversity of choice in cultural products is encouraged by the proliferation of free markets across the globe. Gains from trade encourage niche markets to form for "marginal" cultural expressions such as Inuit art. Specialization and economies of scale allow high-cost, high-quality productions to be made available cheaply to all—as he argues is the case with Hollywood film. The global free-market production of culture, Cowen argues, expands the "menu of choices" available to all. On final analysis, he claims, "just as trade typically makes countries richer in material terms, it tends to make them culturally richer as well" (pp. 12–13). Cowen purposely restricts his analysis to markets for cultural products here, however, leaving no room for discussion of the impact that this or other forms of human communicative interaction may have on preference sets. Culture, in the hands of New Classical economics, has become just another commodity.

New Institutional Economics

Old institutional economics, as we discussed in Chap. 2, presumed human behaviour and tastes to be conditioned and formed by social institutions such as culture. New institutional economics, however, emerged largely out of the new classical school. It begins, therefore, with the assumption of individuals endowed with pre-existing and stable preference sets. Institutions are assumed to be constructed as rational actors seek to correct for market failures that they encounter in their attempts to maximize utility. These market failures are generally associated with incomplete information, transaction costs, or spillover effects from the action of others (Hodgson 1998).

Although not always explicitly associated with new institutionalism, much of the work of Gary Becker exhibits the main qualities of the school. I will focus here on the parts of Becker's work that are consistent with New Institutionalism. His analysis begins almost fanatically with the assumption of a pre-formed rational individual and explains idiosyncrasies in human behaviour as a result of incomplete information and spillover effects. George Stigler (1982) had distilled the Chicago School's credo down to one simple statement: "people act efficiently in their own interests" (pp. 11–12). Gary Becker ran with this idea, attempting to apply it to nearly any imaginable human phenomenon. As Nobel laureate George Akerlof (1990) would describe it, it was as if Becker had learned how to spell the word "banana," but didn't know when to stop. Knowledge of this approach is important for the purpose of this book, since Becker's method at once represents the most purified and far-reaching form of neoclassical economics and perhaps a vehicle within which that discipline could begin to engage with the idea of culture.

Beckers (1976) approach begins with four major assumptions:

1. Human agents always engage in utility maximizing behaviour
2. Human agents are rational, in that they choose one action over another by calculating costs of each option and weighing them against benefits. This may be done consciously or subconsciously.

3. Markets are ubiquitous in all facets of human life.
4. All human agents have a stable set of tastes (preferences), which are "assumed not to change substantially over time, nor to be very different between wealthy and poor persons, or even between persons in different societies and cultures" (p. 5).

The definition of "preference" is important here. The preferences to which Becker refers are "underlying objects of choice that are produced by each household [or individual] using market goods and services, their own time, and other inputs" (ibid.). These "underlying preferences" are biologically determined and "are defined over aspects of life such as health, prestige, sensual pleasure, benevolence, or envy" (ibid.).

If I were to consider telephoning my mother, for example, I would consider rapidly and subconsciously all the benefits—potential bequests of money and emotional benefits of familial contact. The emotional benefits may contribute directly to an underlying preference for social contact with others, but financial bequests may only serve as an input in a production process within which I use my time and mental capacity with the financial bequest to produce goods corresponding to underlying preferences such as prestige and health. In deciding to call my mother, I would weigh these benefits against costs—energy required to remember her number and find the telephone, opportunity costs of the time spent on the phone call, and of course the long-distance charges involved, would be some of the costs implied. With this information, I make my final decision. According to the Beckerian approach, a similar set of preferences, prices, and cost constraints exists for every choice or action undertaken by a human being.

Becker's (1964) concept of ***human capital*** provides an important augmentation to this framework. Human capital is a stock of skills and knowledge that assists in the efficiency of a person or household in producing the commodities that satisfy underlying preferences. Human capital is also knowledge gained in order to increase the efficiency of a person's or household's internal production function—their ability to use goods in the satisfaction of underlying preferences. If I learn to speak English, for example, it could increase the value of the social interaction I have with my mother—especially if this interaction occurs over the telephone. My language education increases my efficiency in producing the fundamental commodity "social interaction." Similarly, if I had decided to sacrifice time earlier to memorize her telephone number, the time-related costs of telephoning my mother would be reduced because I do not have to search for the number. Knowing how to use a telephone allows me to utilize the technology to deliver my mother's voice to my home and to export mine to hers. In Becker's terms, my acquisition of human capital by learning a language, remembering my mother's phone number, and learning to operate a telephone have decreased the *shadow prices* associated with the satiation of my underlying preferences.

The exact delineation of underlying preferences is never clearly undertaken in this school of thought. Since Becker insists that a universal stable set of underlying preferences must exist, it may have made sense for him to present the contents of this set when he established his theory. This was not done, and as a result, underlying preferences are assumed in an ad hoc manner in Beckerian-style studies. Even in Becker's (1976) authoritative book on his own method, he, seemingly without question, includes power-steering, inter-city visits, higher education, wheel-base, altruism, income, profits, power, prestige, genetic transfer, acceptance, and distinction in a universal preference set. Obviously, tautology is the great risk of the economic approach to human behaviour, unless a universal set of underlying preferences may one day be delineated.

It could be conceived that culture enters into this formulation through the idea of human capital. If the act of creating and learning languages in order to satisfy underlying preferences can be called culture, then we have a cultural argument here. Indeed, this is the purpose of language in Becker's (1990) opinion—a classification system that is a public good in that it must be shared in order to allow self-interested actors to coordinate actions. This, however, does not fit with our broad guiding definition of culture as an extra-individual social force that is presumed to impact the preferences, habits, motives, values, and valuations of actors. Underlying human preferences are assumed to be fixed in Becker's framework; language and other forms of human capital are used instrumentally to achieve the maximization of pre-figured utility functions. Culture, then, is far from fundamental in Beckerian economics—it is a secondary phenomenon which has no impact on underlying preferences. As we will see later, all institutions are treated in a similar manner in new institutional economics.

Another important feature that emerges from Becker's (1976, 1996a, b) work is the claim that human action is path-dependent. Since information is limited, and substantial costs must be incurred in gathering it, it is less costly for individuals to utilize information they already have, than to acquire new information. If I have an underlying preference for music, for example, and I have spent a great deal of time learning to appreciate jazz—thus lowering the shadow price for appreciation of that form of music—it is more efficient for me to satisfy my need for music by listening to more jazz than to expend energy in acquiring the knowledge required to appreciate hip-hop. As I listen to jazz subsequent times, it only serves to increase my understanding of the form—locking me further into my penchant for that style of music. Note that my underlying preference for music has not changed here. What has changed is my ability to produce that underlying commodity "intelligible music," which satiates my demand.

In his later work, Becker (1996a) substantially revises his definitions in a way that allows for the greater inclusion of the social in analysis. *Personal capital* replaces human capital in the consumption function. The former comes to include "the relevant past consumption and other personal experiences that affect current and future utilities" (p. 4). The concept of *social capital* is also introduced. This "incorporates the influence of past actions by peers and others in an individual's social network and control system" (ibid.). Human capital comes to signify a person's "stock of personal and social capital" as well as a person's stock of knowledge and skills. The overarching component human capital, then, has been broken down into three constituent parts—personal, social, and (confusingly) human capital. For Becker, "the utility function at any moment depends not only on the different goods consumed but also on the stock of personal and social capital at that moment" (p. 5), as well as human capital (meaning knowledge and skills).

Because the idea of social capital is central to both development and cultural theory, it is important to understand Becker's (1996b) use of the term. "The effects of the social milieu," he argues, are synonymous with "an individual's stock of social capital" (pp. 49–50). And this stock "depends not primarily on [a person's] own choices, but on the choices of peers in the relevant network of interactions" (ibid.), although a person can take actions to impact their own social capital (p. 165). As Fine (2001) has argued, the term "social capital" has become for Becker, "a catch-all for anything that improves life but that has not already been covered by those elements of personal capital" (p. 41). For example, a reduction in racial discrimination can be seen as an increase in social capital for the victim of discrimination, and this reduction will increase opportunities, such as acquiring education and work, to increase overall utility (Becker 1996a, pp. 140–145). Further, Becker (1996b) argues that people have an underlying preference for sociality, and this can mix with underlying preferences for other goods, making some restaurants and types of music more popular, just because they are more popular (pp. 195–202). Individuals who act particular ways are rewarded with social capital and may invest in it themselves. For example, Becker argues that a person,

> can avoid social opprobrium and perhaps ostracism by not engaging in criminal activities; achieve distinction by working diligently at his occupation, giving to charities, or having a beautiful house; or relieve his envy and jealousy by talking meanly about or even physically harming his neighbours. (p. 165)

The concept of social capital is integral to the new institutional economics of development. Although the term has an embattled meaning, it is usually defined more precisely than it is in Becker's catch-all depiction. New institutionalists generally see social capital as a communal resource that is mobilized in the solving of social dilemmas—especially in the presence of market failures. As Bates (1995) explains,

> A social dilemma arises when radical individualism becomes inconsistent with social welfare, namely when choices made by rational individuals yield outcomes that are socially irrational. The core argument of new institutionalism is that institutions provide the mechanisms whereby rational individuals can transcend social dilemmas… Market failures yield social dilemmas and thereby elicit the innovation of institutions. (p. 29)

The classic example of a social dilemma is the common pool resource. When private property rights are not assigned to a stand of trees, for example, each individual in a community has an incentive to cut as much timber as possible without replenishing the stock. Left to itself, this dynamic would result in the total depletion of the resource. Communities may develop means to abate this problem such as the evolution of a norm that regulates tree-cutting practices—perhaps via a religious reverence to the forest. This norm represents a form of social capital. Such institutions can arise in a variety of other situations. To compensate for failing or non-existing capital markets, for example, Bates argues that people,

> Mobilize family ties, religious groups or ethnic associations in support of commerce and trade; the richness of information in such environments facilitates calculations of the appropriate level of trust and the density of social ties increases the cost of the loss of reputation, rendering probity of greater value than opportunism in economic transactions. (p. 36)

It is argued that market failures exist in all economies, but that "the economies of the developing world are characterized by pervasive market failure" (Bates 1995, p. 36). Since incomplete information and common pool resource problems (and similar public goods provision problems) exist in all countries, an enormous literature has emerged with the intent of scouring both micro- and macro-level data for indicators of trust, social cohesion, civic participation, and other informal institutions that are presumed to constitute social capital. In such studies, a lack of any of these key indicators is assumed to be a deficiency in social capital, and therefore to contribute to the problem of underdevelopment in any given locale (Munshi 2006; Morduch 1991; Dayton-Johnson 2001).

Path-dependency provides a complicating factor for these arguments, however. Since human behaviour and institutional evolution are presumed to be path-dependent, outmoded institutions may remain when external technological and political situations have changed. As a result, enduring institutions may be inefficient in that they block the maximization of total productive output. According to North (1995), for example, human actors create "mental models" of the world in order to cope with limits to knowledge and mental capacity for processing information about the actual nature of things. These mental models are "used to interpret the world" and are "in part, culturally derived" (p. 18). They are cultural institutions. North explains the rise of these institutions as follows:

> As tribes evolved in different physical environments they developed different languages and, with different experiences, different mental models to explain the world around them. To the extent that experiences were common to different tribes the mental models provided common explanations. The language and mental models formed the informal constraints that defined the institutional framework of the tribe and were passed down intergenerationally as the customs, taboos, myths that provided the continuity of culture and forms part of the key to path dependence. (p. 20)

With new technological advances, however, "human beings became increasingly interdependent, and more complex institutional structures were necessary to capture potential gains from trade" (pp. 2–21). North continues,

> to the extent that 'local experience' had produced diverse mental models and institutions with respect to the gains from such cooperation, the likelihood of creating the necessary institutions to capture the gains from trade of more complex contracting varied. (p. 21)

Some cultures, this implies, were just not designed to be successful in generating income in a modern global economy. Just as with modernization theory, traditional culture is thought to impede development.

For North and others, it was not simply the path-dependent nature of culture that prevented institutional change. Internal power structures also have their determining impacts, as local elites were perceived to be preventing positive evolution in poor societies due to their stake in the current state of affairs. This, combined with cultural path-dependent arguments, has spurred an alignment of new institutional economics with a brand of social science that has been dubbed "hypermodernism" by Rao and Walton (2004). Key hypermodernist theorists include Francis Fukuyama (2000), who labels some cultures deficient in trust and social capital in general; Robert Putnam (1993), who has produced a number of studies, placing the blame for underdevelopment on a lacking of civic culture; and Harrison and Huntington (2000), who published the principal anthology in the school. In the Harrison and Huntington text, one finds a taxonomy of good and bad cultures, all measured according to their alleged ability to facilitate a tacitly assumed underlying social preference for increased productivity and therefore income—aggregated to gross national product. The new institutional economics, it seems, is a return to modernization theory. This is all built on the presumption of homo economicus endowed with one universal preference set, and the apparent assumption that the universal preference that matters is for something called "income" and is measurable by gross national product.

An extension of this approach appears in cultural economics literature; the most prominent of which appears in the work of Throsby (2001). Here, the new institutionalist idea is clearly adhered to. Throsby claims that, in an economy, "collective action may occur," and that if "markets fail or do not exist, voluntary or coercive collective action may be required in order for optimal social outcomes to be achieved" (p. 13). But Throsby insists that there is another type of human impulse that is distinct from the economic—the cultural impulse—and that this "desire for group experience" mixes with the economic only where strictly defined cultural goods are concerned (ibid.). Such goods may be musical, artistic, or even related to sports, and the behaviour around their production and consumption "reflects collective as distinct from individualistic goals, and derives from the nature of culture as expressing beliefs, aspirations and identification of a *group*" (ibid.). As a result, it seems that cultural economists are at once new institutionalists and old institutionalists. They are the former when discussing the bulk of economic activity; they are the latter when they discuss a strictly quarantined set of 'cultural' goods—such as sound recordings or works of art.

This is not entirely an accurate description, however. Cultural goods are treated by Throsby (2001) as normal economic goods that happen to have a particular penchant for causing market failures. This is a thoroughly new institutional approach which sets cultural goods aside as a brand of misbehaving commodities—a curious exception that must be treated delicately and requires institutional intervention to sustain properly functioning markets. At other times, however, Throsby treats preferences as mutable. This mutability, unaccompanied by a tiering of levels of preferences as appears in Becker's work, violates core neoclassical presumptions (p. 68). This methodological inconsistency is a direct by-product of Throsby's dichotomization of culture and economy. It allows for useful insights, such as the insistence that culture may change "what economic development means" from place to place, culture to culture (p. 66). But Throsby's dichotomy implies that such insights must be only applied to cultural goods which are confined to one part of the total economy. It is likely for this reason that cultural economics has not impacted economic analysis outside of the treatment of strictly defined cultural goods. The remainder of Throsby's analysis, such as the claim that consideration of cultural factors may imply that there are different paths to development (p. 67), is decidedly new institutional since it treats culture as a resource to produce income.

An important insight that emerges from the work of cultural economist such as Throsby's (2001) is that tastes themselves can be path-dependent. A similar argument is integral to Becker's (1996b) analyses of tastes. The argument here suggests that a certain amount of knowledge is required in the consumption of cultural goods. The act of consumption is therefore at once an act of learning. The more jazz we listen too, the more we tend to appreciate the genre. Our tastes seem to have changed, but really we have simply made the consumption of jazz easier by acquiring skills that facilitate its consumption. Our enjoyment of a particular good becomes dependent on the amount of that good that we have consumed in the past. For Throsby, this tendency is noted only in relation to strictly delineated cultural goods. Becker allows this path-dependency to apply to a broader range of goods.

Generally, new institutionalism has provided some welcome theoretical relief from the market utopianism of the new classical school. Work by new institutionalists has allowed for substantial a reinvigoration of interventionist arguments. This has resulted in a post-Washington Consensus regarding policy prescriptions of the major development institutions. As Stiglitz (1998) has suggested, this new development economics is much more holistic as it concentrates more on state–society–economy partnerships as opposed to casting these spheres as oppositional. But if new institutionalism has ejected one form of economic reductionism, it has replaced it with another. New classical economics may have concentrated its effort too much on the economic aspects of development. New institutionalists have corrected for this by suggesting that all action is economic. The social, political, and cultural may be combined in the new institutional approach because they are all presumed to be economic phenomena. These three spheres of human activity are furthermore cast as subservient and epiphenomenal vis-à-vis the economic. Furthermore, the presumed objective-scientific technicians of the new development economics are given extraordinary power to define and adjudicate between social capital and bad tradition—or, in more technical terms, between rational collective corrections for failing markets, and path-dependent suboptimal equilibria. An unqualified trust in markets has been replaced with an unsubstantiated trust in technocrats. And these technocrats, more often than not, presume the measure of the quality on an institution to be its impact on productivity or income. Culture, by definition, is in service of the market.

Another powerful mode of thought exists, which is related to new institutionalism. This *capabilities approach* is usually associated with Nobel laureate Amartya Sen (1993, 1999), but substantial contributions have also been made by Nussbaum (2000), Alkire (2004), and Max-Neef (1993). The model starts with the assertion that there exists a set of core human functionings which are deemed valuable for human existence. Sen has resisted an explicit delineation of these functionings because he feels that they should be prioritized and named only through deliberative participatory discussion amongst the group of people in question. Others have attempted to create lists of core funtionings. Nussbaum (2000), for example, includes "life" and "bodily health," amongst the most fundamental of human functionings. It is argued that humans have differing capabilities in the production of these functionings, and that this depends on material and non-material resources (including things like knowledge and community standing) that they have access to. The similarities to Becker's approach are striking, but the main difference lies in the meaning Sen and others apply to "functionings" compared to "preferences" as used in the Beckerian approach. Whereas preferences stand for a stable set of likes and dislikes internal to each human actor—the satiation of which attributes utility to the individual, functionings are a set of socially held goals that are agreed to contribute to a good life. Where development in the Beckerian tradition comes to mean the expansion of utilities through the consumption of material and non-material goods, in the capabilities approach, it implies the expansion of capabilities to produce functionings, and the removal of "non-freedoms" that impede that production process for the most marginalized groups.

Culture sits in the capability approach in three ways. First, as with other new institutionalist approaches, culture can impact the ability of actors to perform development goals—in this case, the achievement of functionings. Secondly, culture in the form of arts or participation in religious rituals may be a valuable functioning in its own right. Third—and this is where the approach breaks most dramatically with most new institutionalism—culture is assumed to frame what counts as a valuable functioning (Nussbaum 2000; Sen 1999).

In this third respect, however, the capability approach is underdeveloped, and this leads to ambiguities and internal inconsistencies. It also seems to contradict the new institutional claim that human agents have stable preference sets. Sen, for example, asserts that deliberative democracy is important in that it allows communities to not only discover their priorities, but critically reflect on their values in the creation of new priorities in a way that seems to impact preferences themselves:

> [A] proper understanding of what economic needs are—their content and their force—requires discussion and exchange. Political and civil rights, especially those related to the guaranteeing of open discussion, debate, criticism, and dissent, are central to the processes of generating informed and reflected choices. These processes are crucial to the formation of values and priorities, and we cannot, in general, take preferences as given independently of public discussion, that is, irrespective of whether open debates and interchanges are permitted or not. (1999, p. 153)

Although it might appear that Sen considers preferences to be culturally determined and malleable through communication, in reality, he has implied otherwise—that culture simply acts to augment the weight attached to particular preferences, as if a social set of preferences were interacting with an individual one (1977). Resultantly, the way in which the economic actor is constituted is left up in the air for capability theorists. They never seem to address this issue directly. Although deliberative democracy is advocated, and power imbalances related to participation in discussion are noted, the exact nature of participation or the space in which it is to be carried out is not delineated. Finally, although Sen consistently refuses to explicitly create a list of functionings, he often asserts that markets tend to expand capabilities and that "freedom of exchange and transaction is itself part and parcel of the basic liberties that people have reason to value" (1999, p. 6)—that, in other words, market participation is a valuable functioning in itself.

Such diverse and divergent assertions have led many to critique the approach for tending towards both ambiguity and uncritical liberalism. The virtues of the model should not, however, be overlooked. The capability theorists have delicately placed issues of participation and decentralized, non-technocratic policy analysis within the peripheral vision of neoclassical development economists. Perhaps due to its unclear relation to neoclassical method, however, the model has been adopted most enthusiastically by heterodox economists and other social scientists instead of neoclassical economists. Resultantly, the glimmer of hope that a meaningful incorporation of culture into neoclassical thought might be brought by the capability school has yet to intensify into a measurable quantity of light. Often mainstream new institutional-based policy tends to ignore material and structural inequalities and blame the poor for their own poverty by pointing to a lack of civic organization in impoverished communities as the root cause of their poverty.

This is apparent in a fairly recent and ambitious attempt by the World Bank to bring economists and anthropologists together to formulate culture and development policy under a broad capability approach. The result was a plea to theorists and practitioners to focus on a "capacity to aspire" which could be diminished by undue cultural disruption, and a related insistence to pursue a policy trajectory guided by the principle of "equality of agency," which is thought of as a cultural capacity (Rao & Walton 2004). On close reading, this sits uncomfortably close to the standard "hypermodernist" approach that the contributors sought to displace. Some cultural arrangements are maintained as being more conducive to development, with the caveat that unduly rapid cultural disruption could induce a stagnancy that is "beyond poverty" (Douglas 2004, p. 108), and that participatory methods might help to quell this tendency. The theorization of culture is as haphazard and contradictory as it is generally with the capability approach, and only one neoclassical economist was inspired by the concepts introduced by the conference and book to work on one conceptual model, published years later in an abbreviated form (Ray 2006). The Rao and Walton (2004) publication and its singular spin-off do represent a useful incursion into the murky territory of culture and development economics. Its limited impact, especially amongst neoclassical economists, may, however, be testimony to the lack of theoretical coherence endemic to the capability approach.

Conclusion

Culture is not used in any consistent way in mainstream development theory. Some, such as the new classical economists, tended to ignore it outright. When not being ignored, culture was sometimes contorted to fit within neoclassical economic models. New institutional economics allows for this contortion by treating culture as a rational social corrective for market failures based on information imperfections or externalities.

The ethnocentric biases of early modernization theory and its later iterations of hypermodernism have not been successfully avoided via the capability approach. Modernization theory in its early and hyper forms features culture as a traditional curse that subsumes the rationality that is assumed to be necessary for individuals and communities to transcend development problems. These concepts cannot be expected to sit well with indigenous peoples that insist that culture is valuable for its own sake and that it constitutes the human ontological relation with the world—and that it creates ideas of the good life that are the end-point of development.

The capability approach does go some way towards remedying this. Despite notable attempts to reconcile the ideas of culture and development through that approach, however, the combination remains underdeveloped. The concept of "capacity to aspire" is illustrative of this. Within this framework, culture is said to define individual goals, and therefore concepts of development. Culture also provides an ontological roadmap of the world—providing actors with the understandings necessary to navigate from underdeveloped to developed states (both of which can be culturally defined). There is an admission that things such as top-down development projects and natural disasters can disrupt the "capacity to aspire" by creating a mismatch between culturally defined modes of behaviour and knowledge-systems on one side, and the goals of development on the other. The model is unable, however, to distinguish between contentment and apathy, however. In its current form, this mode of thinking, therefore, asks the development expert to mediate between the two states. This brings the idea perilously close to the kind of ethnocentric judgement that was indicative of modernization theory.

There may be a way in which indigenous thought can be expressed in terms of the capabilities approach and capacities to aspire, but this fusion has not yet been achieved. Three things are likely important if this fusion is to ever be successful. First, the habit of presuming economic growth to be essential for development must be abandoned. Second, the habit of assuming markets to be natural and ubiquitous, albeit sometimes malfunctioning, entities must be replaced with ideas that view markets as sometimes useful but non-essential. Third, the capabilities approach must meaningfully incorporate critical ideas that examine multiple forms of inequity.

References

Akerlof, G. (1990). George A. Akerlof. In R. Swedberg (Ed.), *Economics and Sociology, Redefining Their Boundaries: Conversations with Economists and Sociologists* (pp. 61–77). Princeton, NJ: Princeton University Press.

Alkire, S. (2004). *Valuing Freedoms: Sen's Capability Approach and Poverty Reduction*. Oxford: Oxford Scholarship.

Bates, R. H. (1995). Social Dilemmas and Rational Individuals: An Assessment of New Institutionalism. In J. Harriss, J. Hunter, & C. M. Lewis (Eds.), *The New Institutional Economics and Third World Development* (pp. 17–27). New York: Routledge.

Becker, G. (1964). *Human Capital: A Theoretical and Empirical Analysis, with Special Reference to Education*. Chicago: University of Chicago Press.

Becker, G. (1976). *The Economic Approach to Human Behavior*. Chicago: University of Chicago Press.

Becker, G. (1990). Gary S. Becker. In R. Swedberg (Ed.), *Economics and Sociology, Redefining Their Boundaries: Conversations with Economists and Sociologists*. Princeton University Press: Princeton.

Becker, G. (1996a). *The Economics of Life*. New York: McGraw-Hill.

Becker, G. (1996b). *Accounting for Tastes*. Cambridge, MA: Harvard University Press.

Chamberlain, M. E. (1999). *Decolonization*. Malden, MA: Blackwell.

Coleman, J. (1973). *The Mathematics of Social Action*. Chicago, IL: Alder.

Cowen, T. (2002). *Creative Destruction: How Globalization Is Changing the World's Cultures*. Princeton University Press, 2004, 179p.

Dayton-Johnson, J. (2001). *Social Cohesion and Economic Prosperity*. Toronto: Lorimer.

Douglas, M. (2004). Traditional Culture—Let's Hear No More About It. In V. Rao & M. Walton (Eds.), *Culture and Public Action*. Stanford: Stanford University Press.

Dube, S. C. (1988). *Modernization and Development: A Search for Alternative Paradigms*. London: Zed Books.

Escobar, A. (1994). *Encountering Development: The Making and Unmaking of the Third World*. Princeton: Princeton University Press.

Fine, B. (2001). *Social Capital versus Social Theory: Political Economy and Social Science at the Turn of the Millennium*. London and New York: Routledge.

Friedman, M. (1962/1982). *Capitalism and Freedom*. With the Assistance of Rose D. Friedman. Chicago: University of Chicago Press.

Friedman, M. (1968). The Role of Monetary Policy. *American Economic Review, 58*(1), 1–17.

Friedman, M. R. (1998). *Contracts and Conveyances of Real Property* (Vol. 1). Practising Law Institute.

Friedman, M. (2000). On Friedrich Hayek and the Mont Pelerin Meeting. In W. Cran (Producer), *The Commanding Heights*. PBS.

Friedman, M., & Schwartz, A. (1963). *A Monetary History of the United States, 1867–1960*. Princeton, NJ: Princeton University Press.

Fukuyama, M. F. (2000). *Social Capital and Civil Society*. International Monetary Fund.

Harris, R. (2000). Back in Time: Mont Pelerin, 1947. In W. Cran (Producer). *The Commanding Heights*. PBS. Retrieved from http://www.pbs.org/wgbh/commandingheights/lo/story/ch_menu.html.

Harrison, L. E., & Huntington, S. P. (2000). *Culture Matters: How Values Shape Human Progress*. New York: Basic Books.

Hayek, F. A. (1944). *The Road to Serfdom*. London: Routledge & Kegan Paul.

Hazlitt, H. (1977). *The Critics of Keynesian Economics*. New York: Arlington House.

Hodgson, G. M. (1998). Socialism against Markets? A Critique of Two Recent Proposals. *Economy and Society, 27*(4), 407–433.

Huntington, S. P. (1968). *Political Order in Changing Societies*. New Haven: Yale University Press.

Inkeles, A., & Smith, D. H. (1974). *Becoming Modern: Individual Change in Six Developing Countries*. Princeton, NJ: Princeton University Press.

Klein, N. (2007). *The Shock Doctrine: The Rise of Disaster Capitalism*. Toronto: Knopf.

Lerner, D. (1958). *The Passing of Traditional Society*. New York: The Free Press.

Lewis, A. (1955). *The Theory of Economic Growth*. London: Allan and Unwin.

Lucas, R. E., Jr. (1997). *Monetary Neutrality. Nobel Lectures in Economic Sciences.* Singapore: Nobel Foundation.

Martinelli, A. (2005). *Global Modernization: Rethinking the Project of Modernity.* London: Sage.

Max-Neef, M. (1993). *Human Scale Development: Conception, Application, and Further Reflections.* London: Apex Press.

McMichael, P. (1996). *Development and Social Change: A Global Perspective.* London: Pine Forge.

Morduch, J. (1991). Between the State and the Market: Can Informal Insurance Patch the Safety Net? *World Bank Research Observer, 14*(2), 187–207.

Munshi, K. (2006). Nonmarket Institutions. In A. V. Banerjee, R. Bénabou, & D. Mookherjee (Eds.), *Understanding Poverty* (pp. 389–400). New York: Oxford.

North, D. C. (1995). New Institutional Economics and Development. In J. Harriss, J. Hunter, & C. M. Lewis (Eds.), *The New Institutional Economics and Third World Development* (pp. 17–27). NY: Routledge.

Nussbaum, M. (2000). *Women and Human Development: The Capabilities Approach.* Cambridge: Cambridge University Press.

Parsons, T. (1935a). Sociological Elements in Economic Thought I: Historical. *Quarterly Journal of Economics, 49*, 414–453.

Parsons, T. (1935b). Sociological Elements in Economic Thought I: The Analytic Factor View. *Quarterly Journal of Economics, 49*, 646–667.

Parsons, T. (1937). *The Structure of Social Action.* New York: McGraw-Hill.

Parsons, T. (1964). Evolutionary Universals in Society. *American Sociological Review, 29*(3), 339–357.

Putnam, R. (1993). *Making Democracy Work: Civic Traditions in Modern Italy.* Princeton: Princeton University Press.

Rao, V., & Walton, M. (2004). Culture and Public Action: Relationality, Equality of Agency, and Development. In V. Rao & W. Walton (Eds.), *Culture and Public Action* (pp. 3–36). Stanford: Stanford University Press.

Ray, D. (2006). Aspirations, Poverty, and Economic Change. In A. Banerjee, R. Bénabou, & D. Mookherjee (Eds.), *Understanding Poverty.* Oxford: Oxford University Press.

Rostow, W. W. (1960/2000). The Stages of Growth. In J. Timmons Roberts & A. White (Eds.), *From Modernization to Globalization* (pp. 100–109). Malden, MA: Blackwell.

Sen, A. (1977). Rational Fools: A Critique of the Behavioural Foundations of Economic Theory. *Philosophy and Public Affairs, 6*(4), 317–344.

Sen, A. (1993). Capability and Well-Being. In M. Nussbaum & A. Sen (Eds.), *The Quality of Life.* Oxford: Clarendon Press.

Sen, A. (1999). *Development as Freedom.* New York: Anchor.

Stigler, G. J. (1982). Economists and public policy. *Regulation, 6*, 13.

Stigler, G. (1988). *Memoirs of an Unregulated Economist*. New York: Basic Books.
Stiglitz, J. E. (1998). *More Instruments and Broader Goals: Moving Toward the Post-Washington Consensus* (p. 2). Helsinki: UNU/WIDER.
Throsby, D. (2001). *Economics and Culture*. Cambridge: Cambridge University Press.
Thussu, D. K. (2000). *International Communication: Continuity and Change*. London: Arnold.
Tucker, V. (1999). The Myth of Development: A Critique of a Eurocentric Discourse. In R. Munck & D. O'Hearn (Eds.), *Critical Development Theory: Contributions to a New Paradigm* (pp. 1–26). London and New York: Zed.
Van Overtveldt, J. (2007). *The Chicago School: How the University of Chicago Assembled the Thinkers Who Revolutionized Economics and Business*. Agate Publishing.
Van Waeyenberge, E. (2006). From Washington to Post-Washington Consensus: Illusions of Development. In B. Fine & K. S. Jomo (Eds.), *The New Development Economics: After the Washington Consensus*. London: Zed.
Webster, A. (1984). *Introduction to the Sociology of Development*. New York: Macmillan.

CHAPTER 5

Culture in Critical Development Theory

The previous chapter described the place of culture in many strains of functionalist development thought. Although much of this thought has been hegemonic, especially throughout the twentieth century, it may be critiqued as largely Eurocentric, econocentric, linear, and relatively blind to multiple forms of inequality. These traits, although useful in statistical analysis and economic modelling, are unlikely to match well with the indigenous cultural visions of sustainable development emerging from Latin America and other regions of the world. There is a possibility that fruitful theoretical innovation could occur between indigenous development ideas and the capabilities approach, but this has not yet occurred.

This chapter examines the idea of culture from within more critical schools of development thought. Much like many current ideas of indigenous sustainable development, many of these theoretical frames have emerged from Latin America and other parts of the Global South. As such, they should provide a more amenable set of standpoints with which indigenous development ideas can interact.

Critical Political Economy

Critical theories emerged largely from the Marxist tradition in the early postwar period. Led by the structuralists (Prebisch 1950; Furtado 1964; Myrdal 1968), followed by dependency theorists (Amin 1976; Frank 1966; Cardoso 1972), and then world systems theorists (Wallerstein

T. MacNeill, *Indigenous Cultures and Sustainable Development in Latin America*, https://doi.org/10.1007/978-3-030-37023-7_5

1974; Amin 1992; Frank 1981), these approaches tended to replace the functionalism of neoclassical theory with explanations of underdevelopment that were based in exploitation and unequal exchange. For theorists in the neoclassical tradition, markets—despite their occasional dysfunction—were thought to bring opportunity, foreign exchange, benefits from trade, investment, technology, and positive cultural influences to less developed countries. Critical theorists, however, argued that markets tend to bring subordination, exploitation, and homogenization to these countries.

The Structuralist School

Structuralist thought emerged largely in post-WWII Latin America and emphasized the importance of expanding the industrial sector for achieving economic growth. In this, structuralist thinking reflected that of the modernization theorists. Where the structuralists differed, however, was in their assistance that more was required in this process than the simple access to markets, foreign direct investment, knowledge, advanced technologies, and cultural change.

Furtado (1964) argued that structural limitations prevented successful market-based industrialization in the developing world. First, he believed that small domestic markets in many countries were not large enough to sustain the process of industrialization. Domestic industry of small economies, however, was also too weak to compete in global markets with companies from highly industrialized economies. Attempts at free-market-based industrial development, then, would leave domestic business mired in a structural trap that assures domination by stronger, more established, companies from larger economies.

Prebisch (1950) argued that difficulties in industrialization were exacerbated by a legacy of primary commodity production in former colonies. Colonial economies, he claimed, were structured to promote the export of raw materials, while advanced economies were proficient in industrial production. Because of the power of labour unions in industrial countries, and the ongoing technological development of substitutes for primary commodities, Prebisch argued that the value of primary exports compared to industrial imports was constantly decreasing—primary commodity producers in less developed countries faced declining terms of trade. Myrdal (1968) similarly argued that highly industrialized countries could capture asymmetrical benefits from trade because their economies were more internally integrated via forward and backward linkages. Realizing this, structuralists claimed that there existed a tendency for the highly industrialized economies of the core or *centre* to absorb the surplus value produced in the primary-commodity-producing *periphery*. This became known as the *centre–periphery* model (Kay 1989, pp. 29–31).

Inspired by the centre–periphery model, Prebisch (1950), Myrdal (1968), and other structuralists concluded that industrialization in the periphery was necessary in order to combat this problem. However, since they believed industrialization to be impossible in free markets, structuralists advocated for strong management of the process by the state. First, they argued in favour of import substitution industrialization (ISI)—which required trade barriers to be erected which would protect government-supported businesses from international competition. When this programme was found wanting—particularly due to difficulties in higher levels of industrialization—the strategy was changed in favour of export promotion (Martinussen 1997).

Structuralist theory was generally economistic, apolitical, and acultural. An exception to this was the work of Myrdal (1968). Like the modernization theorists, Myrdal cited different cultural traits and institutional forms that existed in poorer economies and were not perceived to be conducive to development. Attitudinal problems cited by Myrdal included lack of work ethic, lack of punctuality, lack of orderliness, irrationality, superstition, inadaptability, submissiveness to authority, and fatalism. Among the most problematic institutional structures was the "soft state" which, Myrdal argued, was unable to uphold the rule of law and could easily be exploited by powerful individuals and groups. Myrdal's work spurred a move away from pristine economism in structural analysis and towards a more complex consideration of internal cultural and political conditions.

Dependency Theory

Perhaps inspired by Myrdal's interdisciplinary analysis, dependency theorists continued the critical tradition and pushed structuralism to encompass more non-economic factors. This expansion of purview was achieved initially by incorporating theories of *internal colonialism* and *marginality* into structuralist economism. The internal colonialism thesis took special note of the racial and cultural character of structurization, noting that subordinate status often corresponded to membership in a particular ethnic group. This seemed to be especially true in Latin American countries with large indigenous populations, such as Ecuador or Guatemala. The argument here was that, contrary to what Myrdal or the modernization theorists might say, the underdevelopment of particular ethnic groups is not due to cultural pathologies. Instead, this condition is actually a class-based domination that is simply more visible in particular populations because those groups have historically been subject to abnormal levels of exploitation. This exploitation has come because of internal unequal exchange relations with national elites, usually of European or mixed lineage, as well as from unequal exchange in the international market system (Kay 1989, pp. 59–87; González-Casanova 1965, p. 33; Johnson 1972). The marginalization thesis similarly posited that modernization policies, whether free market or ISI, tended to marginalize particular populations within a country—excluding them from the benefits of development and exploiting them for the benefit of others (Kay 1989, pp. 88–125; Quijano 1977; Germani 1972).

Andre Gunter Frank (1966) was the first dependency theorist to write in English and therefore presented the view from the South to Western development theorists for the first time. He challenged the modernization view that the development of underdeveloped countries "must and will be generated or stimulated by diffusing capital, institutions, values etc., to them from the international and national capitalist metropoles" (p. 18). Frank augmented *centre–periphery* theory by instead framing relations in terms of *satellite* and *metropole*. Metropoles include the advanced industrial centres of Europe and North America, which establish major trading and industrial centres in less developed countries. Through unequal relationships of exchange, the latter are perpetually subordinated to the former. Just as was the case in the centre–periphery model, the consequence of this relationship is that "metropoles tend to develop and the satellites to underdevelop" (p. 22). Frank incorporates internal factors into his analysis by insisting that each of these satellites, in turn, acts as a regional metropole. As he explains using the case of Latin America,

> The metropolis-satellite relations are not limited to the imperial or international level but penetrate and structure the very economic, political, and social life of the Latin American colonies and countries. Just as the colonial and national capital and its export sector become a satellite of the Iberian (and later of other) metropoles of the world economic system, this satellite immediately becomes a colonial and then a national metropolis with respect to the productive sectors and population of the interior. Furthermore, the

> provincial capitals, which are themselves satellites of the metropolis ... are in turn provincial centres around which their own local satellites orbit ... [E]ach of the satellites ... serves as an instrument to suck capital or economic surplus out of its own satellites. (p. 19)

This thinking leads Frank, along with other dependency theorists, to some stark conclusions. First, he asserts that "underdevelopment is not due to the survival of archaic institutions and the existence of capital shortage in regions that have remained isolate from world history" (p. 22). To the contrary, he argues, "underdevelopment was and still is generated by the very same historical process which also generated economic development: the development of capitalism itself" (ibid.). Through historical analysis, Frank made the case that "the regions which are the most underdeveloped and feudal-seeming today are the ones which had the closest ties to the metropolis in the past" (p. 26). Conversely, "the satellites experience their greatest economic development ... if and when their ties to the metropolis are the weakest" (p. 23). This, and similar analyses, led Frank and other of the more radical dependency theorists (Dos Santos 1971; Amin 1976; Quijano 1977; Marini 1972; García 1972) to conclude that development could only occur with a delinking of the satellite from the metropole. More moderate dependency theorists such as Cardoso (1972), Sunkel (1969), and Furtado (1971) did not disagree with this basic framework, but nuanced it with a focus on internal conditions and insisted that development could occur while maintaining such links—although this development will be characterized by a continuing inequality between the various satellites and metropoles.

Perhaps best thought of as an updated augmentation of dependency theory, *world systems theory* emerged as an increasingly dominant form of critical political economy by the end of the twentieth century. This theory is commonly associated with the work of Wallerstein (1974), and although it did not evolve explicitly out of dependency theory, key theorists such as Amin (1992) and Frank (1981) have adopted its mantle in their later work. Wallerstein (1974) argued that all economies since the sixteenth century must be analysed in relation to their position in a totalizing capitalist world system—to which there is no outside. To the structuralist dichotomy of centre–periphery, he added a semi-periphery, in describing the three relative positions in this system. The latter is useful to the function of the system because it divided the exploited—thus preventing large-scale revolt. Various political and social forms that are often interpreted as being non-capitalist, are, he argued, expressions that represent the different positions that each occupies within the world capitalist system. Even the socialist states of the Soviet Union, he claimed, were institutional reactions designed to make the best of these countries' relative positions.

Cardoso (1972) insists that colonial and neocolonial links had been forged with peoples who "were culturally independent and structurally did not have links with the Western world" (p. 172). For most dependency theorists and world-systems theorists, it is these links, and not cultural factors, that are the cause of underdevelopment. Indeed, this is the core claim in their critique of the cultural explanation inherent in modernization theory. Gereffi (1994/2000), for example, follows Frank and Cardoso in downplaying cultural explanations, insisting that "the impact of cultural variables is most important in outlining an acceptable range of solutions to development problems, rather than in determining specific economic outcomes" (p. 233). Wallerstein (1979/2000) characterizes culture as epiphenomenal—explaining that "ethnic groups, or status groups, or ethno-nations are phenomena of world economies" (p. 201). As a result of the materialist bent that dependency and world-systems theories inherited from Marxism then, culture is often either discounted as a factor and subsequently ignored altogether or characterized as epiphenomenal—to be read-off of economic structures (Kapoor 2002).

There is, however, a substantial tradition of communication research that has drawn from dependency and world-systems perspectives. This literature is neo-Marxist in the critical political economy tradition and focuses on issues such as media imperialism (often generalized as cultural imperialism) and cultural homogenization (Tomlinson 1991). Schiller (1979), for example, argues that the massive media conglomerates of the industrialized countries provide the infrastructure that disseminates a global culture of capitalism. This media network encourages through its programming, a capitalist lifestyle of high consumption, and glorifies the trappings of capitalist modernity. In true Marxian form, Schiller argues that these media serve to encourage a commodity fetishism which serves the interest of capitalist production and blinds its victims to the true nature of their oppression. International media, he claims, act as "inseparable elements in a worldwide system of resource allocation generally regarded as capitalistic" (p. 30). These media, he continues, "create and reinforce their audiences' attachment to the way things are in the world system overall" (ibid.). This involves the creation of audiences "whose loyalties are tied to brand named products and whose understanding of social reality is mediated through a scale of commodity satisfaction" (p. 123). The end result is the formation of colonial subjects who venerate "the capitalist road to development" (p. 31). "The media," he continues,

> now many times more powerful and penetrative than in an earlier time, are the means that entice and instruct their audiences along this path, while at the same time concealing the deeper reality and the long term consequences that the course produces. (Ibid.)

Dorfman and Metellart (1975) claim that this represents a severe form of dependency—one in which former colonies become "exporters of raw materials and importers of superstructural and cultural goods" (p. 97). Dorfman and Mettelart offer the standard dependency critique by holding that, "to service our 'monoproduct' economies and provide urban paraphernalia, we send copper, and they send the machines to extract copper" (ibid.). But the industrialized economies also send Coca-Cola—which Dorfman and Mettelart consider a cultural good. This makes dependency all the more insidious since, as they argue, "behind Coca-Cola stands a whole superstructure of expectations and models of behaviour, and with it, a particular kind of present and future society and an interpretation of the past" (ibid.). Consequently, cultural imports such as Coca-Cola and Disney cartoons are ingested by audiences in the developing world "as instruction in the way they are supposed to live and relate to the foreign power centre" (p. 98).

Salinas and Paldán (1979) reinforce the Marxist argument that cultural imperialism represents the imposition of a hegemonic ideology that promotes the continued domination of those in the peripheral economies by those in the capitalist core. They argue that the cultural institutions such as education and media systems of dependent countries are modelled to serve "the requirements of dependent industrialization" (p. 92). Since this dependent industrialization requires obedient consumers and masses of poor to ensure low labour costs, cultural imperialism can amplify suffering in the Third World by offering a modern lifestyle and denying it at the same time. As some more affluent citizens of less developed countries may be able to live the life offered by the media, "others are submitted to levels of existence that prevent them from exercising minimal cultural rights" (p. 91). They experience "a poverty of culture" (ibid.). Furthermore, argue Salinas and Paládan, the imported culture tends to dominate the indigenous to the point that the latter is pushed to extinction—resulting in cultural homogenization. Hamelink (1983) concurs with this homogenization thesis, offering that,

> In the second half of the twentieth century, a destructive process … threatens the diversity of cultural systems. Never before has the synchronization with one particular cultural pattern been of such global dimensions and so comprehensive. (p. 4)

As Salinas and Paldán (1979) have implied, many in the Third World have seen their culturally ascribed system of meaning eliminated by the power of international capital, only to be replaced by one that they cannot afford to participate in. So, it follows, they work in the factories and plantations that are owned by transnational industrial capital, with the hopes that they will one day earn enough to participate in the new culture from which they are excluded. All the while, the dependency relationship is maintained—the businesses of the centre accrue increasing profits brought by unequal relations of material exchange mixed with asymmetrical cultural power. Breaking this material structural relationship of exploitation is, in the end, largely thought to be a material practice. One who is hopeful for systemic change must wait in orthodox Marxism for the material relations of production to become unstable due to internal contradictions in the economic base. Culture, in the rigidly delineated Marxian tradition, often seems to be depicted as an epiphenomenon, a fetish, and an ideology. This may be an artefact of strict delineation, however. Inspired by adventurous Marxian cultural thinkers such as Gramsci (1957/1971), Althusser (1971), and Williams (1977), for example, critical political economy approaches and cultural approaches have come to share an ambiguous and porous border.

Cultural Approaches

Postcolonialism

Although much thinking in the critical political economy perspective accords most of the responsibility for the propulsion of history to the economic base, Marxism did produce a significant strand that attributed a large amount of power to the ideological. As we discussed in the first chapter, Antonio Gramsci was perhaps the first Marxian thinker to suggest that social change may be incited via interventions in the ideological realm—that cultural change could force systemic change. This insight was taken up with revolutionary fervour, first in anti-colonial struggle by Senghor (1956), Césaire (1953/1972), and Fanon (1952/1967), and then in opposition to forms of neocolonialism by Freire (1970), Said (1979), Bhabha (1986), and Spivak (1988), amongst others. The key tenet of this thought is as follows: "that *representations* and *modes of perception* are used as fundamental weapons of colonial power to keep colonized peoples subservient to colonial rule" (McLeod 2000, p. 17).

Perhaps the most thorough treatment of culture and its relation to human subjectivities in early postcolonialism appears in Frantz Fanon's (1952/1967) *Black Skin, White Masks.* Fanon was primarily concerned with racism, which he perceived to be "a cultural element" (1967, p. 32). Racism, however, was the product of an entire colonial worldview which was produced by the colonizer via language, and then internalized and reproduced by the colonized. Within the colonies, Fanon (1952/1967) argues,

> there is a constellation of postulates, a series of propositions that slowly and subtly, with the help of books, newspapers, schools and their texts, advertisements, films, radio, penetrate and individual—constituting the world-view of the group to which one belongs ... that world-view is white because no black voice exists. (p. 152)

As the quotation suggests, Fanon utilizes a model in which human consciousness, propensities, thoughts, and tastes are produced from without through the communicative innovation of language. Fanon (1952/1967) argues that the production of the human mind, with its beliefs, wants, and desires, "is not dependent on cerebral heredity; it is the result of ... the unreflected imposition of culture" (p. 191). Once subsumed by the world-view of the European, the colonial subject holds "the same fantasies as a European" (ibid.). This is not due to some stable and universal set of attitudes and wants endowed to every human; rather, it is because the colonial subject "partakes in the same collective unconscious as the European" (ibid.).

A psychoanalyst by training, Fanon broke with the tradition of Jung and Freud who tended to accord internal causes to psychological problems. Drawing more on Lacan, Fanon insisted that any neurosis experienced by the colonized was cultural in origin. For him, there was no internal tension or conflict that was not a social one as well. As the colonized subject internalized the values of liberal twentieth-century France, he internalized tension. Lifestyle promises and liberal ideals of equality were delivered with the message of racism. At the same time, colonized peoples became the receivers of culture—being robbed of the confidence and power to create and change it. Thus, the colonized culture "becomes closed, fixed in the colonial status, caught in the yoke of oppression" (1967, p. 34). This runs contrary to the natural character of culture, "to be open, permeated by spontaneous, generous, fertile lines of force" (ibid.). Fanon claimed that the eventual result of this tension and rigidity would be a violent break that would result in both the decolonization of colonized territories and of colonized minds. Fanon advocated that new nations be formed which would be based on true equality and cultural creativity—in which colonial racist binaries would be dismantled.

Similarly, Paulo Freire (1970) holds that human consciousness and unconsciousness are produced communicatively through language. In this way, the economic domination of particular groups is conjoined with a cultural domination. As he argues,

> The oppressor consciousness tends to transform everything surrounding it into an object of its domination. The Earth, property, production, the creations of people, people themselves—everything is reduced to the status of objects at its disposal... [A]t a certain point in their existential experience the oppressed feel an irresistible attraction towards the oppressors and their way of life. Sharing this way of life becomes an overpowering aspiration. In their alienation, the oppressed want at any cost to resemble the oppressors, to imitate them, to follow them. (pp. 58–62)

This infusion of the tastes, beliefs, and ideas of the oppressor is delivered through multiple media, but Freire is most concerned with formal education. The "pedagogy of the oppressed," which creates colonial subjects, must, he argues, be replaced by a "pedagogy of liberation," which involves the creation of a critical space in which the "reality" of this subjugation is "unveiled" and both student and teacher embark on the re-creation of knowledge (p. 69). In this way, the oppressed may chart their own emancipatory course from the domination of capitalist-liberal ideology and racism, towards the regaining of their "humanity" (p. 44). Freire, Like Fanon, posits this humanity as a natural state of man, based in cultural and material equality. The ideology of the oppressor is painted as a false consciousness, a fetish, a dominating ideology, as would be expected with critical Marxist approaches. The difference here—the nuance that makes this a cultural approach—is that cultural relations based in racism and other forms of colonial domination are thought to be injurious in their own right, irrespective of material dependency. Furthermore, Both Freire and Fanon insist that colonialism and neocolonialism can be overturned by interventions in the cultural, even suggesting that such interventions are prerequisites to material emancipation.

The next stage in postcolonial thought was, in many ways, prefigured by the cultural analysis of Freire and Fanon. This was a turn to a post-structuralism which turned on the insistence that all meaningful human experience was made intelligible through language, and consequently, that tastes, thoughts, "material" needs, and ideas are collectively determined through culture. The autonomous self—the economic agent—was for the post-structuralists a decentred subject; a hollow space that is continuously colonized and given substance by multiple discourses that define what liberal philosophers had previously called "the individual."

The form of post-structuralism that was imported into postcolonialism was based around the work of Michel Foucault (1980).[1] Very similar to the Lacanian vision used by Fanon, the cultural world that is produced by language is thought by Foucault to structure the cognitive world of the individual, giving shape to his or her tastes, logics, and desires. *Discourse*, for Foucault, makes the world apprehendable by imbuing it with meaning. By making the world understandable in particular ways, discourse motivates the actions and choices of individuals. Discourse itself is simultaneously discursively constructed, however, as Hall (2002, p. 60) explains:

> Discourse is about the production of knowledge through language. But it is itself produced by a practice: "discursive practice"—the practice of producing meaning. Since all social practices entail *meaning*, all practices have a discursive aspect. So discourse enters into and influences all social practices. (60)

These discourses, for both Hall and Foucault, are co-produced by many individuals—although the extent of an individual contribution to this production is tightly correlated with power. Discourses, however, are not

[1] It should be noted that both Foucault and Derrida were heavily influenced by their experiences during the Algerian War of Independence, which would have inevitably brought them into close contact with much early postcolonial thought—especially that of Fanon—as they formulated their ideas regarding the human experience (Alhassan 2007).

thought to be closed systems (they are always adjusting to influences from without) and are relatively cohesive (never random), although they need not be completely internally consistent or conflict-free. The post-structuralist preoccupation with discourse differs from the use of culture by Fanon and Freire in that the latter maintains an underlying notion that colonial discourses serve to obscure a particular "truth" regarding subjugation. This is consistent with the Marxian concept of ideology. Post-structuralists argue, on the other hand, that, since the world can be given multiple meanings via discourse, a "fact" can be construed in different ways. The task of the social scientist, grassroots revolutionary, or the policy analyst, then, moves away from "deciding which social discourses are true or scientific, and which false or ideological" (Hall 2002, p. 62). What things come to count as true, for Foucault, is the outcome of a struggle for meaning that is weighted by power:

> We should admit that power produces knowledge.... That power and knowledge directly imply one another; that there is no power relation without the correlative constitution of a field of knowledge, nor any knowledge that does not presuppose and constitute ... power relations." (1980, p. 27)

Perhaps the most prominent post-structural work regarding colonial thought is Edward Said's (1979) *Orientalism*. Said draws on Gramsci, Fanon, Foucault, and Lacan in arguing that the lived experience of Western subjects is produced partially by a discourse of Orientalism—a textually produced depiction of the world in which the peoples of the Global South are depicted as degenerate, traditional, and irrational. Said is careful to make clear that this discourse is not to be "mistaken as merely decorative or 'superstructural'," as is the case with the Marxian–Gramscian ideas of hegemony and ideology (p. 25); rather, that the authority it exudes "establishes canons of taste and value" (p. 19). The discourses of Orientalism help to produce the Western individual, complete with his or her preferences and assumptions about the world. Orientalism is tied to political interest for certain, but "it was the culture that created that interest," not the interest that created the culture (p. 12). Said includes all forms of Western writing about the orient in this discourse, but also the messages included in the seemingly objective Western social sciences, such as economics.

Arguments related to postcolonialism are diverse and complex, and they do not suit the current purpose to delve deeply into this literature.

The post-structural insights discussed earlier, however, are important for our interest in culture, since they claim the individual to be a collective construct. Debates regarding the possibility of the subaltern to resist the totality of such discourses pertain to our interest in the concept of development as well. This is the case, as it could be argued that since discourse can provoke feelings of diminishment while validating forms of material subjugation, moves to counter such discourses might be thought to represent development. Resistance is generally thought to imply development in the broadest sense in postcolonial works, and arguments run the gamut between those insisting that resistance is possible (Bhabha 1986; Appadurai 2000; Banerjee 2002) or even ubiquitous, and those who suggest that it may be exceedingly difficult to break from such omnipresent discourses, if not impossible (Spivak 1988; Gates 1992).

Post-Development

If postcolonialism represents a critique of the cultural power exerted over the peoples of Global South through the discursive construction of weighted binaries such as West/rest and primitive/modern, post-development may be thought of as a refined strand of that critique. The linguistically constructed colonial binary at stake in post-development theory is that of developed/underdeveloped. Although much attention is given to Arturo Escobar's (1994) doctoral dissertation *Encountering Development* as a founding text in the field, the discursive force of post-development thought was largely centred on edited readers by Sachs (1991) and by Rahnema and Bawtree (1997) as well.

In these works, the idea of development is attacked as a colonial discourse. Rahnema and Bawtree (1997) reprint a classic work by Sahlins in making the fundamental post-development argument that, in Sahlins' words,

> The world's most primitive people have few possessions, *but they are not poor*. Poverty is not a certain small amount of goods, not is it just a relation between means and ends; above all, it is a relation between people. Poverty is a social status. (p. 19)

Using this logic and basing his argument on historical interpretation, Sahlins argued that the assumptions of the nature of man and poverty that pervade Western thought—Marxist and especially liberal economic—make little sense. When discussing an apparent indifference to poverty amongst hunters and gatherers, Sahlins holds,

> [I]t seems wrong to say that wants are 'restricted', desires 'restrained', or even that the notion of wealth is 'limited'. Such phrasings imply in advance an Economic Man and a struggle of the hunger against ones own worst nature, which is finally then substituted by a cultural vow of poverty.... [Rather], economic man is a bourgeois construction.... It is not that hunters and gatherers have curbed their materialistic 'impulses': they simply never made an institution of them. (p. 10)

Post-development theorists argue that development "experts" entered this milieu, propelled by and propelling the Eurocentric discourse of development. These experts, hailing from the West and privileged castes of the former colonies, began by using discourse to imply "abnormalities" such as "underdeveloped," "malnourished," "poor," and illiterate" (Escobar 1999b, p. 322). To be "developed" came to imply "being like the West." To be "underdeveloped" was to live in any other way. "Traditional" knowledges and ways of life were in this way devalued. Development discourse was internalized by many of the newly defined "poor" under the weight of the authoritative discursive power of Western-trained experts. These ideas of non-Western inferiority were institutionalized through the "professionalization" and "technification" of development. University departments and academic disciplines were established throughout the developed world, where experts sought to,

> Establish the nature of Third World countries, to classify their problems and formulate policies, to pass judgement on them and visualize their future—to produce, in short, a regime of truth and norms about development...[;] a field of control of knowledge, through which truth (and, so, power) was produced. (Ibid., pp. 322–323)

With many similarities to Polanyi's (1944) work, Escobar (1999a) argues that the discipline of development economics sits at the core of this discursive machine which,

> must be analyzed within the context of the establishment of economics as a "positive," "objective," science, thanks in part to the development—during the past 200 years—of a culture in which a specific economic rationality ... became dominant. This process, which one can perhaps call the

> "economization of life," was intimately linked to the development of capitalism; it entailed as necessary prerequisites the establishment of the normative discourse of classical political economy. (Ibid., p. 323)

Rahnema and Bawtree (1997) describe development discourse as a cultural viral infection. This virus, he argues, "penetrates into peoples' minds," propelled by "the school system, the production of addictive needs, and the dis-valuation of indigenous know-how" (p. 119). In human history, he argues, "'economic' man represents a novelty."

> He developed, indeed, in the womb of early capitalism, and his identity card could have been stamped with the words 'white', 'European' and 'male'. Yet he took pride in proclaiming his 'freedom' from belonging to any particular tribe or community, roots or culture, village or oasis. He was an a-cultured, uniform and substitutable person. He perceived himself as an 'individual' rather than a 'member of the community'. (p. 116)

Rahnema argues that the cultural beast, economic man, invaded colonial and postcolonial societies, destroying "the basic institutions of local populations," and that he did this "under the banner of development" (p. 118). It is through development discourse that,

> homo economicus transforms all his prey into 'economic men', like himself, substituting their motives of subsistence and their sense of belonging to the community with those of gain and of full 'individual freedom'. (p. 119)

Those who critique post-development thought often insist that it tends to romanticize poverty and tradition, or that it is hopelessly relativistic. Although it is not true that post-development theorists, or the post-structural theorists they based their work on (Foucault, Derrida), acted without ethics, it does seem that their theoretical construct left little space within which to formulate one. The strength of the post-development critique of cultural and material imperialism, it seems, may have been bought, at least initially, at the expense of any sense of progress. Post-structural assertions that humans engage the world through a largely self-referential, ever-evolving, system of symbols leave themselves open to a critique of cultural reductionism that denies a real material world. The assertion that human values are based in such symbolic systems, similarly, has led to critiques of relativism. Consequently, caricatures of post-structuralism and post-development conjure a theory in which human reality can be changed by pure imagination, even the most atrocious abuses and inequalities can be justified through appeals to culture, and one in which there is simply no such thing as development (Rao and Walton 2004; Pieterse 2000).

Cultural Political Economy

If it were ever true that post-development theorists failed to transcend mere relativistic critique and to forward a substantive ethic with which to conceive social progress, this problem did not last long. Conversely, if political economy approaches to development tended to be irredeemably materially reductionist during the twentieth century, recognition of the autonomy and co-determining power of culture became prevalent into the twenty-first century. In this section, I propose that, as a result of these movements, a meaningful theoretical conversation has taken place between cultural and critical political economy approaches in development studies. With contributions from both the culturalists and the political economists, I suggest that this dialogue represents the emergence of a *cultural political economy* of development.

This is not to deny, for example, that there is a valid and relevant post-development school that contains a subtle, non-relativistic critique that is not mired in cultural reductionism. Nor is it meant to suggest that the political economy of development has not incorporated cultural insights meaningfully into its analysis. The category of cultural political economy is evoked here to recognize that much of the more sophisticated political economy work and more recent permutations of post-development have become strikingly similar—that the schools have converged.

Pieterse (2000) perhaps began the move from the culturalist side by insisting that the focus of the post-development critique is really on modernization theory and the system of development that emerged in the post-WWII period, instead of against the idea of development itself. He also claims that most post-development theorists do not succumb to romanticism and relativism, but partake in a "reflexive development, in which a critique of science is viewed as part of development politics" (2000, p. 343). Consistent with Pieterse's claims, many post-development theorists have advocated the support of grass-roots "new" social movements based on gender and other forms of identity as well as class, and participatory forms of development interventions, policy formulation, and research, instead of technocratic economistic "top-down" development plans instituted by governments and transnational institutions (Nelson and Wright 1995; Alvarez et al. 1998).

Pieterse's assertions may well be true, but they are based in observations of the praxis of post-development thinkers, not on any theoretical advancement that transcends the relativist trap. Through the advancement of what Escobar (2007) calls the "Latin American modernity/coloniality (MC) research program" (p. 179), however, it has increasingly been argued that a modern-style ethic of equality is not necessarily discordant with a cultural approach. Based largely on the writings of Dussel (1980), this school insists first that it is arrogant to assume that modernity was solely a European construction and therefore has little to do with pristine cultures that sit somewhere outside its borders. Second, while Dussel claims his theory to be posmodern, and later transmodern (2012), he insists that this does not imply an idealist world divorced from materiality—rather a cultural world that operates in relation to a material world which, nonetheless, must be symbolically interpreted to have meaning to human actors.

This theoretical innovation buys post-development theorists much in the way of theoretical buttressing for their already existent praxis. "Transmodernity" implies first that there is no outside of modernity in current global semiotic structures, but there are margins from which cultural innovation can, and does, emerge. This concept is accomplished by "locating the origins of modernity with the Conquest of America and the control of the Atlantic after 1492, rather than the most commonly accepted landmarks such as the Enlightenment or the end of the eighteenth century" (Escobar 2007, p. 184). This allows a "world perspective in the explanation of modernity, in lieu of a view of modernity as an intra-European phenomenon" (ibid.). This process did not occur without asymmetries of power, however, as "the domination of others outside the European core" and the "subalternization of the knowledge and cultures of these other groups" typified the process in which modernity was constructed (ibid.). As a result of this line of thought, one can continue to prescribe to a post-structuralism, or post-developmentism, while maintaining a commitment to modern virtues such as equality, human rights, and democracy widely construed.

Material and economic dimensions are not diminished in this perspective. The project, Escobar (2007) argues, has been undertaken with "a persistent attention to colonialism and the making of the capitalist world as constitutive of modernity" which "includes a determination not to overlook the economy and its concomitant forms of exploitation" (p. 184). Modernity, then, was co-built globally by colonizers and colonized, but with a Eurocentrism that was underwritten by military and economic power. This does not mean, however, that other forms of thought do not have interpolating power in this constellation. Development, in fact, requires an equalization of this interpolating power via

> the interpellation which the majority of the population of the planet, located in the South, raises, demanding the right to live, the right to develop their own culture, economy, politics, etc. ... There is no liberation without rationality, but there is no *critical* rationality without accepting the interpellation of the excluded, or this would inadvertently be only the rationality of domination. (Dussel and Mendieta 1996, pp. 31 & 36)

Nearly simultaneous to this theoretical move from relativism and idealism on the part of the post-structuralists has come a meaningful attempt by critical political economists of development to move beyond the depiction of culture as mere materially determined ideology. Central to this is the work of Jessop and Ngai-Ling Sum (2001), who embrace "the post-disciplinary 'cultural turn' for rethinking political economy" (p. 92). This involves supplementing Marxism with a "discursive account of power" which,

> involves the claim that the interests at stake in relations of power are significantly shaped by the discursive constitution of identities, modes of calculation, strategies and tactics and not just by the so-called 'objective' position of specific agents in a given conjuncture (as if they existed outside of discourse); and also [an admission that] that the primary institutional mechanisms in and through which power is exercised, whether directly or indirectly, themselves involve a variable mix of discursive and material resources. Another key feature [concerns] ... emphasis on the social construction of knowledge and truth regimes. (p. 93)

This embracing of the cultural is, however, "subject to certain modifications that re-assert the importance of the materiality of political economy" (ibid., p. 92). Central to this is an emphasis on "the materiality of social relations and the constraints involved in processes that also operate 'behind the backs' of the relevant agents," as well as on the historically contingent evolutionary nature of cultural and other institutions (ibid., p. 94). Resultantly, Jessop and Sum claim that this new political economy can "escape the sociological imperialism of pure social constructionism and the voluntarist vacuity of certain lines of discourse analysis, which seem to imply that one can will anything into existence in and through an appropriately articulated discourse" (ibid.).

What I would like to suggest here is that the simultaneous intellectual augmentations of the post-structuralists and the critical political economists described earlier have resulted in the inadvertent cohabitation of a new school of development thought *cultural political economy*.[2] This school has four main features. First, although it recognizes the discursive constitution of meaning, the school emphasizes the path-dependent nature of linguistic structure—another world is possible, but any world is not possible, since all worlds are only imaginable through the use of already existent semiotic tools. Second, a material, natural world exists outside of culture, although to be made intelligible, it must be discursively interpreted. Third, cultural political economy features a commitment to an egalitarian ethic in both cultural and material terms (although it recognizes both these terms to be little more than abstractions since they are coterminous). Fourth, cultural political economy is interdisciplinary—this has meant engagement with political economy, cultural studies, anthropology, geography, linguistics, and sociology, but not as of yet with neoclassical economics.

The emergence of cultural political economy (CPE) has not simply been an academic pursuit. A cultural political economy approach to development has also been championed by indigenous groups at global, national, and local scales (Mander and Tauli-Corpuz 2006). As Blaser, Feit, and McRae (2004) have elucidated in an edited volume that contains contributions from indigenous leaders, such groups have often rejected modernizationist, neoliberal, externally devised, as well as state- or corporate-led development initiatives. Focus has been placed by indigenous peoples on the realization of *life projects* (as opposed to *development projects*) that emphasize local culturally situated values and goals, solidarity and self-governance. Life projects, according to Blaser, Feit, and McRae, do not, however, distil to a simple romanticization of imagined traditional lifestyles and outright rejection of ideas related to economic growth, development, or social progress. Although the culturally situated nature of human values and lifestyles is forefronted, indigenous groups also seek

[2] This term is explicitly used by Jessop and Sum and also by Best and Paterson (2007), although the latter do not apply the theory specifically to development issues.

material advancement and the acquisition of productive resources—primarily of land—in a struggle for subsistence. Blaser, Feit, and McRae show that assertions related to the primacy of culture coexist in indigenous politics with appeals to universal rights. Furthermore, locally situated projects and politics in indigenous communities are linked inextricably to broader international solidarity and environmental movements.

Culture and Sustainable Development

A cultural political economy approach to development brings together theoretical understandings with praxis just as it allows the co-determined nature of material and cultural elements. One of the areas where CPE can be seen most vividly is in the area of sustainable development. Well before the Club of Rome's (Meadows et al. 1972) assertion that there are environmental limits to development defined strictly as increasing income per capita, a tension between economic development and the natural environment had been noted. Polanyi (1944) spent much time, for example, describing the environmental catastrophe that was apparent in the eighteenth-century economy.

The Brundtland et al. (1987) report formalized this dilemma, using the term "sustainable development" to describe "development that meets the needs of the present without compromising the ability of future generations to meet their own needs." The integration of a CPE approach (along with the strong voices of postcolonial and indigenous movements) requires us to question just what this "development" is that is to be "sustained." Nurse (2006) produced an insightful contribution by insisting that culture be made a "pillar" of sustainable development. By this, he meant that we must understand how culture frames both the production and consumption side of development. On the consumption side, we must not assume to know what the end point of human flourishing is. This opens the door to a grounded redefinition of "the good life" from indigenous and other perspectives. On the production side, this suggests that that there are multiple social practices, actions, and understandings that might produce this development.

As Blaser et al. (2004) and others have documented, indigenous peoples have taken a leading role formulating this new form of sustainable development. This often involves the evocation of indigenous "life projects" that break substantively and ontologically from the mainstream concept of "development." A less radical break from mainstream development is present in the use and valuing of traditional ecological knowledge (TEK) by mainstream developmental and ecological organizations. For example, the International Panel on Climate Change attempts to integrate TEK into its analyses and policy prescriptions, and the Canadian government proposes the use of the intimate ecological knowledge of indigenous peoples in the service of environmental impact assessment. Such uses of TEK are laudable for their admission of the value of indigenous knowledge, but tend to view such knowledge as a resource to be used by non-indigenous agencies to achieve their policy or measurement goals—not as a valuable cultural and ontological contribution to the redefinition of the meaning of developmental and human–environment relations.

A CPE approach allows us to engage with grounded struggles for meanings and material resources implicated when indigenous groups assert their power to redefine the meaning of development itself. It also allows an engagement with the breaking of the human–nature binary that is implied by indigenous worldviews. The hope embodied in a CPE approach is that sociologists, political scientists, anthropologists, indigenous peoples, and economists may be able to use it as a meeting place within which they can form mutual understandings that could lead to positive change in collaboration with indigenous peoples. The necessity of sustainability mandates that this change be embedded in a flourishing ecosystem.

Conclusion

The work undertaken in the last two chapters began with a claim that there exists an uncomfortable silence between cultural and political economy approaches to development on one side, and neoclassical economic approaches on the other. After reviewing the intellectual history of development thinking from the eighteenth century onwards, it is apparent that this failure of communication is the consequence of old disciplinary commitments that have become entrenched due to both methodological expedience and ideological convenience.

For classical political economists beginning with Smith and continuing in varying degrees through to Mill, considerations of culture and ethics were common. These considerations were held separate from economic analysis in all cases, due to a methodological need to assume Smith's self-interested, atomistic personal-gain-maximizing actor—homo economicus—as the primal unit for economic analysis. Only with the assumption of homo economicus would Smith's metaphor of the self-regulating market with its invisible hand make analytical sense. Questions of culture and ethics, although extremely prevalent in the works of the classical political economists, were considered separately so as not to interfere with the elegant functioning of early economic models. It should not be forgotten, however, as Polanyi (1944) has argued, that the segregation of economic and cultural/ethical realms, and the obfuscation of the latter, served the ideological interest of a powerful merchant colonial class whose power rested on the institutionalization of private property rights and market-based economies in the eighteenth century.

These interests and methodological expediencies continued and became solidified through the nineteenth and twentieth centuries. Especially significant in this regard was the marginal revolution which completed the amputation of culture from economy. This was achieved via the methodological adoption of differential calculus which allowed for the mathematization of economics and the disciplines' subsequent ascendance to become the "queen of the social sciences." All the while, it must be remembered, lingering class interests exerted their ideological pressures on the refining of economic thought.

The recognition of cultural difference that accompanied attempts to "develop" newly emergent postcolonial nations in the post-WWII period posed a particular problem for economic theory. The culturally situated actions of peoples of non-European descent did not fit the prerequisites of the economic model. Neoclassical economists responded with a proclamation that traditional culture in the former colonies was exerting a pressure on economic actors in those regions that caused them to behave irrationally. This prompted a temporary alliance with certain sociologists who were enlisted to identify particular cultural pathologies of traditional societies and to devise plans for the cultural cure. They were to then deliver fully formed homo economici to the economists so that the latter could finally actualize their technocratic development plans. Although this seemed to be a period of interdisciplinary cross-fertilization, it could be more accurately described as disciplinary specialization which saw sociologists act in the service of waiting neoclassical economists—subservient social scientists paying discursive homage to the "queen."

With the advent of new classical economics, this interdisciplinary arrangement was terminated. For the Chicago School economists of this tradition all people were considered rational; culture was therefore largely irrelevant, and so was the work of other social scientists. It was (non-cultural) institutional change that was needed to allow the benefits of self-interest to fruitfully accrue, not some sort of cultural engineering. Free markets were the order of the day. It was presumed that rational actors in the Global South would act efficiently within a market-centric institutional setting.

New institutional economists went further in the depreciation of culture vis-à-vis homo economicus as they came to recognize culture as the result of the self-interested action of stable (in their preferences) economic actors. Culture was one of many possible strategic constructions of maximizing automatons in the face of market failures caused by the existence of public goods and associated externalities. Nonetheless, the idea of path-dependency revived modernization theory as it was argued that the once-efficient cultural institutions could become suboptimal equilibriums as technology and other institutional factors change. New institutionalism resultantly invited the intervention of technocrats to legislate between good and bad, efficient and inefficient, culture—supporting the former, while dissuading the latter.

Critical political economists from Marx in the nineteenth century, through to Frank and Wallertstein in the twentieth century, maintained a scepticism towards liberal economics. These thinkers deftly brought attention to the ways in which free-market economies tended to exacerbate inequalities and perpetuate class-based and colonial domination. Culture, however, became separated from, and marginalized in comparison to, what was considered to be a determinant material sphere. This material reductionism was countered by postcolonial and post-development culturalism. These theorist tended to err in the other direction, however, leaving themselves open to critiques of idealism, cultural reductionism, and excessive relativism.

The seemingly incommensurable divide between culturalists and critical political economists has recently been bridged through the advent of various approaches to cultural political economy. By insisting that modernity and the associated ethic of equality were co-produced by colonizers and colonized, and that there was no outside of this cultural formation—just difference at the margins—modernity/coloniality theorists such as Dussel and Escobar escaped the relativist trap. This idea has been increasingly referred to a *transmodernity*. Similarly, through an insistence that a material extra-cultural world existed, yet must be interpreted symbolically, they countered critiques of idealism. Simultaneously, attempts have been made by political economists to take culture seriously by introducing a discursive concept of power and admitting that the cultural and material are co-determining. The familiar intellectual quagmire of relativistic idealism was avoided through an appeal to the path-dependent nature of human language, material constructions, and lived experience. Cultural political economy, it seems, represents a powerful collaborative project of the cultural and critical political economy schools as well as grassroots, especially indigenous, movements.

Communication and cooperation between these groups and neoclassical economists has been much more problematic. The methodological presumption of egoistic, atomistic human actors with stable preference sets seems to preclude any fruitful exchange between neoclassical economists and culturalists. The tendency of neoclassical economists to uncritically valorize and reify markets does not sit well with critical political economists. The most coherent attempt to contribute to cultural political economy from the neoclassical side has come through the capability approach. Perhaps due to the difficulty of this theoretical challenge, however, this approach has yielded a large portion of ambiguity. As a result, the incentive for academic neoclassical economists, as well as those in bilateral and multilateral institutions, has been to borrow from the capability approach piecemeal. This implies the use of broader indicators of development—such as the Human Development Index—for the measurement of development, or the use of participatory approaches to facilitate the implementation of projects that have largely been designed by the economists, or other technocrats, themselves. As a result, the very parts of the capabilities approach that may resonate with cultural political economists—such as the encouragement of genuine grassroots participation, the challenging of power structures, and the recognition of multiple definitions of development—tend to be culled by neoclassical economists (Bebbington et al. 2004).

This book represents an attempt to breach the communication gap between critical political economists and culturalists on the one side, and neoclassical development economists on the other. This is to be done via an integration of indigenous concepts of sustainable development into development theory. The undertaking is not meant to displace or discredit the capabilities approach, but to work towards clarifying it. Such work will entail a contribution to cultural political economy that begins with the neoclassical approach. To be consistent with a cultural political economy approach, this would imply an inductive empirically grounded exploration which privileges the local knowledge of the marginalized—in this case, Latin American indigenous peoples.

References

Alhassan, A. (2007). The Canonic Economy of Communication and Culture: The Centrality of the Postcolonial Margins. *Canadian Journal of Communication, 32* (1).

Althusser, L. (1971). Ideology and the State. In *Lenin and Philosophy and Other Essays* (Vol. 2). Paris: François Maspero.

Alvarez, S. E., Dagnino, E., & Escobar, A. (1998). The Cultural and the Political in Latin American Social Movements. In S. E. Alvarez, E. Dagnino, & A. Escobar (Eds.), *Cultures of Politics, Politics of Culture*. Colorado: Westview Press.

Amin, S. (1976). *Unequal Development: An Essay on the Social Formation of Peripheral Capitalism*. New York: Monthly Review Press.

Amin, S. (1992). *Empire of Chaos*. New York: Monthly Review Press.

Appadurai, A. (2000). Disjuncture and Difference in the Global Cultural Economy. In S. During (Ed.), *The Cultural Studies Reader* (2nd ed., pp. 220–230). London: Routledge.

Banerjee, I. (2002). The Locals Strike Back?: Media Globalization and Localization in the New Asian Television Landscape. *Gazette: The International Journal for Communication Studies, 64*(6), 517–535.

Bebbington, A., Guggenhiem, S., Olson, E., & Woolcock, M. (2004). Exploring the Social Capital Debatess at the World Bank. *Journal of Development Studies, 40*(5), 33–64.

Best, J., & Paterson, M. (2007). *Cultural Political Economy*. Workshop on Cultural Political Economy. University of Ottawa, June 15–17, 2007.

Bhabha, H. K. (1986). The Other Question: Difference, Discrimination and the Discourse of Colonialism. In F. Parker, P. Hulme, & M. Iverson (Eds.), *Literature, Politics, and Theory: Papers from the Essex Conference 1976–1984*. London: Methuen.

Blaser, M., Feit, H. A., & McRae, G. (2004). *In the Way of Development: Indigenous Peoples, Life Projects, and Globalization*. Ottawa: IDRC/Zed.

Brundtland, G., Khalid, M., Agnelli, S., Al-Athel, S., Chidzero, B., Fadika, L., et al. (1987). *Our Common Future*. Brundtland Report.

Cardoso, F. H. (1972). Imperialism and Dependency in Latin America. In F. Bonilla & R. Girling (Eds.), *Structures of Dependency*. Stanford, CA: Institute of Political Studies.

Césaire, A. (1953/1972). *Discourse on Colonialism*. New York: Monthly Review Press.

Dorfman, A., & Metellart, A. (1975). *How to Read Donald Duck: Imperialist Ideology in the Disney Comic*. New York: International General Editions.

Dos Santos, T. (1971). The Structure of Dependence. In K. T. Fann & D. C. Hodges (Eds.), *Readings in U.S. Imperialism*. Boston: Porter Sargent.

Dussel, E. (1980). *The Philosophy of Liberation*. New York: Orbis.

Dussel, E. D. (2012). Transmodernity and Interculturality: An interpretation from the Perspective of Philosophy of Liberation. *Transmodernity: Journal of Peripheral Cultural Production of the Luso-Hispanic World, 1*(3).

Dussel, E. D., & Mendieta, E. (1996). *The underside of modernity: Apel, Ricoeur, Rorty, Taylor, and the philosophy of liberation*. Atlantic Highlands, NJ: Humanities Press.

Escobar, A. (1994). *Encountering Development: The Making and Unmaking of the Third World*. Princeton: Princeton University Press.

Escobar, A. (1999a, November). The Invention of Development. *Current History*, 382–386.

Escobar, A. (1999b). Discourse and Power in Development: Michel Foucault and the Relevance of His Work to the Third World. In T. L. Jacobson & J. Servaes (Eds.), *Theoretical Approaches to Participatory Communication*. Cresskill, NJ: Hampton Press.

Escobar, A. (2006). *Places and Regions in the Age of Globality: Social Movements and Biodiversity Conservation in the Columbian Pacific*. Mimeo: Department of Anthropology, University of North Carolina. Retrieved from http://www.unc.edu/~aescobar/text/eng/places_regions.doc.

Escobar, A. (2007). Worlds and Knowledges Otherwise: The Latin American Modernity/Coloniality Research Program. *Cultural Studies, 21*(2), 179–212.

Fanon, F. (1952/1967). *Black Skin, White Masks*. New York: Grove Press.

Foucault, M. (1980). *Power/Knowledge: Selected Interviews and Other Writings, 1972–1977*. Vintage.

Frank, A. G. (1966). The Development of Underdevelopment. *Monthly Review, 18*(4), 17–31.

Frank, A. G. (1981). *Crisis in the Third World*. London: Heinemann.

Freire, P. (1970). *Pedagogy of the Oppressed*. New York: Continuum.

Furtado, C. (1964). *Development and Underdevelopment: A Structural View of the Problems of Developed and Underdeveloped Countries*. Berkeley: University of California Press.

Furtado, C. 1971. Dependencia Externa y Teoria Economica. *El Trimestre Economico, 38*, 335–349.

García, A. (1972). *Atraso y Dependencia in América Latina; Hacia una teoría Latinoamericana de Desarollo*. Buenos Aires: El Eteneo.

Gates, H. R., Jr. (1992). *"Race," Writing, and Difference*. New York: Barnes & Noble.

Gereffi, G. (1994/2000). Rethinking Development Theory: Insights from East Asia and Latin America. In J. Timmons Roberts & A. Hite (Eds.), *From Modernization to Globalization: Perspectives on Development and Social Change*. Malden, MA: Blackwell.

Germani, G. (1972). Aspectos Teóricos de la Marginalidad. *Revista Paraguaya de Sociología, 9*(30), 7–35.

González-Casanova, P. (1965). Internal Colonialism and National Development, Studies in Comparative International Development. In I. L. Horowitz de Castro & J. Gerassi (Eds.), *Latin American Radicalism* (pp. 118–139). London: Jonathan Cape.

Gramsci, A. (1957/1971). *Selections from the Prison Notebooks*. New York: International Publishers.

Hall, S. (2002). The West and the Rest: Discourse and Power. In S. Schech & J. Haggis (Eds.), *Development: A Cultural Studies Reader*. Malden, MA: Blackwell.

Hamelink, C. J. (1983). *Cultural Autonomy in Global Communications: Planning National Information Policy*. New York: Longman.

Jessop, B., & Sum, N. (2001). Pre-disciplinary and Post-disciplinary Perspectives. *New Political Economy, 6*(1), 89–101.

Johnson, D. L. (1972). On Oppressed Classes. In J. D. Cockroft, A. G. Frank, & D. L. Johnson (Eds.), *Dependence and Underdevelopment: Latin America's Political Economy*. New York: Doubleday.

Kapoor, I. (2002). Capitalism, Culture, Agency: Dependency Theory versus Postcolonial Theory. *Third World Quarterly, 23*(4), 647–664.

Kay, C. (1989). *Latin American Theories of Development and Underdevelopment*. New York: Routledge.

Mander, J., & Tauli-Corpuz, V. (Eds.). (2006). *Paradigm Wars: Indigenous Peoples' Resistance to Globalization*. San Francisco: Sierra Club Books.

Marini, R. M. (1972). Dialéctica de la Dependencia: La Economía Exportadora. *Sociedad y Desarollo*, no. 1.

Martinussen, J. (1997). *Society, State & Market: A Guide to Competing Theories of Development*. Halifax, NS: Fernwood.

McLeod, J. (2000). *Beginning Postcolonialism*. Manchester University Press.

Meadows, D. H., Meadows, D. H., Randers, J., & Behrens III, W. W. (1972). The Limits to Growth: A Report to the Club of Rome (1972). *Google Scholar*.

Myrdal, G. (1968). *Asian Drama: An Inquiry into the Poverty of Nations*. Harmondsworth: Penguin.

Nelson, N., & Wright, S. (1995). *Power and Participatory Development*. London: Intermediate Technology.

Nurse, K. (2006). Culture as the Fourth Pillar of Sustainable Development. *Small States: Economic Review and Basic Statistics, 11*, 28–40.

Pieterse, J. N. (2000). After Post-Development. *Third World Quarterly, 21*(2), 174–191.

Polanyi, K. (1944/2001). *The Great Transformation: The Political and Economic Origins of Our Time*. Boston: Beacon Press.

Prebisch, R. (1950). *The Economic Development of Latin America and Its Principal Problems*. New York: United Nations.
Quijano, A. (1977). *Imperialismo y "Marginalidad" en Amérique Latina*. Lima: Mosca Azul Editores.
Rahnema, M., & Bawtree, V. (Eds.). (1997). *The Post-Development Reader*. London: Zed Books.
Rao, V., & Walton, M. (2004). Culture and Public Action: Relationality, Equality of Agency, and Development. In V. Rao & W. Walton (Eds.), *Culture and Public Action* (pp. 3–36). Stanford: Stanford University Press.
Sachs, W. (Ed.). (1991). *The Development Dictionary: A Guide to Knowledge as Power*. London: Zed Books.
Sahlins, M. (1976). *Culture and Practical Reason*. London: University of Chicago Press.
Said, E. (1979). *Orientalism*. New York: Vintage Books.
Salinas, R., & Paldán, L. (1979). Culture in the Process of Dependent Development: Theoretical Perspectives. In K. Nordenstreng & H. I. Schiller (Eds.), *National Sovereignty and International Communication*. New Jersey: Ablex.
Schiller, H. I. (1979). Transnational Media and National Development. In K. Nordenstreng & H. I. Schiller (Eds.), *National Sovereignty and International Communication*. New Jersey: Ablex.
Senghor, L. S. (1956, June–November). The Spirit of Civilization or the Laws of African Negro Culture. *Présence Africaine*, 8–10.
Spivak, G. C. (1988). Can the Subaltern Speak? In C. Nelson & L. Grossberg (Eds.), *Marxism and the Interpretation of Culture*. Urbana: University of Illinois Press.
Sunkel, O. (1969). National Development Policy and External Dependence in Latin America. *Journal of Development Studies, 6*(1), 23–48.
Tomlinson, J. (1991). *Cultural Imperialism: A Critical Introduction*. Baltimore: Johns Hopkins University Press.
Wallerstein, I. (1974). *The Modern World System: Capitalist Agriculture and the Origins of the European World Economy in the Sixteenth Century*. New York: Academic Press.
Wallerstein, I. (1979/2000). The Rise and Future Demise of the World Capitalist System: Concepts for Comparative Analysis. In J. Roberts & A. Hite (Eds.), *From Modernization to Globalization: Perspectives on Development and Social Change*. Oxford: Blackwell.
Williams, R. (1977). *Marxism and Literature*. Oxford and New York: Oxford University Press.

CHAPTER 6

Origins of a Maya Sustainable Development Movement

Urry (2005) argues that humans and their associated social formations are best viewed as "'transitory hardenings' in the more basic flows of massive amounts of minerals, genes, diseases, energy, information and language" (p. 7). To be consistent with the complexity theory to which Urry subscribes, these hardenings, although transitory, are not arbitrary. The human and social forms that are constructed of basic material, cultural, and energy flows arise from particular histories which cannot be arbitrarily replaced. Everything comes from somewhere—the current forms and future trajectories of human and social forms are dependent on their physical and cultural histories (Prigogine 1997; Oldridge 2003; Urry 2005). In order to best understand the ideas of "development" that have hardened amongst Latin America's indigenous peoples, it would be helpful to look first at their situation amidst a historical sea of discursive and material flows. This is the goal of this chapter. By way of entry, I will be describing the work, position, and thought of one Maya indigenous organization called *El Centro Pluricultual para la Democracia*. Understanding *El Centro* is important because it is the primary organization in Guatemala that has explicitly tasked itself with the creation and promotion of an indigenous idea of sustainable development. This development theory is called culturally sustainable development (CSD) by the practitioners at *El Centro*. In looking at the idea of CSD, and the position of *El Centro*, we can begin to understand the logic of Maya ideas of development in Guatemala, and indigenous ideas of sustainable development in Latin America in general.

T. MacNeill, *Indigenous Cultures and Sustainable Development in Latin America*, https://doi.org/10.1007/978-3-030-37023-7_6

Since the idea of development that is utilized by *El Centro* is communicatively produced by its members, however, I would suggest that we must not look at the organization as an individual form, but as a Habermasian (1984, 1989) public sphere—a conglomeration of human communication in which certain ideas of the world are negotiated, argued, and combined—likely amidst certain types of power asymmetries and incomplete access to information (Durham-Peters 1993). The constituting flows that form the histories of the members of the organization come into contact at *El Centro*, and some of these are favoured, while others are shunned. Just as the organization is an actor that produces discourses which resonate with and militate against a larger discursive formation of global thought on development and progress, it has its own internal discursive negotiating process.

It may be true in many cases that the individuals that make up the organization arrived as products of similar experience with like minds to produce a cohesive idea of what development is and how to get it. But ideas are formed in this location as well. *Maria*, one of the central members of the organization, serves as a good example in this respect. She was trained as a social worker in San Carlos University in Quetzaltenango, Guatemala, coming into contact with various liberal, Marxian, and anti-modern texts. She also takes with her the experience of being an urban indigenous woman in the Western Highlands. But her ideas were more fully formed by interaction with members of *El Centro*. As she explains, "here in *El Centro*, there were also many readings and documents of indigenous peoples and this also created [in me] ways of thinking about the problems that exist."

The work to be done in this chapter, then, is to map out the constituting structures and experiences that help to generate the ideas that are expressed at *El Centro*—to locate it within the tracks of local history and culture, but also within a field of international discourse. But throughout this process, it is important to remain cognizant of internal dynamics and favoured texts as well. The model we must employ here is one in which, *first*, *El Centro* is created by multiple fields of discourse and experience. *Second*, this discourse and experience is interpreted and reformed internally through communication. And, *third*, the ideas generated within *El Centro* are exported in a number of ways as they begin to interact with the very fields of discourse and remembered experience that had worked to constitute *El Centro* in the first place. This model will be kept in mind as we discuss the importance of *Guatemalan national history*, *recent global tendencies*, and the importance of *Maya cosmovision* in relation to the politics and ideas of *El Centro*. There is no space here to discuss all the nuances of Guatemalan history or Maya cosmovision. Nor will it be possible to address the multiple debates and fissures that appear in literature regarding the global tendencies that will be discussed. The goal here is to simply provide enough information to help foster the beginnings of an understanding of the situation of *El Centro* amidst all of these co-causal factors. It is hoped that this will assist in the understanding of the Maya theory of sustainable development that will be elaborated in the following chapter.

Guatemalan History

Following the categorization put forth by Gere and MacNeill (2008) and MacNeill (2014), the history of Guatemala will be divided into five periods in this discussion. These will be the *early colonial period* (1518–1821), the arguably postcolonial[1] period of *exclusive nationalism* (1821–1945), the *Ten Years of Spring* (1945–1954), *La Violenca* (1970s–1980s), and the *postwar period* (1990s–present). As with all historical categorizations, these periods are somewhat arbitrary. They will do, however, for the current purpose of temporally locating the work of *El Centro*. It also should be remembered that although the most current historical periods figure the largest in the felt personal experience of the members of the organization, older periods are presumed to have their own weight—albeit indirectly—on the constitution of *El Centro*.

Early Colonialism

One cannot overstate the multiple impacts of early colonization on the lives, livelihoods, and cultures of the Americas and of Europe (Galeano 1973). The most important observation about this period for our current purpose, however, is that this was the era in which the peoples of what later became called the Americas met their collective Other. Columbus first called the collective peoples of the Americas "indio," quite famously and unwittingly in 1492 (Montejo 2005, p. 2). And especially with the invasion of Central America by Pedro de Alvarado in 1523, peoples of Maya descent, who had previously thought of themselves as *Mam*, *Tzutijil*,

[1] Most members of *El Centro* would argue that Guatemala is still a colonized territory, dominated by colonial Iberian culture and by the economic power of transnational capital.

or *K'iche'* amongst others, became collectively referred to as *Indio* by the white-skinned, bearded colonizers (Galeano 1973; Fischer and Hendrickson 2003). The *native*, or *Indio*, category became at this time counterpoised with the *Spanish*, the *European*, and this categorization became, to various degrees, internalized by the old inhabitants of the *New World* (Montejo 2005). With the dual dynamics of intermarriage and a racialized political economy of status, the names attached to this binary eventually changed in popular discourse. In Guatemala, *ladino*—a genetic mix of *Spanish* and "*Indio*" blood—became the dominant category which was juxtaposed with the subservient *Indigenous* in Guatemala. This relationship was nuanced by the existence of a very small but extremely economically, culturally, and politically powerful third category of virtually pure Spanish descent (Montejo 2005; Casaus Arzú 1995).

The racialized domination and exploitation of Latin America, in general, and Guatemala in specific, has been well documented (Galeano 1973). Disease and conquest reduced the population of the Americas by up to 90% during the sixteenth century (Diamond 1997), as the content was gutted of its natural resources (Galeano 1973). In Guatemala, colonial administration was officially to follow a *two republics* model, as indigenous peoples were allowed their own form of governance alongside an imposed Spanish system (Wittman and Geisler 2005). The seeming acceptance of indigenous culture and governance structure was, however, hardly genuine. As Wittman and Geisler (2005) argue, "the colonial Guatemalan government sought to overrule local law and custom and to gain access to indigenous lands and forests early on" (p. 64). Much formerly communally held territory was expropriated in the name of the crown, and much of this, in turn, was converted to private ownership (ibid.). Still, more than half of the land in Guatemala remained under communal control by the beginning of the twentieth century (Davis 1997, pp. 13–15) and, as Wittman and Geisler suggest, "much current pressure for indigenous community rights in Guatemala is a continuation of the struggle to protect communal lands from long-standing expropriation, privatization, and nationalization" (p. 64).

The complexity of administrative institutions in the Western Highlands deserves a more detailed discussion. At the time of conquest, the indigenous population was divided into a number of *Parcialidades*. This was the Spanish colonial term for *chinamit* or *molab*—which were, "administrative units of 300–600 people and varying amounts of associated territory" (Hill 1989, p. 173). Each *parcialidad* was usually administered by an "aristocratic core family assisted by a council of elders and a staff of messengers" (Ibid.). Since the time of early conquest, argue the members of *El Centro*, these *Alcaldias comunales*—communal mayorships—have become increasingly democratic to the point that their elections now involve nearly 100 percent participation rates of men, women, and children. Now, the *alcaldes comunales* (communal mayors), for example, are elected for one to two years and are unpaid for the work they do in their position. The *alcaldia communal* of each *parcialidad* was responsible for all political, juridical, and administrative functions in the community (Barrios 1988). A higher level of governance—an *amaq'* coordinated the activities of the *alcaldias* and worked to resolve disputes between *parcialidades* (Hill 1989).

Despite the official discourse of *two republics*, the colonizers sought almost immediately to replace the *parcialidades* and *alcaldias* with a Spanish-style system of municipalities (Hill 1989; Wittman and Geisler 2005). Attempts to combine *parcialidades* and move populations into townships which served as municipal centres were common. The municipal administration was, as could be expected, ultimately designed to serve the interest of ladino and Spanish elites and the colonial power (Ibid.). Many of these moves were connected with attempts to exert colonial control over territory as well as juridical control over populations (Ibid.). Largely through creative interaction with Spanish colonial law, and the increasing sympathies of some colonial administrators, the *alcaldias* managed to maintain the significance of their institution—perpetuating the relevance of the idea of *two republics* despite colonial intentions (Barrios 1988; Hill 1989). Not all *parcialidades* and *alcaldias* have survived, however, and those which have, are endowed with varying amounts of legitimacy. In some of Guatemala's 331 municipalities such as *Sacapulas* and *Totonicapan*, the alcaldia communal remains strong, whereas in *Tecpan*, for example, the institution is virtually non-existent (Hill 1989; Wittman and Geisler 2005). As will be discussed in detail in the following chapter, the current work of *El Centro* is an extension of conflict and negotiation between modern/colonial administrative power and communal/indigenous governance institutions.

Exclusive Nationalism

Attempts of marginalization of indigenous culture and institutions, as well as economic domination of indigenous communities, continued through the period of *exclusive nationalism* (1821–1945). The postcolonial experience of most former colonies has tended to be typified by national projects of development that sought to institute a modern capitalist economy mediated by interventions from equally modern nation-state (Tucker 1999). Especially from the late nineteenth century onwards in Guatemala, this implied, "an exclusive nationalism … [that] did not recognize or respect the cultural diversity of the country's Mayan-speaking indigenous population" (Davis 2004, p. 330). Economically, the country's almost entirely agrarian economy was typified by a structural dualism which involved the exploitation of indigenous land and labour for capitalist agricultural development based on export (Ibid.). During this period, Guatemala's political and military elites ruled the country in tyrannical and dictatorial fashion and considered indigenous peoples to represent backwardness and superstition. Indigeneity, for the economic, cultural, and political powers in the country, was the antonym of progress, and therefore indigenous culture, language, and institutions were to be absorbed, marginalized, or otherwise eliminated (Ibid.). The attempted elimination of such elements included continued attacks on traditional social organization around the *alcaldia* communal and *parcialidad* (Barrios 1988).

Ten Years of Spring

This dynamic was systematically challenged for the first time during the *Ten Years of Spring* (1945–1954). With the ousting from office of President *Ubico* in 1944, constitutional and agrarian reforms were initiated in the interest of Guatemala's indigenous peoples for the first time in history (Davis 2004). Political activism was also encouraged amongst the indigenous population, and national leadership of all ethnic groups pushed towards a more substantive multicultural democracy. The presidents presiding over this transition—Juan José Arévalo and Jacobo Arbenz—were determined to address material equalities and to open up political space for dissent and other forms of participation (Davis 2004). Public consultations were held in a process of drafting a new national constitution which:

> outlawed all forms of discrimination (Article 21); called for the providing of adequate housing, sanitation and working conditions for "indigenous workers" (Article 67) … and provided for government recognition and protection of what remained of indigenous communal lands (Article 96). (Whetten 1961, p. 66)

Both the presidents in this period attempted to carry out substantial land reforms—redistributing largely unused portions of the holdings of large landowners to indigenous populations who generally had holdings that were, on average, too small even for subsistence farming (Davis 2004; Handy 1984). These political and economic reforms stimulated a blossoming of indigenous, worker, and *campesino* political participation as "urban and rural unions abounded; congress pulsated with activity; [and] the press criticized freely" (Handy 1984, p. 123). It was in this time, Adams (2004) argues, that Guatemala's indigenous peoples "began to recognize that social change was possible" (p. 158).

Not all groups were happy about these changes, however. These measures were perceived as a threat to both wealthy ladino landowners and foreign multinationals. The United Fruit Company (UFCO), in particular, had been given large tracts of land and government cooperation in labour force suppression by the ousted Ubico dictatorship. The company viewed the reforms during the *Ten Years of Spring* as "an assault on free enterprise" (CIA 1993, p. 16). The United States *Central Intelligence Agency* (CIA) characterized the Guatemalan government as "communist" and feared that the country would "become a central point for the dissemination of anti-US propaganda" (ibid. p. 18). Eventually, enormous countervailing pressure led by ladino elites and UFCO—with substantial support from the US government and the CIA—toppled the democratic government and rescinded its policies via a military coup which forced the resignation of Arbenz in 1954 (Davis 2004). Following this, US President Eisenhower triumphantly claimed that, "in Guatemala, the people of the region rose up and rejected the communist doctrine" (Immerman 1982, p. 178). The truth was that foreign and elite interests had conspired to oust a democratically elected centre-left government and replaced it with corporatist dictatorship (Ibid.).

The Violence

The thirty-two-year war that followed the 1954 coup—a period commonly referred to as *La Violencia*—was waged between a string of American-supported despotic military regimes and the left-wing insurgents of the *Rebel Armed Forces* (FAR) and later the *Unidad Nacional Revolucionaria Guatemalteca* (UNRG). It was the indigenous population, however, that bore the brunt of the violence (Warren 1998; Davis 2004). Caught between the opposing forces of the two European modernizationist ideologies of capitalism and socialism, the indigenous population was often—sometimes correctly and sometimes incorrectly—associated with the socialist insurgents. As a result, during *La Violencia*, the national army inflicted severe damage on indigenous communities (Davis 2004; Warren 1998).

La Violencia was the longest and deadliest civil conflict in the Central American region. It took the lives of over 200,000 unarmed civilians, most of whom were indigenous, and most (but not all) of these lives were taken by national army troops (Treat 2002; Jonas 1996). The anti-communist military doctrine of the Guatemalan government increasingly became anti-indigenous. This is evident in the 1983 statement of one of the last despots, General Mejía Víctores, who bluntly stated, "we must get rid of the words 'Indigenous'and 'Indian'" (Wilson 1999, p. 27). This was attempted systematically as the public sphere was shut down, dissent was frozen, social exclusion became a matter of policy, legislative and judicial branches became subservient to the military, and repression was used as a substitute for law (Gere and MacNeill 2008; Warren 1998, pp. 3–33; Fischer 2001).

This period corresponded to what Hale (2004) refers to as "the state ideology of *mestizaje*," the fundamentals of which he explains;

> Latin American states developed a mode of governance based on a unitary package of citizenship rights and a tendentious premise that people could enjoy these rights only by conforming to a homogenous mestizo cultural ideal. This ideal appropriated important aspects of Indian culture ... to give it "authenticity" and roots, but European stock provided the guarantee that it would be modern and forward-looking. This ideology was "progressive" in that it contested the 19th century thesis of racial degeneration and extended the promise of equity to all; its progressive glimmer, in turn, gave the political project—to assimilate Indians and marginalize those who refused—its hegemonic appeal. (p. 18)

La Violencia, with its physical and ideological attacks on Maya Guatemalans, would have a massive cultural and physical impact on Guatemala's indigenous population. Its force would be felt in the subjectivities of Maya cultural activists in the country (Warren 1998; Gere and MacNeill 2008), and in the life experiences of members of *El Centro*. Many indigenous people in the Western Highlands had lost family and/or friends in the war (Warren 1998), and the members of El Centro were no exception. This experience strongly influenced the ideas internalized by those exposed to it, as the experience of *Louisa*, a field technician at *El Centro*, illustrates:

> We were refugees in Mexico from the armed conflict ... [I learned] from my own experience, my own needs and everything I've lived. I was orphaned when I was very small ... We all felt the need for education, because we all came from the same circumstance, we were experiencing a process of conflict that was very cruel and then felt the need to change, to be different to have other opportunities to grow in another environment and that our children can have a very different fate than we did ... Even when we were kids we had a lot of fear, much fear of war, and we realized how things were, we were fleeing, hiding all the time, we all wanted to do different things but if we do nothing we're not changing anything. So we needed to work, to make changes. There are many philosophers, great writers ... but they did not live what I lived. I lived a very different [life than them] and I've experienced, since early childhood unfortunately, those difficult situations. ... We were persecuted—then you see the need to create change ... We no longer wanted to offer our children the same we live—fear, terror, to be running in another country.

Postwar and Peace Negotiations

This persecution, as we have discussed, was strongly racialized in Guatemala. This meant that the terror of the war was experienced and understood collectively by indigenous Guatemalans. The relatively safe space created by the period of negotiations that preceded the signing of the *Peace Accords* on December 29, 1996, facilitated a collective reassertion of sorts. As many commentators have noted, this environment facilitated a Maya cultural "renaissance" in the form of a national social movement that sought to revalorize and revitalize indigenous culture (Warren 1998; Fischer and McKenna Brown 1996; Montejo 2005). The assertion of Maya culture against the ideology of *mestizaje*, as Hale (2004) argues, "has been the first object of indigenous resistance across the region" (p. 2). Within the political space that appeared around the time of the Peace Accords, a Maya culture that had been blunted for centuries asserted itself again just as it had during the *Ten Years of Spring*. Members of *El Centro* have been deeply involved in this movement through their active positioning within the network of Guatemalan indigenous-based civil society. Members often cite the countering of racism and valorization of indigenous culture as fundamental goals of their project.

Indigenous involvement in postwar politics was immediate. During the Peace Accord negotiations, Maya leaders pressured for the drafting of the national *Accord on Identity and Rights of Indigenous Peoples*, which was signed on March 31, 1995 (Warren 1998, p. 56). The work of *El Centro*, members claim, is carried out "in accordance with" this agreement, and it is indeed evoked often in writings and workshops. The Accord, although not fully legal pending constitutional change that is yet to occur, contained a number of important concessions to indigenous peoples. As Warren (1998) outlines, it included,

> *Recognition of Guatemala's indigenous people as descendents of an ancient people who speak diverse, historically related languages and share a distinctive culture and cosmology. Non-Maya Xinca and Garifuna communities were accorded equivalent status.*
>
> *Recognition of the legitimacy of using indigenous languages in schools, social services, official communications, and court proceedings.*
>
> *Recognition and protection of Maya spirituality and spiritual guides and the conservation of ceremonial centers and archaeological sites as indigenous heritage, which would involve Mayas in their administration.*
>
> *Commitment to education reform, specifically the integrations of Maya materials and educational methods, the involvement of families in all areas of education, and the promotion of intercultural programs for all children.*
>
> *Indigenous representation in administrative bodies at all levels, the regionalization of government structures, and the recognition of localized customary law and community decision-making powers in education, health, and economic development.*
>
> *Recognition of communal lands and the reform of the legal system so Maya interests are adequately represented in the adjudication of land disputes. The distribution of state lands to communities with insufficient land.* (p. 56)

El Centro was founded in the mid-1990s amidst these peace negotiations. Founding members took part directly in *Indigenous Accord* negotiations and indirectly as members of a network of indigenous political activism and civil society. Initially called the *Foundation for Economic, Social, and Cultural Development* (FUNDADECE), the organization was conceived by its five initiating members to serve the purpose of "specifically dealing with projects of infrastructure and production for the benefit of those who had been internally and externally displaced during the war" and was financed by the Swiss organization *Diaconia*. Geographically, the work at this time was restricted to the Western coastal regions near *Champerico* and *Retalhuleu*. But involvement in the politics surrounding the peace process and associated Maya activism facilitated drastic change in the early organization. As *Matea* explains,

> As agreements between the Guerrillas, the Government of Guatemala, and civil society were reached for the signing of the peace, we began to structure a new organizational profile. Specifically, this was because we saw that the people in the Western Highlands had a lot of weakness in participation [in politics in general and the peace process]. This, in conjunction with existing racism and exclusion was strong enough to exclude much of the Maya population. So since the signing of the Peace Accords we began to generate a process of forming a new structure.

With the new structure, came a new name—or rather two: *El Centro Pluricultural para la Democracia* and *Kemb'al Tinimit*—a *K'iche'* name which implies the weaving of the multiple cultures with which *El Centro* works. These two names—the Spanish and the K'iche'—were used side by side to represent the pluricultural focus of the organization. This is also evident in the name given to the four-organization social movement within which *El Centro* was encapsulated. The *Tzuk Kim Pop* Movement was named again around an indigenous metaphor for weaving—*pop*—and this was mixed with an acronym meant to stand for the main cultural groups in the highlands—*Tz'utujil Maya, Kíche Maya, Kakchiquel Maya, Mam Maya*, and *Mestizo* (ladino). *Tzuk Kim Pop* consisted of four main indigenous-run organizations that, in concert with *El Centro*, sought to initiate development projects. Each organization was responsible for a different ambit of this—one undertook community economic development, one multilingual education, one health, and finally *El Centro* would engage in the political sphere.[2] It was to be a holistic concerted effort which, at every step, centralized the idea of "culturally sustainable development."

As is evident with its involvement in *Tzuk Kim Pop*, *El Centro* should not be thought of as a bounded, isolated organization. It is in constant communication with other groups, and this interaction impacts

[2] The Members of Tzuk Kim Pop included El Centro Experimental Para Desarollo de la Pequeña y Mediana Empresa Rural (CEDEPEM), Asoción para la Promoción, Investicación y Educación en Salud (PIES), and Projecto Lingüistico Santa Maria (PLSM).

subjectivities and policies both within *El Centro* and within the network at large. The organization is an active participant in Guatemalan civil society and is changed and changes with this interaction. Besides the member organizations of *Tzuk Kim Pop*, multiple smaller community-level organizations, as well as community, national, and municipal governments, *El Centro* cooperates directly with the following non-governmental organizations:

National and Central American Level:
The Collective of Social Organizations
The National Forum for Decentralization in Guatemala
The Interamerican Platform for Human Rights, Democracy & Development
Dialogue for Central America
The Central American Conference for Decentralization and Development
The Guatemalan Conference for Decentralization and Development
Social Forum of the Americas
The National Council of the Peace Accords

Region of the Western Highlands:
Regional Network for Bilingual and Intercultural Education
Departmental Commission of Women
Coordinating Board for Basic Institutes of Cooperation
Organization of Indigenous Women's Development in the Basin of El Rio Samala.
Association of Farmers of the Basin of El Rio Samala.
Association of Mam Indigenous Women.
Forum of Civil Society and Commonwealth of Huehuetenango.
Council of the Peoples of the West
Roundtable of Totonicapán

Members of *El Centro* also make regular visits to small and large organizations in communities throughout the highlands, as well as those of national scope. These visits are designed to extend knowledge and a spirit of cooperation amongst organizations who work in political, economic, cultural, agricultural, health, or education-related realms. As a result of this, *El Centro* should be thought as a social subject that is situated within a vast and nebulous organic system of civil society—one which is characterized by regular flows of information which transform each of its subjects to varying degrees. *El Centro* is constantly transformed by these relationships but also helps to transform the whole of civil society. *El Centro*, therefore, can be thought of as a window through which we can see the workings of the entire Maya indigenous rights movement as it constitutes, deliberates, and reconstitutes itself. The organization has worked as a node through which knowledge and experiences are passed by indigenous *campesinos* and *alcaldas tradicionales* to the national-level Maya movement, and vice versa.

Global Considerations

The culture and rights-based activism that inspired the language of the *Indigenous Accord* as well as the politics and ideas of *El Centro* must not be thought of as the product of only a unique Guatemalan historical political-cultural-economy. A number of global tendencies have emerged more recently which have had notable impact on the Guatemalan political, cultural, and economic climate as well as on the membership of *El Centro*. First, a discourse around *human and cultural rights* was gaining force globally. Second, and connected to this, there was a *global indigenous movement* which had particular force in Latin America. Third, the neoliberal policy climate of the major international donors slowly moved to a *post-neoliberal* or *post-Washington Consensus* model. Fourth, there was rise of the global environmental movement. Finally, fifth, there were global movements for gender equality. Members of *El Centro* have combined these global phenomena with critical development discourse that stems from *Marxism*, *feminism*, and *environmentalism*, and, more importantly, with their own felt sense of *Maya cosmovision*.

Rights Discourse

Indigenous activists in Guatemala, including members of *El Centro*, have been embedding their activism in the language of *human and cultural rights* for at least fifteen years (Warren 1998), and members of *El Centro* are also implicated in this tendency. When asked to depict the essence of what it is to be human, for example, members of *El Centro* insist that whatever else a human being is—it is always a citizen with "rights and responsibilities." The instrument most evoked by Guatemalan indigenous activists (ibid.) as well members of *El Centro* is *International Labour Organization Convention 169*—regarding the collective rights of indigenous and tribal peoples. The convention includes protections for "traditional life styles," "culture and a way of life," "consultation and participation," and the right to,

> decide their own priorities for the process of development as it affects their lives, beliefs, institutions and spiritual well-being and the lands they occupy or otherwise use, and to exercise control over their economic, social and cultural development. (p. 1)

Guatemala is one of twenty countries to have ratified the Convention (ibid.), although its interpretation within Guatemala jurisprudence and relation to the National Constitution is contested. Similar language, claims, and ambiguities hold true for the *Accord on Identity and Rights of Indigenous Peoples* which were negotiated as part of the Peace Accords in 1995 (Ibid.).

Despite such uncertainties of implementation, Guatemalan indigenous activists, including those at *El Centro*, make heavy use of these agreements to assert their collective and cultural rights. Such activists must not be thought to be simply reacting to these human rights instruments, however. That is to say, Maya indigenous activists are not simply the opportunistic products of international convention. Indigenous Guatemalans were instrumental in the negotiation of *ILO 169* and, of course, the national peace accords (Warren 1998). Former members of *El Centro* were involved directly and indirectly in these processes as well.

Marxism and Dependency Theory

Although, they tend to distance themselves from Western modes of thought, all of the organization's members are somewhat familiar with Marxist strands of social theory, and especially variants related to Latin American dependency theory. As a result of this, and the experience of their communities, they are highly critical of capitalism and neoliberal economics. In Marxist-inflected terms, *Roberto* claims that free-market capitalism is a "hegemonic" structure that is equated often with imperialism and domination for example. He continues,

> [Regarding] the theme of the neoliberal theory of development, there is a concept of development, perhaps it suggests an individualistic concept of development, but it is not a concept of development that benefits the collectivity. For example, when they talk of free markets, the free competition benefits those who have the means of production—those who have all the capital. However, this does not benefit the economically poor for example—it does not benefit the indigenous peoples.

One should not overstate the importance of Marxian political economy for members of the organization, however. Such thought is present, and, if fact, control over the "means of production" is an important element of culturally sustainable development. But there are other intellectual and cultural traditions that overshadow that of Marxism for the members of the organization. As *Juan-Carlos*, a *Ki'che'* field technician for *El Centro*, told me regarding critical Marxian theory:

> I have studied some of Marx's ideas, but I would say [that my ideas come] a bit more from the Maya—from the Maya worldview. I do not want to disparage El Senior Marx, but more of my ideas come from the Maya Cosmovision.

Global Indigenous Movement

Connected with human and cultural rights discourses, has been the powerful emergence of a global *indigenous movement* since the 1990s. Some have suggested that these movements emerged as a direct result of the development of instruments such as *ILO 169*. This, however, would overlook the immense involvement of indigenous organizations in the construction and negotiation of those very agreements (Cowan et al. 2001; Warren 1998). Yashar (2005) locates the roots of the movement in the wave of democratization that occurred globally following the end of the Cold War, and on neoliberal reform which eased corporatist restraints on assertions of indigenous autonomy while exacerbating the economic woes of indigenous communities. Whatever the foundational forces of the movement might be, Guatemalan Maya have been central to the movement. The most striking example of this would be the awarding of the Nobel Peace Prize to Rigoberta Menchu—a *K'iche'* woman from the Western Highlands—in 1992. Menchu's prize was symbolically significant to the global indigenous movement, especially since 1992—the 500th year anniversary of the conquest of the Americas—had been marked at the *First Continental Conference on 500 Years of Indian Resistance* in Quito, Ecuador, in July 1990, to commemorate "continual resistance" and "liberation" on the part of the continent's indigenous peoples (IAA 1990). Members of *El Centro* are well aware of Menchu of course, and her name is evoked in numerous conversations between members. On a less notable scale, members of *El Centro* have been involved in a number of international indigenous peoples conferences and meetings and have participated in university exchange programmes such as those offered through the Department of Indigenous Studies at the University of Regina, Saskatchewan, Canada.

The Post-Washington Consensus

The turn of global donors to a *post-neoliberal* or *post-Washington Consensus* model has been based on the *New Institutional Economics* that was discussed in Chap. 3. Key to this, now the mainstream in development thought are ideas such as social capital and human capital mixed with the privileging of free markets which are to be mediated occasionally by benevolent governments (Fine and Jomo 2006). In this context, ethnicity and culture—especially indigenous culture—have come to signify a form of social capital and a facilitating agent for the building of human capital. This is consistent with the new institutional presumption that cultural forms are the manifest result of concerted action by egoistic human actors in the presence of market failures based on public goods. As a result, donor funding strategies have come to target indigenous groups. As Hale (2004) has explained in the case of Guatemala, following the signing of the Peace Accords, "the country was soon awash in international aid, with Maya civil society as the privileged recipient" (p. 20). In Guatemala, as with much of the world, indigenous civil society and rights-based organization are a "donor driven" priority (Ibid.).

El Centro has drawn primarily from funding by the *European Union*, the *Ford Foundation*, and the *Soros Foundation*—all which target indigenous groups explicitly. Donors must be chosen carefully, however. As *Matea*, a founding member of *El Centro*, argues, at the point of project implementation, parameters of funding agreements—especially those of the EU—tend to "limit somewhat the actions" of the recipient "in accordance with their policies." On-the-ground freedom of action is limited in such cases, she continues to explain, as "cooperation starts to generate an accumulation of policies, a mountain of meetings, of monitoring."

This is not a benign process. The World Bank website on "Social Capital and Ethnicity" offers the following:

> Ethnicity can be a powerful tool in the creation of human and social capital, but, if politicized, ethnicity can destroy capital. … Ethnic diversity is dysfunctional when it generates conflict. (n.p.)

This line of thought emerges directly out of new institutional economics which lauds the benefits of culture-as-social capital while insisting that some cultural formations can become inefficient or destructive. The selection between the two is, of course, left to the technocrat in government or the donor agency. Hale (2004) has argued that such policies have resulted in exacerbating the problem of "Indio Permitido" (authorized Indian) in Guatemala. This implies that particular kinds of culture-based organization—those which facilitate democratic processes, cultural tourism, or community public-goods projects—are good. Those which disturb the functioning of markets, natural resource exploitation, or capitalist production through protest or attempts at territorial control are not acceptable. *El Centro* is very much caught in the politics of *Indio Permitido*. As a result, although the organization has close relations with indigenous activist groups that seek to disrupt markets and threaten political–economic power in such ways, it is careful to distance itself from such practices. As *Matea* explained to me when asked about *El Centro*'s involvement of such political acts,

> We don't organize protests. We have tried to generate the space in which [people] can dialogue, discuss, and we have facilitated processes in which there is dialogue between two sectors that may have different interests—for example, dialogues in which the national organizations of justice meet with communal authorities.

As we will see in the next chapter, *El Centro*'s involvement with more radical political activism is somewhat more blurry than this. The point for the time being, however, is that *El Centro* is articulated and constrained by a national politics of *Indio Permitido* which is reinforced by a donor climate that is informed by new institutional approaches to international development policy.

Environmentalism

Also connected with the post-Washington Consensus is the idea of environmental sustainability. Members of *El Centro* have been influenced by related discourses as is evidenced by their common use, almost verbatim, of the Brundtland Report (WECD 1987) definition of sustainable development when addressing environmental issues. The report's claim that sustainable development "implies meeting the needs of the present without compromising the ability of future generations to meet their own needs" has become an integral part of the mainstream development discourse of the post-Washington Consensus (Fine and Jomo 2006). When asked to define sustainable development in interviews, Brundtland Report discourse was common amongst members of *El Centro*. So too was the tendency to connect the protection of the environment with the protection of indigenous culture.

Such a depiction correlates strongly with mainstream post-Washington Consensus environmentalism, which depicts indigeneity as a form of social capital that serves to mitigate the types of market failures that lead to environmental damage. The World Bank page on "Social Capital and Environment," for example, argues that indigeneity is a collective resource that allows communities to "address their concerns, such as land scarcity and environmental degradation" (para. 2). The Bank's page on "Indigenous Peoples" forwards the argument that "Indigenous Peoples are distinct populations in that the land on which they live, and the natural resources on which they depend, are inextricably linked to their identities and cultures" (para. 5).

Such ideas—common in both indigenous rights and mainstream development discourse—appear often in the work of *El Centro*. "We the Indigenous peoples," claims *El Centro* in the preamble to a document advocating for community participation in the planning of mining projects, "have our own ways of conceiving development, focused on the search for equilibrium with our ecosystem" (CPD no date1, p. 5). In a focus group I organized on this topic with members of *El Centro*, the fundamental marker of Maya culture was claimed to be "the relationship with nature and the cosmo." In Guatemala in particular, *Matea* argues, it is only the Maya who have the cultural and organizational (social capital) resources to achieve sustainable development:

> The population that at the moment has the proposals to make life sustainable in the region is the indigenous population—the Maya population. Why? Because, for example, the have norms, and they have created acts and accords that come from the communities that direct the ways to manage the forest, to manage resources like water for example.

Such statements do not provide evidence of a unidirectional causal relationship between mainstream development discourse, global indigenous movements, and *El Centro*. Given the close relations that the organization has with both these global discourses, however, a certain complex articulation or co-resonance of these ideas might reasonably be assumed to exist. That is to say, the Maya relationship with nature has a deep and meaningful history. It may, however, be reinforced by its relation to global discourses of social capital and indigeneity. It must be allowed as well, however, that Maya belief systems have a tangible impact on these global discourses through sympathetic resonance and articulation.

Discourse on Gender Equality

A similar dynamic can be noted regarding gender equality. Members use international instruments such as the *Universal Declaration of Human Rights*, which emphasize gender equality, in their work. They utilize more so the national *Agreement on Identity and Rights of Indigenous Peoples*, which specifically addresses the rights of indigenous women. Section *B1* of the agreement states:

> It is recognized that indigenous women are particularly vulnerable and helpless, being confronted with twofold discrimination both as women and indigenous people, and also having to deal with a social situation characterized by intense poverty and exploitation. The Government undertakes to take the following measures:
>
> (a) Promote legislation to classify sexual harassment as a criminal offence, considering as an aggravating factor in determining the penalty for sexual offences the fact that the offence was committed against an indigenous woman;
>
> (b) Establish an Office for the Defense of Indigenous Women's Rights, with the participation of such women, including legal advice services and social services; and
>
> (c) Promote the dissemination and faithful implementation of the Convention on the Elimination of All Forms of Discrimination against Women.

The impact of such rights discourses on the ideas of those in *El Centro* is likely given the extensive use of these instruments in workshops and information sessions. The situation of *El Centro* in a complex network of Guatemalan civil society and the resultant direct and indirect involvement of associates in the negotiation of the national agreement particularly should caution us on assuming a direct top-down causal relation here, however. Indeed, it is a common claim by Maya cultural revivalists that gender equality and complementarity has always been integral to Maya culture (Warren 1998). This will be explored more thoroughly in the following section.

Maya Cosmovision

As influential as the national history and the various discourses discussed earlier have been on thought in *El Centro*, the strongest influence, according to the members interviewed, comes from Maya cosmovision itself. Internationally and nationally situated ideas surrounding development and rights, however, mix, articulate, and resonate often with deeply held cultural beliefs. The structure of Maya cosmovision facilitates the use of the concept of the "natural environment" as the central focal point of the Maya political subjects that *El Centro* is interested in nurturing. It also imbues a sense of egalitarianism, community cooperation, and gender equality. Within *El Centro*, and the communities with which it works, Maya cosmovision is fused with felt local history and international discourses to create a distinctive worldview and idea of development.

Any attempt to represent cultural meaning of perceived "Others" is bound to be laden with problems. In order to minimize this, my interpretations of *El Centro*, its work, and of Maya cosmovision were presented to a focus group composed of members of the organization. After I presented my interpretation of the cosmovision, the necessary question emerged—can Maya Cosmovision be understood and properly represented by a Western academic? The quick answer was "no." After a short period of discussion amongst the members (myself excluded), however, it was announced by the group of field technicians, office administrators, and Maya spiritual guides that although it would take me years to truly understand the cosmovision, my current interpretation was accurate enough for the purpose at hand. What follows, then, is an approximate representation that will serve reasonably well the task at hand. To limit my own interpretive interference, I will rely heavily on direct quotations.

Upon explaining Maya cosmovision to me, *Mario*, who is a Maya spiritual guide who works with *El Centro*, made it clear that the universe is to be understood as an "indivisible whole." Any division between concepts such as nature, human, man, woman, cosmos, or culture is simply an abstraction. The planets, sun, and moon, for example, are interconnected with menstrual cycles, harvesting schedules, and human reproduction. This interconnectivity, claimed *Mario*, is central to all aspects of the cosmovision. This can be understood with reference to the concept of *Ajaw*, which is a singularity that is interpretable as a duality. It consists of "Heart of Sky"—"an immaterial and incomprehensible energy or force and transcendent space" or a "mysterious something [that] precedes everything else" (Molesky-Poz 2006, p. 46). But also of "Heart of Earth" where "Heart of Sky … abandons the spiritual dimension and enters [creates] the material world" (Cabrera qtd. In Molesky-Poz 2006, p. 46). "Heart of Heaven" and "Heart of Earth" are both equal and one. They are connected because they are part of a whole, one representing the masculine, and the latter the feminine—two not-separate, but complimentary categories (Ibid.).

Humans, in this conception, as part of *Ajaw*, are to be "givers of praise, givers of respect, providers, and nurturers" (Ibid., p. 38). They live in dialectic with the cosmos and natural environment and consequently must both give to and receive from nature.

"In this worldview," explains Molesky-Poz (2006),

> a person connects intuitively with the Rhythms and thoughts of the universe, with ancestors, and takes on a responsibility to others. One navigates from cultural and psychological constructions in which one inhabits his or her body and experiences it, and perceptions of life, in ways very different from those shaped primarily by Western reason and rationality. (p. 74)

"To understand the relationship that the human being has with the land, nature and the cosmos," *Roberto* suggests, "is profound." He continues,

> Perhaps you are not going to understand me … The life of the human being in the perception of the Mayan peoples is connected with the land, nature. Conception for example. When a parent conceives a child it says: "Good, child, the fetus grows in the belly of the mother—in the body of the mother—as one lunar cycle passes, and another." There are eight moons of conception, and it is for this reason that the human being has a relation with the moon and it is conceived by many people to be the grandmother of everybody.

Roberto offers another example:

> To cut a tree down in a community, you must cut when the moon has waxed for the wood you cut to be functional, for it to be resistant, to be durable for many years. But if I am going to cut a tree down when the moon has waned, the wood will not serve me. This wood will only serve me for five or six years.

The moon, then, must be thought of as being connected to all things terrestrial and human. "It is the same with the sun," explains *Roberto*: "with the sun began all of the ideas around the Mayan calendar, the solar calendar—all that can be had can be seen with the solar cycle."

Members of *El Centro* explain that these types of connections—or rather oneness—should be respected in all human activity according to the cosmovision. *Roberto* offers an example:

> when they say "I am going to cut down a tree"—this is for a service that is primordial, principal, and fundamental in the community or for the family. The people say that [the tree] "is a living being equal to me, therefore I must ask the permission of the tree."

Louisa explains the central logic of this belief system:

> In Mayan Cosmovision respect is the most fundamental value. I respect all that exists, whether they be people, nature, animals—all of them. … The Mayan Cosmovision is based on fundamental values and one of them is harmony. I must live in harmony and I cannot destroy that which serves me. I have to respect, but I also have to have equilibrium between all that there is, in a horizontal system. Nothing above and nothing below, but everything in a horizontal system in which equilibrium is important. I must be good with God, good with my family, good with nature, good with my surroundings because this helps me to be tranquil … If one applies it in their life, they can be living very much in harmony with all else.

Sofia conceptualizes this more succinctly, saying that "as indigenous, the land is us, it gives us food, and we are the land." *Matea* does not believe that such beliefs exist in the more Euro-culture saturated *ladina* or *Mestiza* population of Guatemala. What is lacking in *Mestiza* culture, she argues, "is the theme of the trilogy that exists between the human being, the spirit, and the natural world." This way of seeing, she argues, is part of a "distinct form of life" shared by all the different Maya communities in Guatemala. Although each of these groups "has its own cosmovision," all share a similar "essence" that requires a "spiritual co-habitation with nature and other human beings."

This "spiritual co-habitation" can be seen in El Centro's depiction of the idea of gender equality in Maya cosmovision. Regarding this, *Roberto* explains,

> The philosophy of the Mayan peoples [is] the theme of duality. The theme of complementarity in this case is the same as talking of a focus on gender equality. When we speak of complementarity of men and women, when we speak of the duality of men and women, we say, good, the sun and earth are dual. They are complimentary. The moon as well. Or when we see as well that the man has feminine aspects but also male aspects, this is part of the concept of indigenous peoples as well.

Roberto's position is nuanced by one of *El Centro's* publications:

> In Maya culture there are philosophies, theories, in relation to the life of men and women, such as: the collective work, mutual help ... to look for council [from both genders] ... values that should orient personal life, family life, community life, social life and political life. Taking as the base, the principle of duality: in Maya thought, differences [in gender] are complimentary. That is to say that opposites (for example day and night, fire and water, happiness and sadness, man and woman), cannot exist without the other. (CPD no date3, no page number)

The text continues to explain that Maya women have traditionally carried out roles inside the family but also played other roles in the public realm, such as within the communal mayorship. Consistent with this, when asked if Maya culture is patriarchal, *Mario* insisted that some ancient Maya political centres were governed by women. He continues, "when we talk of Maya culture, we say that there is mother and father—mother is nature and father is heaven" (Heart of Earth; Heart of Heaven). Further, he insists that "when patriarchal tendencies emerge," in indigenous communities, "it is nothing more than an imposition from Western culture."

Matea's comments in this regard are telling. When asked if Maya culture is patriarchal, she offered the following:

> Would you like a political position or a personal position? Because the political position that has developed is that throughout the existence of the Mayan people there has existed a process that promotes the complementarity or equality in which the human being exists. This belief system promotes equality between men and women. And they complement each other because one is masculine and the other feminine. One is the day and the other is the night. One is life and the other is death and therefore the will compliment each other in relation to all that exists.

"This is the political idea," *Matea* continues, "but in reality I believe that there has been too much change, and not only in the Mayan culture." When asked to account for this change, she suggests that "the catholic religion and evangelism have created the idea of the superiority of men over women and this has influenced the relations in the communities."

Matea's comments may be thought to place the "truth" about Maya cosmovision in doubt. One might ask if the claims regarding gender equality and environmental harmony that are intrinsic to the cosmovision are nothing more than politically expedient constructions. Do Maya peoples really believe and feel such things? And if they do not, how can it be claimed that these are essential elements of Maya culture?

To ask such questions is to miss the point, however. Maya culture is interpreted and reinterpreted. It, like any culture, is forever changing. The members of *El Centro* are interpreting a Maya culture, which does contain strong elements of environmental respect and gender harmony. This interpretation is undertaken in resonance with many of the ideas regarding gender equality that have emerged internationally—such as those which are imbedded in the policy of every funding institution that *El Centro* deals with, *ILO 169*, the *Indigenous Accord*, and most international human rights instruments. This interpretation of Maya culture has been produced under the discursive force of such instruments and in collaboration with Western anthropologists as well as the global indigenous movement (Molesky-Poz 2006). Such global discourses of equity, indigeneity, and environmentalism have resonated with similar pre-Colombian sensibilities in the current culture in Maya communities. To encourage such sensibilities, and dissuade others, are part of an environmental-egalitarian ethic that has itself resonated with members of *El Centro*.

Promoting this, as we will see in the next chapter, is central to the conception and implementation of culturally sustainable development. The important thing to take from this section, however, is that the cosmovision—amidst the other things already discussed—has had an important impact on the subjectivities of the members of *El Centro*. "Let me give you an example," says *Juan-Carlos*,

> When I grew up you could never throw away an ear of corn from the time it began to grow. Corn cannot be thrown away or people will scoff. This is because in the Mayan worldview it is our food, it is our rise, it is our root. [You see] I have, not with the clarity we should have, but I have many of the

> values and principles of the Mayan worldview. For example, I live with my parents, and I have been taught that when you salute them you must tip your head. For many, this might seem ridiculous, but for us this all makes sense from a Mayan worldview. It is a respect for the elderly—for those who have not studied but have a wisdom of life. That is most important. I believe that all of my ideas, concerns, hopes and all I have is based in this [fundamental respect for the wisdom of the elderly]. Thanks to that—thanks to all … that I have been taught from the family, I am able to contribute here [at *El Centro*].

As we will see in the next chapter, the concept of culturally sustainable development is rooted substantially in such orally transferred cultural inheritances of thought. CSD, then, cannot help but be to a large extent an expression of Maya cosmology. Certainly, as *Juan-Carlos* argues, the Maya worldview "unfortunately is not given much importance" in global discourse surrounding development, equality, rights, environment, and gender. But, he argues, "many of these principles, many of these values, are right from Maya cosmology." There is a felt resonance here between these international discourses and the orally transmitted Maya worldview.

Conclusion

The goal of this chapter was to situate the Maya idea of sustainable development articulated at *El Centro* vis-à-vis a long history of colonialism, a felt cultural heritage, and a number of more recent global discursive tendencies. *History* and *cosmovision* are highly important constituting factors for the thoughts, ideas, and subsequent policies of the members of the organization. So too are the global discursive tendencies of *post-neoliberalism*, the *indigenous movement*, *human and cultural rights*, *Marxism*, *feminism*, and *environmentalism*. The relationships between *El Centro* and these global discourses are not simply causal, however. They are reciprocal. That is to say that it should not be presumed that there is a one-way relationship in which these discourses interpolate the organization, or cause it to happen. This is not a simple relationship in which a number of global dependent variables exert formational pressure on an independent variable. Although it could be assumed that Maya cultural activism has been impacted more by the global indigenous movement than it has impacted that movement, for example, it should not be forgotten that the actions of *El Centro* have the power to change the international movement as well. *El Centro* is embedded in a network of Guatemalan civil society in which all these variables are again transformed and negotiated. It is a discursive sphere through which the national Maya movement speaks to indigenous *campesinos* and *alcaldas comunales* in the creation of a sustainable development project that is rooted in Maya cosmovision.

A final thought must be added here regarding internal dynamics of the organization. All of the swirling discourses, sedimented histories, and cultural proclivities that were addressed are interpreted, discussed, and reorganized within *El Centro*. The output of this process is a policy package that seeks to achieve what we have been calling "Culturally sustainable Development." The communicative process that creates this output must not be presumed to occur in a purely egalitarian public sphere that is devoid of power imbalances of its own. From my observations, at meetings with core members, there is a tendency for women to be less vocal, and although the organization is "pluricultural," ladino representation is very low in most meetings and workshops. Furthermore, certain members of the organization tend to carry more persuasive weight in meetings. Beyond this, members of *El Centro* are often looked upon as experts and authorities when they organize meetings with communities, for example.

Every communicative act, Habermas (1984) has reminded us, is in danger of being infused with such power differentials. The point, for those who seek to implement democratic processes, is to mitigate these as much as possible. The structure of *El Centro* is designed in a non-hierarchical fashion. "Directors" and "coordinators" are joined at meetings and workshops by "office administrators" and "field technicians"—all who, at least officially, have equal weight attached to their utterances. The majority of the core 20 members of *El Centro* are women, and women are just as likely to hold key positions as are men. Ladinos are underrepresented but not in proportion to their small population in the Western Highlands. Furthermore, language of the ladinos—Spanish—is used as the primary language at all meetings and in all publications.[3]

As *Matea* claimed to me regarding gender power differentials, these structures "do not change from night to morning." But members of the organization have made deliberate efforts to address such issues internally. Furthermore, as we will see in the following chapter, addressing many of these power issues in communities is integral to their development

[3] This is expedient since members do not all speak the same indigenous languages.

programme. As an observer, I am not in a position to interpret properly every nuance of internal communicative democracy, or lack thereof. Furthermore, the purpose of this work is to outline the ideas of *El Centro*, not to map internal power dynamics. Despite this, these things must be recognized here. As with any organization, there are problems regarding internal power structures, and I do respect the efforts put forth organizationally to address such issues, however. There is a tangible awareness of the potential dangers of such inequalities in the organization. As a result, there are constant attempts to mitigate them.

References

Adams, R. H. (2004). Remesas y pobreza en Guatemala.

Barrios, L. (1988). *La Alcaldía Indígena en Guatemala: de 1821 a la Revolución de 1944*. Guatemala City: Instituto de Investigaciones Económicas y Sociales (IDIES): Universidad Rafael Landivar.

Casaus Arzú, M. (1995). *Guatemala: Liniaje y Racismo*. Guatemala City: Facultad de Latinoamerica de Sciencias Sociales.

Central Intelligence Agency (CIA). (1993). *#756; Operation PBSUCCESS: The United States and Guatemala 1952–1954*. Declassified May 15, 1997. Washington, DC: Central Intelligence Agency.

Cowan, J., Benedicte Dembour, M., & Wilson, R. (Eds.). (2001). *Culture and Rights: Anthropological Perspectives*. Cambridge: Cambridge University Press.

Davis, S. (1997). *The Guatemalan Peace Accords and Indigenous Communal Lands*. Paper Prepared for Colloquium Series, Program in Agrarian Studies, Yale University.

Davis, D. E. (2004). *Discipline and development: middle classes and prosperity in East Asia and Latin America*. Cambridge University Press.

Diamond, J. (1997). *Guns, Germs and Steel*. New York: WW Norton.

Durham-Peters, J. (1993). Distrust of Representation: Habermas on the Public Sphere. *Media, Culture and Society, 15*, 541–571.

Fine, B., & Jomo, K. S. (2006). *The New Development Economics: After the Washington Consensus*. London: Zed Books.

Fischer, E. F. (2001). *Cultural Logics and Global Economics: Maya Identity in Thought and Practice*. Austin: University of Texas Press.

Fischer, E. F., & Benson, P. (2006). *Broccoli & Desire: Global Connections and Maya Struggles in Postwar Guatemala*. Stanford: Stanford University Press.

Fischer, E. F., & Hendrickson, C. (2003). *Tecpán Guatemala: A Modern Maya Town in Global and Local Context*. Oxford: Westview Press.

Fischer, E. F., & McKenna Brown, R. (1996). *Maya Cultural Activism in Guatemala*. Austin: University of Texas Press.

Galeano, E. (1973). *The Open Veins of Latin America. Five Centuries of the Pillage of a Continent*. New York: Monthly Review Press.

Gere, E., & MacNeill, T. (2008). Radical Indigenous Subjectivity: Maya Resurgence in Guatemala. *The International Journal of Diversity in Organizations, Communities, and Nations, 8*(2), 97–106.

Habermas, J. (1984). *The Theory of Communicative Action, Vol. 1*. Thomas McCarthy (Trans.). Boston: Beacon Press.

Habermas, J. (1989). The Public Sphere: An Encyclopedia Article. In S. Bronner (Ed.), *Critical Theory and Society: A Reader* (pp. 136–145). New York: Routledge.

Hale, C. (2004). Rethinking Indigenous Politics in the Era of the "Indio Permitido". *NACLA Report on the Americas, 38*(2), 16–22.

Handy, J. (1984). *Gift of the Devil: A History of Guatemala*. Toronto: Between the Lines.

Hill, R. (1989). Social Organization by Decree in Colonial Highland Guatemala. *Ethnohistory, 36*(2), 170–1998.

Immerman, R. (1982). *The CIA in Guatemala: The Foreign Policy of Intervention*. Austin: University of Texas Press.

Indigenous Alliance of the Americas (IAA). (1990). *Declaration of Quito, Ecuador*. Quito: IAA.

Jonas, S. (1996). Dangerous Liaisons: The US in Guatemala. *Foreign Policy, 103*, 144–160.

MacNeill, T. (2014). Culturally Sustainable Development: Maya Culture, Indigenous Institutions, and Alternative Development in Guatemala. *Cultural Dynamics, 26*(3), 299–325.

Molesky-Poz, J. (2006). *Contemporary Maya Spirituality: The Ancient Ways Are Not Lost*. Austin: University of Texas Press.

Montejo, V. (2005). *Maya Intellectual Renaissance: Identity, Representation, and Leadership*. Austin: University of Austin Press.

Oldridge, M. (2003). The Rise of the Stupid Network Effect. *International Journal of Market Research, 45*(3), 291.

Prigogine, I. (1997). *The End of Certainty*. New York: The Free Press.

Treat, J. (2002, November 25). *Guatemala's Landless Movement*. NM: Interhemispheric Resource Centre. Retrieved from http://americas.irc-online.org/pdf/focus/0211landless.pdf.

Tucker, V. (1999). The Myth of Development: A Critique of a Eurocentric Discourse. In R. Munck & D. O'Hearn (Eds.), *Critical Development Theory: Contributions to a New Paradigm* (pp. 1–26). London and New York: Zed.

Urry, J. (2005). The Complexity Turn. *Theory, Culture and Society, 22*(5), 1–14.

Warren, K. (1998). *Indigenous Movements and Their Critics: Pan-Maya Activism in Guatemala*. Princeton, NJ: Princeton University Press.

Whetten, G. (1961). The Land and the People. *Whetten208Guatemala: The Land and the People*, 208.

Wilson, R. (1999). Maya Resurgence in Guatemala: Q'eqchi' Experiences. University of Oklahoma Press.

Wittman, H., & Geisler, C. (2005). Negotiating Locality: Decentralization and Communal Forrest Management in the Guatemalan Highlands. *Human Organization, 64*(1), 62–74.

World Commission on Environment and Development, & Brundtland, G. H. (1987). Presentation of the Report of the World Commission on Environment and Development to the Commission of the European Communities, the EC and EFTA Countries... 5 May 1987, Brussels. World Commission on Environment and Development.

Yashar, D. (2005). *Contesting Citizenship in Latin America*. New York: Cambridge University Press.

CHAPTER 7

The Maya Idea of Culturally Sustainable Development

The concept of *culturally sustainable development*, as it is articulated by *El Centro Pluricultural para la Democracia*, will be presented in this chapter. The method of analysis here will involve the depiction of conceptions that have emerged out of my interviews and focus groups, as well as texts of *El Centro*. Specifically, concepts related to the following questions will be presented: *what is the relationship between humans, nature, and culture? What is Mayan culture? What is development? How do you do development?* The goal here is to depict, as closely as possible, the thinking of *El Centro* regarding these concepts.

Clearly, issues related to the ability of Western trained academics to represent the thinking of indigenous activists must be addressed here. A multifaceted and participatory methodology was developed in an attempt to address these issues. The process of interpretation involved, first, a three-month period of participant observation at *El Centro*; second, a thorough reading of all of *El Centro's* publications; third, individual interviews with members of the organization; fourth, a preliminary interpretation of the concepts; fifth, a presentation to members of *El Centro* of this preliminary interpretation; and, finally, a focus group discussion of these interpretations was held in which members changed, critiqued, and approved or disapproved of the author's representations and interpretations. The following depiction of the theory of *culturally sustainable development* is the result of this process.

T. MacNeill, *Indigenous Cultures and Sustainable Development in Latin America*, https://doi.org/10.1007/978-3-030-37023-7_7

Human, Nature, Culture

When beginning the process of discerning the meaning of *culturally sustainable development* in the initial phase of fieldwork, it seemed logical to first establish the properties of the fundamental unit of development—the human being. To do this, it would be necessary to hold the concept of culture to the side. It became clear early in the interview process, however, that to sever these concepts from one another would be to do violence to the idea of CSD. Of course, in the construction of the categories and typologies that are necessary for academic work, we regularly make somewhat arbitrary distinctions. The trick is to know when such distinctions cross the line between reasonable categories for analysis and unacceptable misrepresentations. In the course of investigation, it became increasingly apparent that treating culture and human as separable would be to cross that line. The same, it should be understood, could be said for creating a false distinction between humans and nature, or culture and nature for that matter.

Considering this, it is important to remember the words of *Matea* when she was asked to explain what she thought a human to be. "Everything to do with the human being," she said, "has to do with the spirit; has to do with nature." Similarly important is the example that *Mario* used to convey the inseparability of natural materials and cultural understandings of them. "Take the stone in the vision of the Mayan world," he suggests,

> In the Western world it is a material, a mineral that has no value. In Mayan culture, the stone, if it has use, it has use because it is complementary to the culture; and it is complimentary to the culture because we use it.

In *Mario's* comments, we see a claim that use-value is imbued on an object by the virtue that it has cultural value. But it is not presumed to be a unidirectional relationship. There is dialectic here—the cultural meaning of a material thing stems from its usefulness, and its usefulness is culturally determined. To speak of one is to speak of the other. As we address issues of culture and humanity here, then, we must be cognizant that we are speaking at the same time of the hard materiality of the natural world, of culture, and, as *Matea* suggests, of "the spirit."

Similarly, the division between individual and community is ambiguous. When the members of *El Centro* speak of human beings in the context of their work, they speak of "social subjects." True to the sense of ambiguity around the concepts of human and culture, a social subject can be a single person or a group of people. Each of the members of *El Centro*, for example, would be considered a social subject, but so too would the organization itself. Social subjects are "social" both in the sense that they may actually be a group of people, but also in that, as Matea suggests, "culture provides the elements for the formation of subjects." The culture, community, and person are inseparable. As Sofia understands it,

> much of what is a person, of what is a community, is the culture. Therefore you cannot separate it. ... You cannot say, "good, I am going to leave the culture here and develop over there". This is impossible because the culture is part of you; of your ideology; of your form of being. And therefore, if you propose ideas of how to generate development in your community, you will do it from the place of your culture, because you are there, and you identify with it, and it is from this point of view that you have generated an idea of how to generate changes that include the culture. You cannot pose questions that are not in accordance with the reality in which you live. Therefore into all of all you propose goes the culture. It is part of you and you cannot leave it to one side.

Matea elaborates more on the elements of culture, describing culture as "the social organizing processes that are given at the level of the community." These include "expressions that mark differences from other cultures based on the form of life, the form of sustenance, the spirituality, the customs," as well as "traditions and all the organization that you have at the level of the villages."

Cosmovision is an integral part of culture. Whereas culture represents the totality of meaning in a locale, cosmovision, *Matea* continues, is "the form of seeing all themes that are given in the world—perception. This exists in every part of the world ... there is a cosmovision in all places." Cosmovision is a subject's understanding of the way in which the world functions, and it is constructed of the pieces of culture. As *Roberto* explains, your culture is "your language, [and] your clothing," but also "your way of thinking—you have to see with your cosmovision." And, he continues, your cosmovision informs "your own way to conceive of your relation to the natural world."

But to say that subjects are socially formed is not to say that they are simply determined by their cultural environment. More than this, as *Mario* explains, subjects,

> are those who act. Who do [things]. … The subject is an element, is a cognitive subject that has experience, has ideas, has thoughts. And a subject is a motor. The motor of his or her own development. … The subject is the people. [The subject and the culture] are the same thing; subjects are the members of a culture.

Similarly, *Maria* insists that culture is created by "the population"—that it is created by subjects with agency. This is done, however, "in accordance with [a community's] thoughts and customs." It is with cognitive tools based on "the practices that have developed," she continues, "that the culture of a community is made."

For the members of *El Centro*, such assertions are much more than attempts to conceptualize structure and agency problems in academic theorizing. Cultural devaluation or cultural loss is necessarily a personal imposition. It is personal devaluation. It is a felt personal loss for members of communities who hold such cultural practices. Culture, for the members of *El Centro*, is valuable in itself, and must therefore be protected. This is evident in *Maria's* response when asked why it is important to protect culture:

> Because the culture forms part of the person, therefore the culture carries values, carries principles and this must not be forgotten in the development process but must be maintained, and because it forms part of the identity of the people, the view of the culture must not be lost.

It would be easy to misinterpret this as an assertion that cultures must not change—that they must remain static. This would not be consistent with the thinking of members of *El Centro*, however. *Sofia*, for example, holds that cultures do change—just not "from night until morning." After evoking the idea that the "essence" of Mayan culture is in the cosmovision, *Matea* draws attention to the tendencies of cultures to change, and what she perceives to be the true problem related to this—inequality:

> I think that all cultures should have independence. Not that they are going to be static or that they will maintain uniformity. But that they will not change their essence. When they lose their essence, they become debilitated and fall into the other culture. I feel that this should be changed, because at the level at which we are working there exists a large culture, but also a small culture. And often what happens is that the large culture absorbs the small culture. Like ideology, I speak of all the subliminal messages that provoke

> consumerism in us but also of more radical things that are possessed by other cultures. I speak of wars, I speak of impositions through financial resources. These things impact the entire country and prevent it from advancing. Therefore the cultures do not seem equal. It is this way because the one that has greater resources and greater numbers, greater financial resources, is often the one that maintains the hegemony. The survival of the small one is hard to achieve, and a lot of struggle is required if it is to survive.

Although it is not clear if the "larger" culture *Matea* refers to is Western culture, or ladino culture, or both, the statement draws attention to the hard material and cultural realities related to CSD in Guatemala. "Cultures are going to change," she continues, "depending on the moments and the processes in which each of these peoples exists." It is in this way, she argues, "that we have had to be learning from other forms." However, she insists that this process of cultural interchange has, "in some cases, done much damage to us."

The cases in which damage has been inflicted have occurred amidst great material and hegemonic power imbalances according to *Matea*. *Roberto* expands on the co-determining nature of material and cultural power, and the difficulty of the subordinated to engage in the production of culture. An idea of development that is culturally sustainable, he argues, must come from the people, but "sadly," he explains, "we don't have one to tell you about." Furthermore,

> The theory of development from the perception of the indigenous Mayan peoples in Guatemala is [non-existent] because there are no conditions, resources, or means of production. Otherwise it would be possible in this moment to have all the conditions necessary to initiate it.

Such an assertion brings the struggle for development undertaken by *El Centro* not just into the realm of the cultural or ideological, but into the material simultaneously, as is evident in the following statement from *Roberto*:

> The international economy or free market or international market has its own strategy of enrichment, of accumulation of resources. The strategy is to generate consumerism in the population. This is not development. If I am earning four thousand *Quetzales* and at the end of the month I buy a big television, or a large sound system, or other things, I have already spent my paycheck. I think this is a way in which local people spend money on items

> that are not useful for survival in this society. Survival and achievement of a better life do not depend directly on these things. Therefore I think that the strategy of consumerism in the population has been generated only for the benefit of foreign capital.

In *Roberto's* opinion, cultural and material imperialism not only rob indigenous Maya of their culture, but of the fundamental sustenance necessary to assert their own culture and their own idea of development. A form of development is nurtured in such a situation, but it is one in which "I have nothing to eat, I have nothing for education, I have nothing for health, but I am interested in equipping my house." In such a situation, members argue, the fight for development is lost. Indigenous culture is devalued, and indigenous people become subordinately integrated into a global economy that is structurally bent on material exploitation and cultural domination. Subjects have been nurtured in this situation—but they are of the wrong kind. They are not the "political subjects" that CSD requires, as *Maria* explains,

> When we speak of political subjects it is when they already have a greater capacity—of participation, of decision, of impact. Therefore the culture may create subjects, but [not] political subjects, [which] are created at the level of leadership.

Both cultural and material domination, then, are thought to undermine the creation of subjects which would be endowed with the agency required to conceive of, and then direct, their own development. Hegemonic messages of global consumer culture are presumed to bury and devalue local indigenous culture, while diverting material resources away from the reinforcement-through-use of local culture and towards the purchase of mass-produced consumption goods.

The concept of culture, and the politics that surrounds it, can now be more clearly delineated in a way that attempts to depict the meaning ascribed to it by members of *El Centro*. In a publication on *culturally sustainable development*, culture is described in this way by *El Centro*:

> Culture is a form of life, a manner of being, a way of thinking and feeling, and a different style of doing things throughout the day. That is to say, it is the solution that every community or group of humans gives to their relation to one another and with nature. Understood in this manner, culture is a social product that unites values, beliefs, attitudes, and behaviours of a

> society determining its development. Therefore, culture is dynamic, that is to say, it changes. (CPD 2008, p. 21)

The appearance of the word *solution*, and culture's depiction as a *product* that *unites* values in a society, thus *determining its development*, might lead one to assume this to be an instrumentalist definition of culture. That is, it may look like something akin to new institutional economics. When contextualized with the interview materials presented earlier, however, it seems more probable that the *solution* here is not to the problem of "how do I get more of what I want?" Rather it is a solution to the questions, "how do I make sense of the world?" "how should I act in the world?" and "what do I value?" The answers to these questions change, but not "from night until morning," and such changes can most likely be thought of as positive if they are undertaken in an environment that is relatively devoid of material and discursive inequalities such as income inequality or racial prejudice. This is to say that culture and cultural change are judged positively when the social subjects that are composed of, and compose, culture have "equality of agency" in the construction of that culture—to borrow a term from Rao and Walton (2004).

The *development* that is *determined* in this definition of culture is not a quantitative measure such as a level of gross national product or aggregated community income. It is qualitative—culture informs the kind of development that is sought. Culture is not subordinate, nor is it separable from the material world. There is great concern at *El Centro* that the urge to purchase Western consumer products can cause subjects to misallocate their resources away from the provision of healthcare, food, clean water, or education, for example. A culture of consumerism is chosen here at the expense of what are seen to be the fundamental elements that provide for life. Even this, however, does not reduce to a critique of "good" indigenous culture versus bad consumer "culture." *Roberto*, for example, reluctantly admits that this is "a type of development." The more fundamental issue for members of *El Centro* is that one of these "cultures" is exorbitantly strong, dominant, hegemonic. In such instances, *Matea* explains, "there is a psychological bombardment on us, therefore we learn another distinct form of life, that we consider better than our own." This undermines the capacity for the local culture to adapt in a democratic way—one in which values can be reevaluated and problems can be negotiated in a climate of relative discursive and material equality.

What becomes apparent from this discussion is that for any action to be "culturally sustainable," it must facilitate a discursive equality in which indigenous culture and knowledge are not subordinated, overpowered, or dominated. Market-led development is perceived to carry with it Western consumer culture that is backed by material power. Development of this sort is not considered to be culturally sustainable because of the felt devaluation of indigenous culture and its submersion in the hegemony of Western capitalist consumer society. The same could be said of development plans that emanate in a top-down manner from Western-trained development practitioners—be they rooted in liberal or Marxian theories. Such interventions, well-intentioned as they may be, carry with them a discursive force that is backed by economic power. They, therefore, threaten to devalue local knowledge and culture. For development to be culturally sustainable in Guatemala, *Roberto* claims, it must "come from the perception of the indigenous Mayan peoples … from the communities; the majority of which are indigenous communities."

The "perception" of indigenous communities is thought still to be rooted in Mayan cosmovision. Members of *El Centro* maintain that despite cultural and material intrusions from Spanish colonialism, Christianity, consumer culture, resource-extracting corporations, and civil war, the core of Maya cosmovision remains intact, if buried, in the subjectivities of the residents of indigenous communities. The continued existence of the communal mayorship in most communities is offered as proof of this. So too is the use of traditional clothing and the perseverance of indigenous languages throughout the highlands. All of these institutions and practices, it is argued, have changed somewhat with external interaction, but have been maintained, almost miraculously, throughout over 500 years of what members characterize as planned and deliberate ethnocide. This cultural maintenance in the face of planned destruction has been done through a creative incorporation and blending of cultural elements as *Matea* explains regarding religion:

> In Chichicastenango, for example, inside the church are all the [Christian] images and pictures, while the altar outside is Mayan. Both the churches and Mayan alters were put on the highest points in town—the same places. And you see a combination of the two traditions. You see Mayan priests and the people doing Mayan ceremonies, and then go to the church. Or they may just go to the church but engage in Mayan ceremonies.

Mayan cosmovision, then, is thought to remain embedded to varying degrees in the subjectivities of contemporary indigenous Guatemalans, even those who practice Christianity. As discussed in the previous chapter, a felt connection to the natural world and cosmos, as well as egalitarian, harmonious tendencies, is assumed to be integral to that belief system.

Participation, Democracy, Development

The very fact that the cosmovision has become subordinated to colonial belief systems represents a fundamental inequality to the members of *El Centro*. Attempts to re-valorize the cosmovision in the eyes of ladino and Maya populations are, therefore, fundamental to CSD. This "principal objective," as *Mario* calls it, has been integrated into every part of *El Centro*'s operations. But perceived damages to nature are also threats to CSD—not simply in that they may compromise the abilities of future generations to realize their own development, but because nature and culture are one according to the cosmovision. To damage nature is to damage part of the culture, and to damage culture is to damage the person that is integral to that culture. As was discussed in the last section, only a development that takes place in an environment of discursive and material equality can, therefore, be considered culturally sustainable, as *Mario* suggests:

> Culture has its own value. ... When the people already value and come to value their own form, then a great measure of development with culture will have been achieved. This is because without respecting their own culture, the people will be alienated. That will be monocultural—looking for only one culture and not diversity. Diversity is force. With diversity there are various visions of the world, for example, you can not submit me to your vision of the world, and I cannot submit you to mine. ... If we know how to achieve diversity with respect, with harmony, with coexistence in peace, then development is better.

To recapitulate a fundamental point, CSD does *not* imply the freezing of culture (or nature, or politics, or the economy for that matter). Nor does it suggest a complete reversion to some imagined pre-Columbian state. It involves the equalization of discursive and material power relationships between indigenous peoples with their nature/cultures and hegemonic Spanish colonial and global capitalist systems. Sustainability means continuity amidst constant cultural and natural change. CSD, therefore, does not imply a particular cultural or economic form, but rather a transformative participatory process of deep democracy, as the organization explains in one of its publications:

> If we understand participation as an essential element democratic system, we can say that this makes all the people and the political community as a whole, the protagonists of different social processes. All must be involved closely in the cultural, political, economic, and environmental aspects of group life. It is this involvement that, more or less, marks the advance of democracy in a given society. (Chávez Cayax 2003, pp. 8–9)

During *El Centro's* workshops that are set to promote democratic participation, traditional elements of the cosmovision are encouraged. The intimate relation of indigenous peoples to the land is reaffirmed often, for example. This is done not to "freeze" a primordial culture but to attempt to counter the hegemonic imposition of Spanish-colonial and Western capitalist ideologies which have conspired to devalue indigenous belief systems for 500 years. The value of pre-Colombian institutions such as the communal mayorship is reasserted in an attempt to revalorize Mayan culture as well. But so too is the value of international human rights architectures, democracy, and positive change. These are all things that are commonly associated with "modern" or "Western" culture, and they are things that do not imply stagnation.

The core of the goal of *El Centro's* development work is, in fact, to encourage a culture and politics of "transformative participation"—not a cultural ossification. It is hoped that this transformative process would go beyond the "pseudo-participation" of stakeholders being simply invited into the decision-making process "for the photo," or merely being consulted, being given charge of delegated tasks in larger processes that have been conceived from "above," as Chávez Cayax (2003) argues in one of *El Centro's* publications. As Chávez Cayax (2003) continues to explain, "transformative participation" requires political subjects who are "actors, not spectators" in decision-making processes at all levels, and this involves the building of capacities of traditional and local institutions and countering discursive structural barriers by valorizing indigenous culture and combating racism (pp. 10–12).

A legal architecture does exist, which provides a framework from within such participation can take place. And these legal texts are utilized extensively by *El Centro* in its interaction with communities. In *Article 46* of the

Guatemalan constitution "it is established as a general principal in matters of Human Rights, that the treaties and conventions accepted and ratified by Guatemala have preeminence over internal rights." Often referred to by members of *El Centro*, *Articles 20* and *21* of the *Universal Declaration of Human Rights*, ratified by Guatemala in 1994, establish "freedom of association and the right of participation in governing the country" (Chávez Cayax 2003, p. 22). Members insist that this right is not restricted to voting but to "participate in the decisions that are made in the State, and to obtain the form of organization desired by all the inhabitants that form the country" (Chávez Cayax 2003, p. 23). The Guatemalan Constitution also guarantees the right of meeting and manifestation of collectives that may present petitions and grievances to government, the right of free association (*Articles 34, 35*, and *44*), the right of a person to participate in the creation of their cultural identity (*Articles 57, 58*, and *66*), and rights of collective participation (*Articles 136* and *136*).

As discussed in the previous chapter, *ILO 169* is commonly evoked by *El Centro* in texts, interviews, and meetings. The agreement contains language protecting culture, traditional lifestyles, consultation, participation, and control over economic, cultural, and social development processes. Although some of the interpretation of the agreement has been contested in the Guatemalan context, it is insisted at *El Centro* that *ILO 169* contributes to the creation of space in which political participation can be undertaken.

Agreements negotiated under the *Peace Accords* also provide space for wide political participation in Guatemala. The interrelated agreements of the *Accords* convey a deep discourse of indigenous rights, decentralization, cultural affirmation, and community self-management. Guatemala agreed to become a signatory of the *Universal Declaration of Human Rights*, as a part of the *Peace Accord* negotiations in 1994. The *Guatemalan Accord for the Identity and Rights of Indigenous Peoples* was signed in 1995. The *Accord of Agrarian Socioeconomic Aspects and Situation* and the *Accord for Strengthening Civil Power and the Function of the Exercise of a Democratic Society* were signed in 1996. The *Law of Councils of Urban and Rural Development, the General Law of Decentralization*, and the new *Municipal Code* were signed in 2002.

The purpose of this chapter is not to go into detail on arguments regarding legal interpretations of these accords and conventions. The essential point regarding these instruments is that they all attempt in some way to create legal space for direct participation of communities in politics and policy via their own culturally situated political institutions and social organizations. Many contain strong wording in this regard. Section III.1 of the *Indigenous Accord*, for example, states:

> The Maya, Garifuna, and Xinca are authors of their cultural development. The role of the state is to help said development, eliminate obstacles to the exercise of this right taking the legislative and administrative measure necessary to fortify indigenous cultural development in all areas corresponding to the state and to assure the participation of the indigenous in the decisions relating to the planning and execution of cultural programs and projects through their own organizations and institutions.

The *Accord* continues in part IV.B.3:

> Recognizing the role that corresponds to the communities, in the framework of municipal autonomy, to the exercise of the right of the indigenous peoples to decide their own priorities with respect to the process of development and in particular with relation to education, health, culture, and infrastructure. The government is committed to affirm the capacity of said communities in this manner.

In such a way, the concept of culture is mixed with the concept of development in national and international law. Both concepts are tied to human rights and with the idea of civic participation. A legal space for decentralized participation of indigenous peoples is provided by such instruments. This is not a sufficient condition, argue members of *El Centro,* however, to assure that such participation will occur. There is more involved in participation than the simple granting of the right to participate, as an *El Centro* document suggests:

> Participation, in all its manifestations, must be a transformative action and practice of liberation initiated by the person, not for them, in which the oppressed and the excluded encounter conditions in which they can discover themselves reflexively as a subject of their own historical destiny. In this way, people discover paths to their own liberation through their own research and planning, and simply because freedom to meet in such a way is freedom to become master of your own decisions. In this sense, participation is not something that is granted, as one might mistakenly think, it is something that is won through constant struggle. (Chávez Cayax 2003, p. 21)

True democratic transformative participation, this suggests, cannot occur without the formation of political subjects. Active groups of persons must initiate the processes of participation in which they discover and redefine themselves amidst the rubble of colonial and neoliberal ideology in which they may be currently trapped. The formation of political subjects, even within such an expansive legal architecture of participatory rights, requires the exertion of energy—a "constant struggle" (ibid.).

Intervention, Organization, Political Subjects

According to *El Centro*, the struggle to create active indigenous political subject is undertaken through social organization. As Bulux (2003) argues in one of the organization's documents:

> Social organization is a comprehensive development process, which facilitates the study and understanding of the local context in formulating solutions. It also provides mechanisms that enable a community to meet collective challenges while maintaining its own identity, unity and solidarity. (p. 15)

Communities are not thought of as currently existing in a state of dysfunctional disorganization, however, and CSD does not require the imposition of organizations and institutions by outside experts. As Bulux (2003) explains:

> In the community there exists a diversity of forms of organization—those which come from the communal authorities, associations, committees, cooperatives etc. ... It is from these cultural values of organization that culturally sustainable development must be realized. In this sense, sustainability must be understood as a value of the culture in that cultural practices already exist as responses that have been created and recreated through experiences of life and cohabitation with neighbors and with nature throughout their historical social development. (pp. 21–22)

Maya cultural institutions of governance, such as communal mayorships, then, can be employed as the main driver of CSD. This is not as simple a solution to problems of development as it may appear, however. Bulux (2003) explains that,

> Because of colonial policies of slavery and forced labour, the organization of Maya society suffered the disintegration of its social nucleus and therefore its social organization, which had been based in the value of common good and collective work. (p. 12)

Furthermore, as discussed in the previous chapter, both Maya cultural tradition and human rights conventions encourage the direct participation of women in political and planning processes. There are few organizations of Maya women existing in most communities, however. Considering this, "organization must be promoted amongst those sectors, such as youth and women, which may not be organized" (Bulux 2003, p. 15).

It is in these areas that the work of *El Centro* is situated. Through various interventions, the organization seeks to strengthen existing forms of social organization and to encourage the formation of political social subjects where they may not exist. These interventions do not simply target indigenous peoples and institutions, however, but also seek to create an acceptance of indigenous forms of social organization, in the spirit of mutual support, with official, modern, *ladino*-dominated state institutions such as municipal governments. This work is undertaken through four distinct projects at *El Centro*.

Four Programmes

In attempting to foster CSD, *El Centro* mobilizes four programmes in the Western Highlands. These are the *Communal Mayorship* programme, the *Municipalities* programme, the programme for *Women and Youth*, and the *Research* programme. All of these utilize participatory processes in the formation and building of capacities of local and municipal institutions and organizations. This is done through arranging information sessions, participatory workshops, diploma programmes, as well as community- and municipal-level meetings on topics that are important to the people of the Western Highlands.

The Communal Mayorship Programme

As discussed in the previous chapter, at the time of conquest, Mayan government involved communal mayorships which would undertake all the political, juridical, and administrative duties connected with *parcialidades* (administrative units of 300–600 people). These mayorships would convene from time to time at a regional level in an *amaq'* council. As a result of hundreds of years of Spanish colonial administration and institutionalized racism, the *amaq'* had disappeared by the time of the *Peace Accords*, and, although their existence remains widespread, the communal mayorships had been reduced to largely ceremonial status in a system dominated by a colonially imposed municipal governance structure (Hill 1989; Wittman and Geisler 2005; Barrios 1988). The *Communal Mayorship* programme is designed to remedy this by reasserting the cultural and political relevance of the institution in the eyes of indigenous peoples, ladinos, and official national, regional, and municipal governance institutions.

The initial step of this is called "first contact" by field technicians and coordinators at *El Centro*. In this step, a number of indigenous mayors from geographically close communities will be invited to a meeting at a nearby location. Members of *El Centro* will deliver a talk that is designed, first, to educate the mayors of the rights provided to them and their institution by the legal architecture discussed earlier in this chapter. Emphasis here is on the assertion that the communal mayorship has as much, or more, legal power than does the municipal mayorship. This is generally an unexpected revelation to the communal mayors.

Second, the communal mayors are asked to list all of the duties they currently perform in the communities. This list is usually substantial and covers juridical, political, and administrative responsibilities. Finally, the session concludes with an emotionally charged speech by the *El Centro* field technician who praises the resilience of the institution in the face of hundreds of years of colonial attempts to dissolve it, the cultural significance of the mayorship, and its democratic nature. "They tried to erase you," as *Matea* said in such a situation, "they still say you don't exist—but here you are." The purpose of *El Centro*—to assist the communal mayors—is asserted, and those mayors in attendance are asked what they would like *El Centro* to do for them. Often the mayors simply want to "know more about these laws."

After the first contact is completed, the communal mayors are often asked if they would like to attend a larger meeting—one which approximates an *amaq'*—of many communal mayors from across the region. These meetings are issue-based—perhaps covering topics such as health, education, or environmental degradation, but most commonly, of late, regarding the problems that communities are having with transnational mining companies. Information regarding the issue is provided by a member of *El Centro*. The mayors are split into a number of groups and are asked to construct strategy proposals regarding the issue. The merit of each proposal is discussed by the group, and consensus is sought regarding an overall strategy. All participants are paid enough to cover their travel, and they are fed. The meetings may last an entire day, so remuneration is essential given the loss of time that the mayors would otherwise have been spending on farm-work.

Although policy outputs of such meetings are important, the cultural and social significance of the meetings themselves must be emphasized. I was lucky enough to attend a regional meeting of mayors only two weeks after first contact had been established with five participants. I had also attended the first contact with these participants. What is striking anthropologically is that this, just as much as it is a policy meeting, is a social ritual in which subjectivities may be reformed. As a thought experiment, we could imagine what it could be like to be one of these communal mayors who just a few weeks before had accorded little value to their positions, then to be told that their institution was powerful enough to stand up to hundreds of years of planned ethnocide, and then told that their power is equal to that of the municipal government under national and international law. Finally, these mayors attend a meeting with forty to fifty other indigenous mayors who are actively constructing policy.

It is beyond the scope of this chapter to assess impacts of such activities. This would provide fertile ground for further study. But it should be made clear that this type of activity is designed to be "transformative" for participants. This type of participation is not consistent with liberal or republican forms of citizenship which presume a pre-formed human actor with stable beliefs and preferences as it engages in political participation. It is more congruent with thinking of Habermas (1984) or Rostboll (2008), who focus on the way in which such forms of participation act to transform subjectivities as they seek policy outputs, and assert that the overarching goal must be that all such participation be as egalitarian as possible. The goal for *El Centro* is to facilitate the creation of active political subjects who gain increasing respect for their own culture and institutions. Policy decisions created in such meetings are secondary to this "primary goal."

The Programme for Women and Youth

This programme is similar to the *Communal Mayorship* programme in that it seeks to transform subjects into political subjects through rights education and social organization. The difference here is that the focus is on groups who are less likely to have pre-existing organizations and institutions. Women and Youth, it is insisted, have been excluded from political participation due to the importation of colonial cultural and political norms. The goal of the *Programme for Women and Youth* is to remedy this.

The first step undertaken by this project is to locate women's or youth groups that may be pre-existing in communities. Members of *El Centro* will ascertain through community interviews if such organizations are inclusive or exclusionary. Depending on this, activities will be organized within existing organizational structures or outside of them. In either case, the first order of business is rights education similar to that of the Communal Mayors Programme except that the focus is more on rights accorded to women and children within the national and international legal architecture. A second step is the organization of workshops based around a community issue. Similar to the case of the Communal Mayors, consensus on policy will be sought. Free access diploma programmes in democratic participation and rights are also offered. Again, the focus here is not so much on the policies agreed on, or number of diplomas awarded, but on the transformative nature of political participation.

The legitimacy of the Communal Mayorship is an important point that is maintained in this programme as well. The full electoral participation of all men, women, and children is located as a source of legitimacy. It is also reinforced that Mayan societies have historically sought equality and complementarity between genders and that women have the legal right to participate equally in the Communal Mayorship. Some communities have, in fact, elected woman mayors since *El Centro* began its work in the highlands, although this representation at meetings of Communal Mayors remains very low.

The Municipalities Programme

Similar to the other programmes, the *Municipality Programme* is centrally concerned with rights education. The increased autonomy granted to municipalities under national law is focused on, of course, but so too is the power granted to the Communal Mayorships. Great effort is taken to sensitize the municipal authorities to the equal status of the Communal Mayorships and the necessity that they be integrated into the municipal governing process. Assistance is provided by *El Centro*, when requested, with everything, from budgeting to the integration of community groups to conflict resolution and legal interpretation.

To have a municipalities programme was not of initial priority to *El Centro*, but members of the organization soon realized it to be necessary. As *Sofia* explains,

> When we began work, we worked only with the population, with civil society, with organizations, with the communal authorities, but only with the population. Therefore it seemed illogical to work with municipal governments. But the municipal government is a place where people take proposals. Therefore the work of our program now is to make the municipal governments aware of the need to open spaces [to dialogue and receive proposals from the population]. The problem is that many municipal governments are authoritarian, and remain closed. They do not accept proposals from the population. So our work involves facilitating a space for dialogue between the municipal government and the population, and to create acceptance of these proposals with the departmental and national governments if need be.

This sensitization of the need of municipal, departmental, and national governments to dialogue directly with the population regarding policy is now a fundamental part of *El Centro's* CSD strategy. Most of the focus in this regard is concentrated in the relationship between the communal mayorships, women's and other civil society groups, and the municipality. The idea is not to replace the state and municipality with a romanticized pre-Columbian institution, but to create a space in which all of these institutions may dialogue and engage in mutual change, exchange, and support. It is with respect to the municipalities programme that we can see a fundamental goal of *El Centro*—to create an organic and mutable form of decentralized democracy which combines indigenous and modern (state) institutions in a sphere of dialogue and mutual change. This implies that indigenous culture and cosmovision be integrated into policymaking beginning at the municipal level, but at departmental and national levels as well.

The Research Programme

El Centro has a need to investigate its own activities and evaluate their effectiveness. This, however, is not the primary purpose of the *Research*

Programme. This initiative is more centrally interested in facilitating a transformative form of participation through participatory research within communities, and encouraging knowledge-sharing amongst them. This is clear when we consider the following text, contained in the prologue of one of *El Centro's* research documents on community conflict over water, which outlines the five main goals of the research process:

> The first, to reconstruct the history of the experience; the second, to approximate the collective reflection of those subjects who participated in the same [events], third; to communicate the results so that they can serve as inspiration, orientation and foundation for the attitudes and actions of future generations; fourth, for the construction of collective knowledge; and fifth, so that it may serve as orientation and example for other communities in the solution of their own conflicts, from their own reality, cosmovision and practice. (CPD 2008, p. 7)

The process of research and distribution of published materials is at least as important as their textual content. The research process is participatory—involving focus groups and qualitative interviews. The final representation of events is presented and validated or changed by community members. In the end, travel is paid for to allow community members to attend a publication release event in which each attending member is presented a copy of the research.

The case of the (2008) publication of *Conflictos Comunales por el Derecho al Agua* (Community Conflicts over the Right to Water) serves as a fitting example. A number of communities in the municipality of *Palestina do Los Altos* were involved in a long-standing conflict over rights of access to a natural water source. The conflict, which lasted from approximately 1988 to 2002, was typified by violence, incarcerations, kidnappings, split communities and families, as well as public protest. The issue cut across the jurisdiction of several communal mayors, two municipalities, and involved a development plan implemented with little consultation by an international development organization (CARE). After years of sometimes violent conflict, a solution was created with assistance from *El Centro*. Through cooperation, negotiation, and compromise, an agreement between municipal (viewed as "State") authorities and the communal mayors was achieved. The agreement was the result of several workgroups, meetings, public consultations, and participatory budgeting initiatives (CPD 2008).

The history of the conflict was then researched in a participatory manner by *El Centro*. The resulting document recounted the history as constructed by participants. A number of conclusions were also formulated. These included an assertion that state action is often "an imposition … with respect to community-based forms of organization." This, it was argued, "contrasts with the communities own forms of organization, specifically the communal mayorship which has its own norms, principles, and values with which to resolve disputes" (p. 53). It was also argued that the time of conflict was also a time of learning for local authorities, as they

> learned to negotiate with the institutions of the state, with all of its difficulties, something that none had done before the conflict. They also learned to coordinate the actions of state institutions with the ancestral institutions represented by the communal mayorships. (p. 53)

Furthermore, it was explained that "the communities undertook participatory budgeting, something that had not even crossed their minds before" (p. 56), and that, throughout the process, "the Communal mayor did not complete a roll only as 'auxiliary' to the municipal mayorship" but was engaged as equal partner (p. 56). It was argued that the conflict and resolution fostered not only the "construction of social capital" (p. 58), but also the "construction of collective conscience [as] … the experience served to promote the understanding that collective well-being should always prevail over individual interest" (p. 59). The analysis ended with a strong affirmation of the authority and legitimacy of the communal mayorship:

> The efforts made to reclaim the role of communal Mayors reflect the roles they are playing today. The institution has transcended the role of assistant to the municipal mayor to perform roles of local leader and administrator of the community in the political aspects and administration of justice. This is evidence that it is not the laws that are imposed by the state that govern the development of communities, but is their own historical evolution that is shaping social relations according to their own culture. (p. 59)

The way in which these findings are disseminated is of upmost importance. The history and analysis were published in a small book. A public event was planned in Quetzaltenango—Guatemala's second-largest city—and nearly 100 delegates were invited from all of the communities involved. Travel expenses were covered for attendees, and food was provided during the half-day event. The communal mayors and municipal mayors involved in the conflict spoke about the experience, as did members of *El Centro* and other community members. In the end, community members in attendance were called, each by name, to receive a personal copy of the book, complete with handshakes from members of *El Centro*, and a photo in each case. Recipients were men, women, and children from the communities. They were receiving what amounted to an award for their ingenuity and achievement. The point, as was explained to me later, was to instil confidence in local communities of their competence and ability to direct their own development. Copies of the book were also given to community representatives for free distribution in the communities. Finally, such publications are distributed to other communities in the highlands—especially to communal mayors—in order to share these lessons.

Maya versus the Mine

The issue of mining has become central to the activities of *El Centro*, so it serves well as example within which the theory and practice of the organization may be contextualized. The Central America region, Guatemala in particular, is witness to a continuing proliferation of conflicts between communities and transnational mining interests. Since the 1996 Peace Accords were signed, for example, there have been 380 solicitations for mining rights to the government of Guatemala (CPD 2009, p. 22). No attempt will be made here to explore the issue deeply in all its facets nationally, internationally, or locally. What will be presented is a brief overview of the relationship of *El Centro* to the mining conflict involving the municipality of *Sipacapa* in the department of *San Marcos*.

El Centro began working with women, youth, and the communal mayorship of *Sipakapa* in 2004. It was not until the following year that the issue of mining arose, and at this time it was the communal mayorship that brought it to the attention of the organization. In 2003, the Canadian mining company *Montana* (a subsidiary of *Glamis Corp.*, and then *GoldCorp*) had been granted, without community consultation, a large gold-mining concession in the Western Highlands. In all, 85 percent of the concession lay in the municipality of *San Miguel*, and 15 percent in *Sipacapa*. A total of 1 percent of the proceeds from the concession was to be accrued by the national government, and the remaining 99 percent to the company. No royalties from the resource extraction were to be granted to the community (CPD 2009; Yagenova and Garcia 2009).

In 2005, aided by investment funds from the World Bank, Montana began construction of the Marlin Mine in *San Miguel*. In the time between the granting of the concession and the beginning of construction, residents of *Sipacapa* had begun to educate themselves about the environmental and health risks associated with mining, and about their legal rights of consultation in the granting of such concessions. This community-led research was facilitated by *El Centro* and a number of other human rights and environmental organizations such as *Madre Selva*. As Roberto explains, they were trying "to generate a process of understanding in the population, and to give them the elements necessary to defend their collective rights." Growing community concern led to activism against the development of the mine in nearby *San Miguel* and its planned expansion into *Sipacapa* (CPD 2009). The precautionary concerns, which soon manifested in reality in *San Miguel*, were material and cultural as Roberto explains:

> When we have 30 kilometres of mining exploitation, it will imply that we are going to see 30 kilometres of territory in these municipalities without natural areas, without natural resources, without forests, without biodiversity, without fauna, without flora, without anything. And apart from this with certain contamination of water—not just the rivers but the water table, the subterranean water will be contaminated as well. More than this, there are illnesses; these have actually appeared [in San Miguel]. Many illnesses of the skin have appeared and we believe this to signal a great risk to the lives of the people. In the theme of culture, for example, as well: there is a destruction of the land and the land is conceived as the mother for the indigenous peoples because it is what produces all that sustains and provides nutrition for the population … [This therefore] can affect as well spirituality, cosmovision. We speak of a culturally sustainable development from the perspective in the indigenous peoples—in these municipalities everything is the opposite.

This corresponds with the assertions of lawyers working with the community, who argued that,

> the company is in flagrant violation of the UN International Covenant on Economic, Social, and Cultural Rights and ILO Convention 169 Concerning the Rights of Indigenous and Tribal Peoples in Independent Countries. The company has also infringed local property rights, including the use, posses-

> sion, and administration of local indigenous land and territory. The mining project has also trampled on the patrimonial right of San Miguel and Sipacapa to decide on whether to issue mining licenses that pose risks to health, the environment, security, social and cultural life as well as the right to the free self-determination of the people. (Yagenova and Garcia 2009, p. 165)

In addition to this, physical damage from blasting at the mine has appeared in the form of cracks in housing structures (Marroquín 2009).

The communal mayors and other community groups sought help from the municipal mayor's office, but received only the response that the mining issue was beyond its jurisdiction. All the while, connections were being established between local community groups, national organizations such as *Madre Selva*, and international groups such as the *Indigenous Peoples Council of Central America*. Concerted activism was apparent in 2005 as citizens of Los Encuentros—a municipality hours from *Sipacapa*—cooperated in a protest which blocked the transport of necessary materials for the construction of the mine. In that same year, the community of *Sipacapa* held a public consultation in which they declared a ban on mining under the auspices of ILO 169 and the authority of the traditional communal authorities (CPD 2009; Yagenova and Garcia 2009).

The legality of the consultation was challenged on many levels by the mining company. The most notable of these challenges was a grievance filed on the grounds that the consultation was unconstitutional. The Guatemalan Constitutional Court on 8 May 2007 granted that the consultation was legal, but only as just that—a consultation—and was not legally enforceable since subterranean resources are constitutionally the property of the national government (OCG 2010). Shortly after this, the same court found, however, that the national mining law was unconstitutional in that it violated environmental stipulations in the constitution. In 2010, a group of over 80 civil society organizations including *El Centro* officially petitioned the national government to suspend mining operations in the country, pending community consultations and impact assessments (Prensa Libre 2010). Later that year, just as members of *El Centro* were meeting in Canada with indigenous peoples who had conflicts with resource extraction under the invitation of the Canadian Ambassador to Guatemala, a Canadian Supreme court ruling required Canadian extractive industries to abide by stricter ethical and environmental guidelines (Ljunggren 2010). Finally, in June of 2010, the Guatemalan government officially enforced the closure of the *Marlin Mine*, pending more research into the environmental and social consequences of mining (Marroquín 2009). This closure was suspended in 2011 when the mine resumed full production. The Marlin Mine finally closed permanently in 2017, somewhat due to political pressure, but more so due to the near-complete extraction of all gold. All mining equipment has been moved to a new mine, which is currently beginning production in Cerro Blanco, Guatemala.

The saga of opposition to the Marlin Mine is complex. There are many researchers that will no doubt craft exemplary accounts of the issue. There are two import points for the current discussion that involve, *first*, the way in which mining was perceived as a threat to CDS in the Western Highlands, and, *second*, the way in which communities, and especially communal mayors, organized with the assistance of a large network of rights organizations—a processes to which *El Centro* was integral.

Regarding the first point, there were five main damages that emanated from the mining project which were perceived by the community and *El Centro*. First, there was the damage of disrespect associated with the community not being consulted regarding plans to initiate mining on communal territory. Second, there were damages associated with contamination of water supplies and associated illness. Third, there were physical damages to housing structures. Fourth, there were environmental damages, as the ecosystem near the mine was completely destroyed. Finally, and related intimately to this, is the personal felt cultural damage inflicted indirectly as environmental degradation impacted indigenous subjectivities which have a close felt relationship with their natural environments, as *Roberto's* earlier statement suggests. These damages are material, spiritual, and cultural, but each is perceived as real and important. And, as *Roberto* has suggested, they all run contrary to a development that is culturally sustainable, despite promises of potential employment. Importantly, at no point has community opposition to the project been undertaken with the goal of receiving economic proceeds from the mining. This reveals that economic incentives are low on the list of priorities of community members compared to the other damages listed earlier.

The second point—regarding the reaction or the communities to these perceived damages—is equally revealing of the multifaceted nature of *El Centro's* theory of development. Resistance to the project was undertaken in multiple ways—through press, through protest, through the judicial system, but key to this was the building of capacities of pre-existing cultural institutions such as the communal mayorship. *El Centro* does not measure success in the conflict by noting constitutional court decisions, but by recognizing the capacities of environmental monitoring and political action that have been developed in the communities during the process, as well as the increased status of the communal mayorship that has been achieved (CPD 2009). Underlining this, it was the community that introduced mining as a problem to *El Centro* in the first place, and the community of *Sipacapa* and many others in the Highlands have made this point strongly enough that mining has become the main issue around which CSD work revolves at the organization.

Conclusion

Any attempt to succinctly summarize the thinking of *El Centro* must begin with the cosmovision. The essence of Maya cosmovision is that the three discursive, analytical categories of nature, culture, and human are inseparable—that they are one. Cosmovision is practically inseparable from culture—it is the way of seeing that is predominant in a particular cultural setting. It also prescribes, however, ways of acting, and all ways of acting are thought to be consistent with the cosmovision, since it is the core of the culture. Appeals by *El Centro* to Mayan cosmovision may be thought as attempts to point out that threats or damages to culture or nature are interpreted as real human damages by subjects that are situated within Mayan culture, and that Mayan subjects, by virtue of their intimate relationship with nature, are culturally predisposed to be effective stewards of the local natural environment.

The "subjects" that are evoked here may be single persons, but are just as likely to be groups of persons. This ambiguity exists partly because the concept of an individual, which is divisible from the community, is not consistent with Maya cosmovision. Subjects are created by their material and cultural environment. Importantly, this implies that values, valuations, beliefs, tastes, and utility functions (to use the language of neoclassical economics) are viewed as the products of culture, and this culture is not understood simply as the product of self-interested interaction as new institutional economics tends to suggest. Culture exists for culture's sake. "It has its own value," as *Mario* has suggested.

This depiction need not imply that cultures and subjects are stagnant and immutable. Cultures are constantly mutating, and subjects may have agency to change their cultural situation, just as they may have agency to change their material situation. Cultures, it is asserted, are constantly informed and re-formed from their interaction with their "outsides"—through the blurring of their edges. It is the agency of social subjects within this process that is thought to determine the outcome of the interaction.

It is argued by members of *El Centro* that agency, however, is not equally distributed across the globe, within Guatemala, or within the Western Highlands. Material deficiencies are thought to impact the agency that a subject has to change its discursive and material environments, so are less tangible elements such as racism and cultural devaluation. The agency of indigenous Mayan subjects is promoted by the organization through measures that attempt to assure that food, health, and clean water are attainable to subjects but also through increasing indigenous peoples' self-valuation of their own culture and sensitizing ladino subjects and state institutions to the same. This is attempted through *El Centro's* four major programmes which deal with communal mayorships, women and youth, municipalities, and research.

It is essential to note that claims that Maya subjects are culturally predisposed to environmental consciousness should not be taken to imply that all indigenous Maya men, women, children, or even communal mayors exhibit this behaviour and feel this connection. Of course, it is understood by members of *El Centro* that many do not. But the underlying logic of CSD is this: the cultural tradition of the Mayan cosmovision gives much more credence to the unity of human/culture/nature and the place of humans as "givers of praise, givers of respect, providers, and nurturers" than do Western enlightenment culture with its Newtonian model of the universe, consumer capitalist culture with its view of the environment as a resource (whether or not that resource must be sustained for the benefit of future generations), or related forms of Christianity which tend to depict the natural world as a gift from God to be exploited by Man (Molesky-Poz 2009, p. 38). The simultaneous work of valorizing Maya culture while opening space for indigenous political action is undertaken in order to create political subjects that value Maya cosmovision more intensely. These resultant Maya political subjects, it is assumed, will therefore be environmental subjects by virtue of this increased valuation of the cosmovision.

This is simultaneously cultural change and cultural continuity, and it would not be possible if Maya cosmovision was not already ingrained, if only partially, in the subjectivities of indigenous people. For proof that it is, members of *El Centro* point to the continued existence of a wide variety of Maya cultural practices—from the widespread use of traditional clothing and language to the persistence of indigenous religious practices and the continued relevance of the communal mayorship. The programmes of cultural valourization are not considered impositions because they resonate with the existing cosmovision of the indigenous peoples of the Western Highlands. In cases where the cosmovision is lost to a greater extent, such as could be argued to be the case in the town of *Tecpan* (Hill 1989; Wittman and Geisler 2005), decentralization would be instead promoted via the municipal government.

The revalorization of Mayan culture, the amplification of indigenous political agency, and the reassertion of rights to resources and territorial control that are implied in this process are linked to the promotion of grassroots democracy which is thought to be the prerequisite to any meaningful sustainable development plan. Centuries of racism, colonialism, and neocolonialism have robbed indigenous Maya not only of their culture, and their political voice, but also of the fundamental sustenance necessary to assert their own culture and their own idea of development. The programme of *El Centro* is designed to promote a foundational level of discursive and political equality which includes access to material resources—or at least not the continued degradation of existing resources (by mining operations, e.g.). The guiding principal is that of equality of the capacity to participate in decision-making, policy, and planning processes, as well as the communicative production of culture. Only once this is achieved will culturally sustainable development initiatives be possible.

In such a climate, it is argued by members of *El Centro*, development plans, governing policies, and systems of cultural understanding implicated in development processes would be authored substantially by the communities of the Western Highlands themselves. This does not necessarily suggest that this authorship not be undertaken in cooperation with the Guatemalan State, foreign donors, or transnational corporate interests, nor does it prescribe insulation from global cultural flows. It does suggest a fundamental and ongoing commitment to struggle for equality so that such interactions remain democratic.

In this we can see the solving of a suggestive riddle: why would an organization that is centrally concerned with *culturally sustainable development* be called the *Pluricultural Centre for Democracy*? The answer is that CSD is predicated on democracy in the deepest sense. Or, rather, that development *is* democracy. This democracy is not limited to the formal liberal architecture of municipal, national, and departmental elections with free press and active civil society which exerts pressure on decision-makers in government. This Maya form of democracy involves the devolution of decision-making power to local communities, as well as the valorization, continued transformation, and respect for diverse cultural institutions and schemes of understanding. It is a decentralized and *pluricultural* democracy—one in which human agency and human subjectivities are in constant flux, but also rooted meaningfully in the past. It is also a democracy whose maintenance requires constant struggle.

References

Barrios, L. (1988). *La Alcaldía Indígena en Guatemala*. Guatemala City: Instituto de Investigaciones Económicas y Sociales (IDIES): Universidad Rafael Landivar.

Bulux, C. R. G. (2003). *Organización y Desarrollo Culturalmente Sustentable: Refleciones a Partir de Ambito Municipal*. Quetzeltenango: El Centro Pluricultural para la Democracia.

Chávez Cayax, E. O. (2003). *La Participación Democratica para el Desarollo Culturalmente Sustentable*. Quetzeltenango: El Centro Pluricultural Para la Democracia.

El Centro Pluricultural para la Democracia (CPD). (2008). *Conflictos Comunales por el Derecho Humano al Agua*. Quetzeltenango: CPD.

El Centro Pluricultural para la Democracia (CPD). (2009). *Systemitización de las Experiencias de Consultas Comunitarias sobre El Tema de Minería, en Los Municipalidades de Sipacapa, San Marcos y Colotenango, Huehuetenango*. Quetzeltenango: CPD.

Habermas, J. (1984). *The Theory of Communicative Action, Vol. 1*. Thomas McCarthy (Trans.). Boston: Beacon Press.

Hill, R. (1989). Social Organization by Decree in Colonial Highland Guatemala. *Ethnohistory, 36*(2), 170–1998.

Ljunggren, D. (2010, May 14). Canadian Court Ruling Clarifies Mine Permit Process. *Reuters*.

Marroquín, A. (2009, November 16). Responsabilizan a Montana Exploradora Por daños en Casas. *Prensa Libre*.

Molesky-Poz, J. (2009). *Contemporary Maya Spirituality: The Ancient Ways are not Lost*. University of Texas Press.

On Common Ground Consultations Inc. (OCG). (2010). *Human Rights Assessment of Goldcorp's Marlin Mine*. Vancouver: OCG.

Prensa Libre. (2010, April 6). *Unas 80 Organizaciones Piden Suspender Actividad Minera en el País*.

Rao, V., & Walton, M. (2004). Culture and Public Action: Relationality, Equality of Agency, and Development. In V. Rao & W. Walton (Eds.), *Culture and Public Action* (pp. 3–36). Stanford: Stanford University Press.

Rostboll, C. F. (2008). *Deliberative Freedom*. Albany: State University of New York Press.

Wittman, H., & Geisler, C. (2005). Negotiating Locality: Decentralization and Communal Forrest Management in the Guatemalan Highlands. *Human Organization, 64*(1), 62–74.

Yagenova, S. V., & Garcia, R. (2009). Indigenous People's Struggles Against Transnational Mining Companies in Guatemala: The Sipakapa People vs Goldcorp Mining Company. *Socialism and Democracy, 23*(3), 157–166.

CHAPTER 8

Garifuna Sustainable Development

The last two chapters described a Maya idea of sustainable development that has been emerging from Guatemala's Western Highlands. This involved a detailed look at the cultural, discursive, historical, and material roots of the idea, as well as a description of the idea itself. This chapter uses the same method, but moves the focus southward into the contested Garifuna territories of coastal Honduras. Much of this chapter is based on ongoing fieldwork that I have undertaken since 2011. This work is beginning to show a complex and contested Garifuna sustainable development ideal that is emerging around the concept of food sovereignty. Just as with the study of Maya sustainable development, an indigenous political institution will be used as a locus around which to describe an indigenous idea of development. In this case, the story will revolve largely around ideas and activism associated with the Black Fraternal Organization of Honduras (OFRANEH). The story of Garifuna activism stands as another exemplar of the transmodern nature of indigenous development ideas that are merging in Latin America during a period typified by neoliberal multiculturalism.

The Historical Construction of Garifuna

The Garifuna case study allows, more than most, a clear example of the co-constructed nature of indigeneity and modernity. Processes of colonialism actively created the Garifuna subjectivity while Garifuna subjects

T. MacNeill, *Indigenous Cultures and Sustainable Development in Latin America*, https://doi.org/10.1007/978-3-030-37023-7_8

helped build the modern nation of Honduras while possibly adding force to the percolation of European enlightenment ideals such as national sovereignty, personal freedom, and human rights. Currently, Garifuna activism contributes to environmental, indigenous rights, and food sovereignty movements while being, at the same time, at least partially, created by them. There is no distinct pre-Columbian Garifuna culture, rooted in a deeply associated territory, to appeal to in this discussion. It was colonialism, and resistance to it, that produced the Garifuna.

In 1675, a ship carrying Mokko people, destined to be slaves, from present-day Nigeria, was wrecked near the Caribbean island of St. Vincent. The indigenous *Kalinaku* were known for resisting British and French attempts at colonialism. The widely known success of this resistance attracted escaped slaves from throughout the Caribbean, and within a few generations of intermarriage amidst an increasing Afro-heritage population, an emergent Garifuna culture began to take form—combining elements of African and *Kalinaku* culture. Perhaps due to the historical shock of the Mokko escape from slavery, and the famous resilience of the *Kalinaku*, the islanders were fiercely independent and resistant to colonialism. St. Vincent continued to be a beacon for anti-slavery movements as *Kalinaku* and Garifuna worked together to repel attempted invasions by both the French and English in the eighteenth century (Taylor 2012). Although the island was officially granted to Britain by the French in the Treaty of Paris of 1763, continued resistance of the local inhabitants delayed the British colonization of the island until 1796. St. Vincent was the last of the Caribbean islands to be subjugated by colonial rule (Taylor 2012; Anderson 2009).

When British colonial rule did arrive, it was brutal. Although the population of St. Vincent was intermixed by 1796, the colonial administration chose to abruptly and arbitrarily disrupt the solidaric community. The population was sorted along a binary of lighter and darker skin colour, and 5000 of the latter were deported. This tore both immediate and extended families apart, but also solidified the separate indigenous category of Garifuna. These darker coloured Mokko/*Kalinaku* (mixed with other Maroon Afro-descendants) were relocated by force to the smaller island of Roatan—just off the coast of present-day Honduras. Only half made it there alive. Those who survived the perilous forced migration, increasingly identified as Garifuna as they faced harsh conditions on Roatan, which had limited arable soil.

At this time, the Spanish were intent on maintaining their land holdings in Central America. After the injuries of Spanish colonialism all but depopulated the North Coast of Honduras, the Empire was in a tenuous situation—having to hold on to a large expanse of land without a settler population. Creating an unlikely alliance, the Garifuna petitioned the Spanish to allow them to occupy the mainland of Honduras. Since the Spanish were eager to fill the underpopulated territory with Spanish subjects, the majority of the country's North Coast was granted to the Garifuna (Taylor 2012). Although Garifuna life on the North Coast was disrupted from time to time by colonial trade, their de facto title to the North Coast of Honduras was relatively stable until the late twentieth century.

This colonial history created the Garifuna through the fusing of Mokko and *Kalinaku* DNA and culture. The injustice and injury of colonialism based on slavery, conquest, and forced relocation also forged Garifuna subjectivity. The Garifuna are at once an indigenous African people and an indigenous Caribbean people who have been dislocated to new territory in Northern Honduras, with which they have developed a deep felt relationship. As a result, Garifuna remain fiercely independent—often reiterating that they are the only Afro-descendent peoples in the Americas that have never been slaves. They consider themselves as indigenous, and are legally recognized as such. The Garifuna also have a deep cultural relationship with the land of the North Coast—to which many insist they still hold title.

These historically driven proclivities are obvious in interviews of Garifuna villagers who often assert their independence as never having been slaves, as inheritors of indigenous land title, and as having relative autonomy within the Honduran state. Many of these assertions find their official home in OFRANEH—the main Garifuna political organization in the country. Although OFRANEH is the largest, most active, and most radical Garifuna organization, it is not the only one. The Garifuna do not have a singular voice. OFRANEH is, however, the main conduit through which ideas of indigenous Garifuna sustainable development are articulated. It therefore holds a central role in this chapter.

Often speaking through OFRANEH, Garifuna activists strongly assert their indigenous culture. For them, this is an essential part of their cultural and political identity. This is vital for the movement, as there has been a move by the national government to deny the indigenous part of the identity by designating Garifuna as simply "Afro-decedent" in national statistics. This is a discursive move that threatens to bleed into popular culture, putting into question claims to indigenous status, along with land title. These important implications for land tenure and political rights are apparent in an OFRANEH (2013) memo:

> In the decade of the 30s, the Trujillo intellectual *Sixto Cacho* maintained that the Garifuna people were black skin but indigenous culture. To date we have managed to preserve a good part of the cultural heritage despite the homogenization promoted by the state, through the education system and the mass media … In recent decades, the cultural scam has been promoted to eradicate the Garífuna identification to replace it with the vague term of Afro-descendant, discarding the cultural patrimony of our ancestors by a simple identification of supposed race, denying this form the genetic hybridism of which we are carriers … The difference of visions between the Garífuna and those who call themselves 'Afro-descendants' is abysmal, the first ones seek territorial autonomy and defense of our communities, the second ones are satisfied with an insertion within a corrupt system and the power handouts of the satraps (foreign-controlled dictators).

This memo suggests that the cultural hybridity implicit to Garifuna identity is both a valued cultural trait and a political resource to many Garifuna. The identity encapsulates a felt history of independence and resistance that propels the political activism of a people who have never been slaves and still refuse to become so. This is combined with an understanding of cultural distinctiveness and indigenous cosmovision. This political identity is evident in the words of Mirian Miranda, OFRANEH's president:

> Things like spiritual recognition and cultural identity are important to our people. We think our cultural identity can also be a route to revolution … in a country where we have a uniform model of living, where there is definitely a tendency to believe everything white is better, that white is perfect. (Brigida 2017)

This Garifuna Afro-indigenous identity is entangled with territory as well. This assures that this indigenous resistance is not limited to the cultural sphere, but inhabits the material one as well.

A Threatened Land Base

In interviews, North Coast and Garifuna assert a strong historical right, and cultural connection, to the land. Stories of the survived attempt at enslavement, the expulsion from St. Vincent, and the granting of title on Honduras' North Coast are common. Alfredo Lopez, a Garifuna leader, articulates the relationship with land clearly:

> The Earth is our mother; the sea is our father. When this relationship is broken, we are no longer Garifuna peoples. We make our living from fishing and navigation. We don't use fertilizers because we don't want to offend the earth. What do we do? There is a model of working, its called *Barbecho.* We work five years in one area, then we let it ferment and fertilize, and then we occupy another space. This is why our property is collectively owned. Because we need this space, which relates to our functional habitat ... so the cultural and ancestral life we are accustomed to can continue. Rights are collective; there is no private property in our way of thinking. (Matamoros 2016)

As the following statement by OFRANEH's leader shows, the organization works actively to protect indigenous title while underlining the connection between the land of the North Coast and Garifuna culture:

> Without our lands, we cease to be a people. Our lands and identities are critical to our lives, our waters, our forests, our culture, our global commons, our territories. For us, the struggle for our territories and our commons and our natural resources is of primary importance to preserve ourselves as a people. (Miranda 2015)

Anthropological studies have noted this connection between land and identity while describing the indigenous Garifuna tenure system. Garifuna beachfront communities were traditionally built at a distance from agricultural and hunting lands, so that food sources were separated from living spaces. This left much Garifuna land to appear unsettled and unused in the perception of non-Garifuna. The *barbecho* rotating crop system that involved leaving farming plots fallow for numerous years contributes to this impression (Brondo 2010).

All Garifuna land was traditionally tenured collectively, creating vast territories that were governed internally via Garifuna communal councils and tribal leaders. According to Garifuna norms, no land is transferable without the approval of local councils. These internal governance and subsistence practices had the historical effect of distinguishing Garifuna territory from the dominant Mestizo society with its European-sourced national governance structure and private tenure traditions (Taylor 2012). This common title, cultural identity, and territorial distinction were reinforced through repetition and lived experience. The distinct Garifuna language, kinship structures, matrilineal inheritance patterns, subsistence farming, fishing and hunting practices, governance structures, dance, and other cultural practices all created a repeated lived experience rooted in the land (Euraque 2003).

Garifuna tenure was challenged, especially in the late twentieth century. This was often interpreted by Garifuna as a direct attack on the people and culture. Although the large territorial grant of the North Coast was essential in the establishment of the Spanish colony and later the state of Honduras, the state did not officially recognize Garifuna title or customary law. Nor were subsistence practices thought to be important when compared to production for international markets. As a result, the state granted large amounts of Garifuna territory to international banana companies in the early twentieth century. This injury was met with strong Garifuna opposition. Garifuna preferred to continue subsistence practices on limited land rather than to join the Mestizo-dominated labour force (Euraque 2003). As a result of Garifuna resistance, the *Instituto Nacional Agrario* (INA), which administered titling nationally, began to recognize the collective right of Garifuna to their remaining lands in the 1970s. This was officially only a permission for occupation of the land, not ownership. This legal ambiguity facilitated multiple and continued encroachments on Garifuna land by local elites and foreign investors (Brondo 2010).

As neoliberal development policy became hegemonic in the late twentieth century, the push for clear land-ownership institutions became stronger in both Honduras and in the rest of the world. With this, official titling on Garifuna lands began in 1990 (Brondo 2010). These policies privileged individual title as the primal component of market-led development. A UNHP project at that time mapped and demarcated Garifuna communal land—limiting it to those tracts that were most obviously settled and recently used. Due to the prevalence of *barbecho*, this restricted the Garifuna land base a great deal.

Official collective title meant that Garifuna land could not be sold without community agreement, but this title was applied to a very limited geography. It has been estimated that as much as 80 percent of Garifuna traditional land was lost by the end of this titling process (MacNeill 2017). In addition, Decree 90–90 was enacted in 1990 to develop the North Coast as a Caribbean tourism destination by allowing foreigners to own beachfront land. The privilege was formerly limited to Honduran nationals. This decree, therefore, brought a new threat to Garifuna territory—foreign capital aimed at tourist industry investment.

This history of land titling and dispossession has had a major impact on Garifuna indigenous development and political identity. Leaders, especially those associated with OFRANEH, describe a continual history of "land stealing" by "colonizers" who use their economic power to bend the Honduran state and judiciary to their advantage. For example, Garifuna protesters at a trial of Canadian investor Randy Jorgensen in November 2015, shouted, "no more sales of Garifuna land; no more theft of Garifuna land" (Rights Action 2015). The lawyer representing the Garifuna at the trial cited reaffirmations of Garifuna title in 1901, 1934, and 1995 by the Honduran government. Garifuna activists claim that dispossession is the result of a failed state and judiciary that have been corrupted by wealthy elites and foreign capital, despite official protection by law. "We could say the rule of law in Honduras is corruption," said Garifuna protestor Carmen Alvarez, "All the way from the Supreme Court to the local court here in Trujillo, and everything in between, is corrupted ... but we Garifuna are not going to give up" (Rights Action 2015). OFRANEH continues to hold the ultimate return of all traditional lands as an explicit goal (OFRANEH 2019).

Oligarchy, repression, and dictatorship were the prominent forms of government in Honduras historically. By 2008, however, the Honduran resistance movement, including OFRANEH and other Garifuna groups, had become powerful enough to influence national politics (Shipley 2013). This inspired the then president Manuel Zelaya to pursue numerous progressive policies. Honduras joined socialist and social democratic national governments in the *Bolivarian Alliance for the Peoples of Our America* (ALBA). The minimum wage was raised by 60 percent. Numerous pro-poor policies were undertaken. A moratorium was placed on the granting of mining concessions until environmental impact assessments were completed. The lands of poor *campesinos* were increasingly protected, and some was redistributed (Gordon 2010). The Garifuna were not explicitly mentioned in land reform initiatives, but drew hope from these conciliatory politics (Brondo 2013).

These reforms threatened the interests of national elites as well as Canadian and American investors who were heavily involved in the mining, agricultural, tourism, and manufacturing sectors. These elements conspired and successfully removed Zelaya via military coup in 2009. Successive oligarchic post-coup governments reversed the changes of the Zelaya administration. This inspired poverty rates to increase from 58 percent before the coup, to 68 percent in 2016, and then to drop slightly to 66 percent. Unemployment rates moved from 3 percent to 7.3 percent in that same period, dropping to 6.5 percent in 2018 (INE 2019). Social spending was also dramatically curtailed, the minimum wage was reduced to pre-Zelaya levels, and the proportion of people employed below that wage increased from 28.8 to 43.6 percent (Johnson and Lefebre 2013).

Sustained political crisis and repression have permeated post-coup Honduras. This has famously inspired large numbers of Honduras to flee their country towards the United States. Politics on all levels have traditionally been controlled by an oligarchic group of ten powerful families. This control was solidified with the coup. Additionally, national policy has regularly been influenced by foreign governments and business interests (MacNeill 2017). This too intensified after the coup. Oligarchic and foreign capital control was extended via the assassination, torture, and repression of large numbers of oppositional politicians and activists, including members of the Garifuna community. For example, North Coast Garifuna residents have accused Canadian investor Randy Jorgenson of having Garifuna land rights activist Vidal Leiva shot three times in 2015 (Cuffe 2015). More recently, the resistance movement's de facto leader, Berta Caceres, was assassinated in 2016, followed by two other high-profile members, Lesbia Janeth Urquía and Nelson García (Lyengar 2016; Agren 2016).

Violence and corruption have become an understood inevitability in the country. Post-coup Honduras became the most violent in the world outside a war zone. Political and legal systems are so extensively compromised that the national government is instituting a plan to carve out multiple localities from the official Honduran judicial and political system in order to offer stability in some areas to international investors (Government of Honduras 2017). Most Hondurans consider their government to be highly corrupt, while it ranks as one of the worst in the world when regarding the abuse of public power for private gain. Transparency of government finances is characterized with the lowest distinction of *scant or none* and the country rates extremely low on *Press Freedom* and *Voice and Accountability* (Transparency International 2017).

Garifuna land tenure has been a notable flashpoint in the post-coup climate. Much Garifuna activism has been occurring in the Trujillo area, and complaints are largely aimed at the Canadian investor Randy Jorgensen, and his companies *Life Vision* and *Banana Coast*. Complicating this local confrontation, there are established links between this investment consortium and the post-coup government. OFRANEH and local Garifuna claim that these links have facilitated foreign acquisition of Garifuna lands (MacNeill 2017). Specifically, OFRANEH has accused Canadian investors of illegally usurping lands belonging to the villages of *Cristales* and *Guadalupe*. Furthermore, Garifuna activists charge that the entire population of *Rio Negro* was illegally evicted to allow for the construction of *Life Vision*'s Banana Coast cruise ship port.

Construction of the port began in 2011, and it was completed in 2014. Former residents are difficult to find locally. According to local accounts, many have scattered to other parts of Honduras or have fled the country. To OFRANEH, who insist that "the majority of these transactions were carried out under pressure," the usurpation of *Rio Negro* is a "fraud carried out against the inhabitants" of the town (OFRANEH 2011). The writ of *eminent domain*, used by Jorgensen in the eviction, was obtained through bribery and corruption according to OFRANEH. Jorgensen, and the Canadian investors, insist that the town had been "a waterfront eyesore and a habitat for disease." They also insist that the town had been legally removed to make way for "a project that would create community wide benefits" (Jorgensen 2014).

Jorgensen's nearby *Campa Vista* housing project is subject to similar accusations of land grabbing. In this case, it is traditional Garifuna hunting and farming territory just south of the community of *Cristales* that is in dispute. Both ILO 169 and the Honduran constitution require Garifuna community consensus prior to the sale of pertinent land. Jorgensen claims that a consultation was held in which the community allegedly agreed to sell 20 hectares to a third-party business associate of Jorgensen (Jorgensen 2014). This associate paid the community president of the time, Omar Laredo, $5000 US dollars for the land. Community members allege that they never received this money. Laredo immediately left town and has not returned. Jorgensen then purchased the land for $20,000 from his associate and actually fenced-off 62 hectares of land. Over the next few years, he sold the lands, parcel by parcel, to Canadians as vacation home lots, for a total of approximately $8.5 million.

There are other land disputes between Jorgensen and Garifuna communities in two other barrios in the Trujillo area. There are also disputes involving other Canadian land investors (Aqui Abajo 2017). Jorgensen is adamant that the land in each case was legally obtained, and that it was not being productively used by the Garifuna anyway. He also rejects the authenticity of Garifuna land rights saying, "they are foreigners; they are immigrants to Honduras" (Hadden 2016). Local Garifuna and OFRANEH insist that they have the same rights of any indigenous group in Honduras, that the lands were essential to their subsistence food practices, and that they were illegally sold (Cuffe 2015).

Accusations of police intimidation and state corruption and violence are also related to these land disputes. One Garifuna, a self-proclaimed "land defender," claims she was arrested and tortured by Honduran police and military for opposing a Canadian tourism project (Aqui Abajo 2017). Others claim to have been shot and/or intimidated by Jorgensen's "hitman" (Rights Action 2015). The barrios of Cristales and Rio Negro have attempted to bring criminal charges against Jorgensen for illegal possession of Garifuna lands, but these charges were granted a five-year stay in a Trujillo court (Rights Action 2015). Truth and legality are difficult to discern in these murky events. However, it is clear that many local Garifuna assume as a quotidian fact that the police, local government, and Honduran state are corrupt and operating in the interest of foreign investors and local elites. This implies that any indigenous Garifuna development project will need to be undertaken via strong mobilizations towards Garifuna territorial autonomy and self-direction.

Food Sovereignty, Environmentalism, and Indigeneity

The 1990s saw the erosion of Garifuna territorial rights due to neoliberal reforms and the encroachment of foreign tourism interests. Perhaps precipitated by the Zapatista movement in Mexico and the now global Via Campesina movement, a global indigenous rights movement emerged in this period as well. Garifuna thought on indigenous sustainable development both informs and is animated by this movement. The Honduran ratification of the International Labour Organization's Convention 169 Concerning Indigenous and Tribal Peoples, in 1995, granted the Garifuna official indigenous status (ILO 2017). Importantly, it contains protections for language and culture while asserting indigenous control over economic development and territorial administration. These territorial rights were not limited to regularly used human settlements, as any lands used in traditional subsistence practices are also protected (ILO 1989).

In 2007, these commitments were reaffirmed via Honduras' adoption of United Nations Declaration of the Rights of Indigenous Peoples. These conventions require that development projects be designed "with respect to peoples' right to healthy food, to water, to forests for foraging …, and ability to continue traditional small-scale agricultural customs" (ILO 1989, p. 183). The Garifuna, especially through OFRANEH, fought hard to pressure the Honduran state to become a signatory to these international indigenous rights conventions. Their adoption is an essential part of Garifuna sustainable development, and the discourse contained in the conventions has become essential to Garifuna ideas of indigenous development.

Adding to the discursive power of indigenous rights instruments, UNESCO took an unprecedented step in 2001 when it recognized Garifuna culture as the first "masterpiece of oral and intangible cultural heritage." The UNESCO proclamation explicitly noted the cultural centrality of land and subsistence practices (UNESCO 2001). These conventions and international recognitions are key to Garifuna sustainable development initiatives. True indigenous development, Garifuna leaders claim, is not possible without the land protections integral to ILO 169 (Rights Action 2015). It is clear that OFRANEH considers such conventions to be protections from the imposition of culturally and environmentally destructive development projects. A 2012 memo clearly articulates this:

> The Right to Consultation in Honduras, and we can say in the rest of the continent, has become a defense mechanism for indigenous people in the face of the advance of 'development' based on the ideology of the accumulation and the destruction of the environment and the planet. (OFRANEH 2012)

Local Garifuna that I interviewed in the Trujillo area were all aware that their culture had been designated a "masterpiece of cultural heritage." One local, for example, asserted that, "there is no culture like the Garifuna. We have our *punta* [dance and music], *serre* and *hudut* [foods]. We are original in the world." OFRANEH makes these claims explicit by citing the UNESCO designation repeatedly on their website (OFRANEH

2019). This distinction gives force to the idea that development organized from within Garifuna culture would be substantially different from development imposed from without.

Given the cultural significance attached to *Barbecho* and the determined resistance to territorial loss exhibited by Garifuna activists, the concept of food sovereignty has become central to Garifuna sustainable development. In October 2015, OFRANEH was awarded the 7th annual Food Sovereignty Prize from the U.S. Food Sovereignty Alliance. The prize purposefully emphasizes grassroots culturally appropriate organization of local food systems in juxtaposition to the homogenizing, environmentally destructive, and disenfranchising practices of the neoliberal world food system.

OFRANEH insists that locally controlled subsistence practices have been severely threatened by modern development. In some areas, such as the marine coastal reserve at Cayos Cochinos, subsistence practices are relatively strong. In others, they are greatly diminished. In Chachahuate—the main Garifuna settlement on Cayos Cochinos—47 percent of those I surveyed in 2016 practised subsistence farming or fishing. Some traditional fishing rights have been protected, although the loss of land and subsistence there has been severe (Brondo 2013). In contrast, only 17 percent claimed to engage in these traditional food production practices in Garifuna settlements in the Trujillo area. No traditional fishing remains in the Trujillo bay, and much farmland has been lost.

As this note from OFRANEH's director Miriam Miranda suggests, autonomous food production based on traditional practice is key to Garifuna sustainable development:

> Our liberation starts because we can plant what we eat. This is food sovereignty. We need to produce to bring autonomy and the sovereignty of our peoples. If we continue to consume [only], it doesn't matter how much we shout and protest. We need to become producers ... It's also about recovering and reaffirming our connections to the soil, to our communities, to our land. (USFSA 2015)

She continues:

> Without our lands, we cease to be a people. Our lands and identities are critical to our lives, our waters, our forests, our culture, our global commons, our territories. For us, the struggle for our territories and our

> commons and our natural resources is of primary importance to preserve ourselves as a people ... There's more pressure on us every day for our territories, our resources, and our global commons ... [T]hey're taking land that we were using to grow beans and rice so they can grow African palm for bio-fuel. The intention is to stop the production of food that humans need so they can produce fuel that cars need. The more food scarcity that exists, the more expensive food will become. Food sovereignty is being threatened everywhere. (USFSA 2015)

The idea of food sovereignty was cited as a goal by Garifuna leaders in the Trujillo area during interviews I conducted in 2014. For example, speaking of actions being taken by local Garifuna to reclaim traditional lands, one leader stated "this land contains our cultural heritage, without our lands we cannot have food sovereignty, we cannot be self-sufficient, we lose our traditions." The village of Vallacito, east of Trujillo, is actively attempting a Garifuna sustainable development programme, which has food sovereignty as its centrepiece. The village is under regular attack from drug cartels, palm-oil plantation owners, and charter cities—a government-directed plan to usurp local land and form islands of modern development. Even in this volatile locale, communal kitchens, organic gardens, and a coconut plantation have been established with plans to grow medicinal plants, rice, and beans in adjacent areas according to the practice of *barbecho*. The idea, according to Garifuna leaders associated with OFRANEH, is sustainable development based on self-sufficiency (Clark 2018).

Food sovereignty is central to Garifuna activism and ideas of development. The national resistance movement, of which OFRANEH is an important member, has been built around an existing national civil society network that centralized and even incubated the concept of food sovereignty. Boyer (2010), for example, has shown that the Honduran resistance movement has played a vital role in the creation and popularization of La Via Campesina—the global movement that is most commonly associated with food sovereignty. From 1996 to 2004, La Via Campesina maintained its international headquarters in Honduras in the offices of CONOCH (The Honduran Coordinating Council of Peasant Organizations). CONOCH included Garifuna activists and was attached to the civic Council of Popular Indigenous Organizations of Honduras (COPINH). COPINH, which includes Garifuna groups such as OFRANEH, emerged from Honduran indigenous coalitions of the 1970s and has centralized the idea of food sovereignty since the 1990s (Frank 2010; Boyer 2010).

In May 2016, La Via Campesina reaffirmed their connection with Garifuna in particular when they issued a statement of solidarity with the "Afro-Indigenous" Hondurans. The statement affirmed that La Via Campesina was "extremely troubled by repeated violations of … human rights" against the Garifuna. They continue to denounce "violations of the human right to life as well as of the right to food sovereignty" in Garifuna Honduras (La Via Campesina 2016).

As with most indigenous groups, environmentalism is deeply connected to Garifuna politics of indigeneity and food sovereignty. One of the major concerns made by Garifuna representatives about land titling projects reflects this. A 2006 report from the World Bank's Honduras Land Titling Project documents Garifuna dissatisfaction with land titling. The report shows how Garifuna considered World Bank designed title, instituted under the guise of an indigenous development project, a limitation of their "functional habitat" as opposed to a protection of title. The Garifuna complaint was partially connected with environmental concerns—asserting that Garifuna had preserved the land of the North Coast for centuries, and the titling project would leave the territory open to environmental degradation. Garifuna livelihoods and culture, according to the complaint, are connected intimately to the natural environment. Therefore, Garifuna patrimony equates to environmental protection (World Bank 2006).

Being one of the largest indigenous groups in Honduras, the Garifuna are appropriately active in the Council of Indigenous Peoples of Honduras (COPINH). COPINH is central to the Honduran environmental movement, considering itself and members to be "environmental defenders." In the current political climate of the country, such environmental activism is incredibly dangerous. Consequently, numerous COPINH members have been assassinated, tortured, jailed, and surveilled. COPINH is not alone in its struggle for territorial and environmental defense, however. The groups are connected to a network of organizations that are integral to the global environmental movement.

Global witness is an organization that exists to "protect human rights and the environment by fearlessly confronting corruption and challenging the systems that enable it" (Global Witness 2019). In a 2017 report, the organization pronounced Honduras to be "the deadliest country in the world for environmental activism," claiming that 120 environmentalist had been assassinated since 2010 (Global Witness 2017). OFRANEH

(2019) and its leaders reiterate this distinction regularly, purposefully positioning themselves on the frontline of the global fight for indigenous and environmental defense. In addition to the Food Sovereignty Prize, the organization has recently won the Nota Sol Award for defending human rights and promoting sustainable development, and the Carlos Escaleres Environmental Award after OFRANEH launched its "Defense without Fear" environmental and territorial protection campaign. Following this, a diversity of large global environmental organizations have used Garifuna as an exemplar of strong environmental activism and indigenous stewardship. Some of the more notable of these organizations are the Sierra Club (Gibler 2017), the Rainforest Action Network (2016), Friends of the Earth (2017), and the World Watch Institute (2019).

This positioning of Garifuna culture and land tenure as positively related to ecological protection is not fanciful. Multiple studies have found evidence that indigenous farmers tend to maintain more ecologically diverse farms than do their non-indigenous counterparts (Brush & Perales 2007; Perreault 2005). This has been found to be true with Garifuna communities in particular (Williams 2016). This does not necessarily mean that Garifuna culture is essentially pro-ecological diversity, however. It would be more accurate to say that Garifuna identity is a node upon which global food sovereignty, indigenous rights, environmental movements, a felt history, and marginalizing political economy exert significant interpolating pressure. These pressures form and are formed by Garifuna subjectivities in a way that substantiates—in fact—that Garifuna-controlled agriculture tends to promote ecological diversity.

Conclusion

Garifuna is a people and subjectivity forged in both colonialism and resistance to it. Their resistance on the island of St. Vincent, along with slave revolts in other locales, is likely to have had a larger impact on the British anti-slavery movement and discursive force of enlightenment ideals than Eurocentric histories will admit. Their very existence helped to secure the land required to forge the modern state of Honduras. There heritage is simultaneously indigenous and modern in a more obvious way than is the case with any other group.

Territorial claims based on international rights agreements such as ILO 169 are commonly used in Garifuna politics. Furthermore, the Garifuna also hold on to an idea of development—one rooted in food sovereignty and political autonomy within modern Honduras. Garifuna culture has clearly been forged via colonialism, and this colonialism continues in the form of land grabs. Thus, Garifuna politics constitutes, and is constituted, in relation to "modern" ideals such as freedom, rights, and progress as they mix within global indigenous, environmental, and food sovereignty movements.

Garifuna sustainable development requires cultural, economic, and political autonomy. This stems as much from their independent history as much as the coercive weight of the current Honduran and international political economy. Garifuna, like most people, strive for a better life—some form of development. But development controlled by national elites and foreign investors has only depleted their land base without yielding local benefits (MacNeill and Wozniak 2018). They feel that a distinct Garifuna form of development will naturally embody environmental protections because of their cultural relation to nature.

Connecting to, and caring for, the land of the Honduran North Coast is integral to this idea of development. Similar to Maya ideas of sustainable development, the Garifuna have had little opportunity to enact their own version of culturally embedded progress. The idea involves food sovereignty, but this programme is embroiled in a politics of land protection as a prerequisite to the flourishing of local indigenous ideas and policies. This land protection, as with the Maya, is the first order of business in the quest for a culturally embedded sustainable development. Only then, when what Garifuna activists call their "functional habitat" is protected, can a sustainable development based on collective title, food sovereignty, and the revival of *Barbecho* be established.

References

Agren, D. (2016, July 7). Honduras Confirms the Murder of Another Member of Berta Caceres' Activist Group. *The Guardian*. Retrieved from https://www.theguardian.com/world/2016/jul/07/honduras-murder-lesbia-janeth-urquia-berta-caceres.

Anderson, M. (2009). *Black and Indigenous: Garifuna Activism and Consumer Culture in Honduras*. Minneapolis: University of Minnesota Press.

Aqui Abajo. (2017, February). *One Land Defender's Story of Repression, Criminalization and Arrest: Young Garifuna Woman Arrested for Reclaiming Ancestral Land*. Retrieved from Aqui Abajo http://www.aquiabajo.com/blog/2017/2/8/one-land-defenders-story-of-repression-criminalization-and-arrest-young-garifuna-woman-arrested-for-reclaiming-ancestral-land.

Boyer, J. (2010). Food Security, Food Sovereignty, and Local Challenges for Transnational Agrarian Movements: The Honduras Case. *Journal of Peasant Studies, 37*(2), 319–351.

Brigida, A. C. (2017, February 23). *Garifuna Flee Discrimination and Land Grabs in Record Numbers.* Retrieved from Telesur http://www.telesurtv.net/english/news/Garifuna-Flee-Discrimination-and-Land-Grabs-in-Record-Numbers-20170223-0002.html.

Brondo, K. (2010). When Mestizo Become (Like) Indio ... or Is It Garifuna? Negotiating Indigeneity and Making Place on Honduras' North Coast. *Journal of Latin American and Caribbean Anthropology, 15*(1), 171–194.

Brondo, K. V. (2013). *Land Grab: Green Neoliberalism, Gender, and Garifuna Resistance in Honduras.* University of Arizona Press.

Brush, S. B., & Perales, H. R. (2007). A Maize Landscape: Ethnicity and Agro-biodiversity in Chiapas Mexico. *Agriculture, Ecosystems and Environment, 121*(3), 211–221.

Clark, C. (2018, August 28). Honduran Minority Fights for a Threatened Way of Life. *Reuters.* Retrieved from https://www.reuters.com/article/us-honduras-landrights-garifuna/honduran-minority-fights-for-a-threatened-way-of-life-idUSKCN1LD168.

Cuffe, S. (2015, December 12). The Struggle Continues: Garifuna Land Defender Shot in Honduras. *Truthout.* Retrieved from http://www.truth-out.org/news/item/33976-the-struggle-continues-garifuna-land-defender-shot-in-honduras.

Euraque, D. (2003). The Threat of Blackness to the Nation: Race and Ethnicity in the Banana Economy. In S. Stiffler & M. Moberg (Eds.), *Banana Wars* (pp. 229–252). Durham: Duke University Press.

Frank, D. (2010, May). *Out of the Past, a New Honduran Culture of Resistance.* NACLA Report on the Americas. Retrieved from https://nacla.org/news/out-past-new-honduran-culture-resistance.

Friends of the Earth. (2017, June 28). *In Solidarity with OFRANEH and Social Activists in Honduras.* Retrieved from https://www.foei.org/features/solidarity-ofraneh-social-activists-honduras.

Gibler, J. (2017, February 2). *Honduras: The Deadliest Place on Earth to Defend the Planet.* Sierra Club. Retrieved from https://www.sierraclub.org/sierra/green-life/honduras-deadliest-place-earth-defend-planet.

Global Witness. (2017). *Honduras: The Deadliest Country in the World for Environmental Activism.* Global Witness. Retrieved from https://www.globalwitness.org/en/campaigns/environmental-activists/honduras-deadliest-country-world-environmental-activism/.

Global Witness. (2019, July 11). Retrieved from https://www.globalwitness.org/en/.

Gordon, T. (2010). *Imperialist Canada.* Arbeiter Ring Pub.

Government of Honduras. (2017). *Zonas de Employo y Desarollo Economico.* Retrieved from Zonas de Employo y Desarollo Economico http://zede.gob.hn/.

Hadden, G. (Director). (2016). *Lands to Die For* [Motion Picture]. Retrieved from https://america.cgtn.com/2016/12/20/lands-to-die-for-the-garifuna-struggle-in-honduras.

ILO. (1989). *ILO 169—Indigenous and Tribal Peoples Convention.* International Labour Organization. Retrieved August 16, 2017, from http://www.ilo.org/dyn/normlex/en/f?p=NORMLEXPUB:12100:0::NO::P12100_ILO_CODE:C169.

ILO. (2017, August 16). *Ratifications for Honduras.* Retrieved from International Labour Organization http://www.ilo.org/dyn/normlex/en/f?p=1000:11200:0::NO:11200:P11200_COUNTRY_ID:102675.

Instituto Nacional Estadistica (INE). (2019). *Estadisticas Nacional.* Government of Honduras. Retrieved from www.ine.gob.hn.

Johnson, J., & Lefebre, S. (2013). *Honduras Since the Coup: Economic and Social Outcomes.* Washington, DC: Center for Economic and Policy Research.

Jorgensen, R. (2014, January 3). Personal Communication with the Author (T. MacNeill, Interviewer).

La Via Campesina. (2016, May 18). Honduras: Statement from the CLOC-La Via Campesina Central America in Reaction to the Increasing Criminalisation of the Peasant Movement. *La Via Campesina.* Retrieved from https://viacampesina.org/en/honduras-statement-from-the-cloc-la-via-campesina-central-america-in-reaction-to-the-increasing-criminalisation-of-the-peasant-movement/.

Lyengar, R. (2016, March 16). Two Weeks After the Murder of Berta Caceres, Another Activist Killed in Honduras. *Time.* Retrieved from http://time.com/4262328/honduras-activist-nelson-garcia-berta-caceres-shot-dead/.

MacNeill, T. (2017). Development as Imperialism: Power and the Perpetuation of Poverting in Afro-Indigenous Central America. *Humanity & Society, 41*(2), 1–31.

MacNeill, T., & Wozniak, D. (2018). The Economic, Social, and Environmental Impacts of Cruise Tourism. *Tourism Management, 66*, 387–404.

Matamoros, B. (Director). (2016). *OFRANEH* [Motion Picture].

Miranda, M. (2015, October 7). *Defending Afro-Indigenous Land: Black Fraternal Organization of Honduras Wins Food Sovereignty Prize.* Retrieved from Upside Down World http://upsidedownworld.org/archives/honduras/defending-afro-indigenous-land-black-fraternal-organization-of-honduras-wins-food-sovereignty-prize/.

OFRANEH. (2011). *Garifuna Communities of Trujillo Take Legal Action against Canadian Porn King.* Retrieved from Oragnizacion Fraternal Negra Hondureño http://friendshipamericas.org/ofraneh-garifuna-communities-trujillo-take-legal-action-against-canadian-porn-king.

OFRANEH. (2012, March). *Honduras: El Banco Mundial, REDD y el Derecho a la consulta de los pueblos indígenas.* Retrieved from OFRANEH https://

ofraneh.wordpress.com/2012/03/13/honduras-el-banco-mundial-redd-y-el-derecho-a-la-consulta-de-los-pueblos-indigenas/.

OFRANEH. (2013, September 16). *Afrodescendientes o Garifunas?* Retrieved from OFRANEH https://ofraneh.wordpress.com/2013/09/18/afrodescendientes-o-garifunas-raza-o-cultura/.

OFRANEH. (2019). *Organizacion Fraternal Negra Hondureño.* Retrieved from http://www.ofraneh.org/ofraneh/index.html.

Perreault, T. (2005). Why Chacras (Swidden Gardens) Persist: Agrobiodiversity, Food Security, and Cultural Identity in the Ecuadorian Amazon. *Human Organization, 64*(4), 327–339.

Rainforest Action Network. (2016, March 10). An Open Letter to Secretary of State John Kerry. Retrieved from https://www.ran.org/the-understory/an_open_letter_to_secretary_of_state_john_kerry/.

Rights Action. (2015). *Canadian Porn King on Trial for Tourism Projects in Honduras.* Retrieved from https://www.youtube.com/watch?v=wWqoB5GTfm8.

Shipley, T. (2013). The New Canadian Imperialism and the Military Coup in Honduras. *Latin American Perspectives, 192*, 44–61.

Taylor, C. (2012). *The Black Carib Wars: Freedom, Survival, and the Making of the Garifuna.* Jackson: University Press of Mississippi.

Transparency International. (2017). *Corruption by Territory: Honduras.* Retrieved from Transparency International www.transparency.org/country#HND.

UNESCO. (2001). *First Proclamation of Masterpieces of Oral and Intagible Heritage of Humanity.* Retrieved from UNESCO http://unesdoc.unesco.org/images/0012/001242/124206eo.pdf.

USFSA. (2015). *Food Sovereignty Prize.* Retrieved from US Food Sovereignty Alliance http://foodsovereigntyprize.org/portfolio/international-winner/.

Williams, N. E. (2016). The Political Ecology of 'Ethnic' Agricultural Biodiversity Maintenance in Atlantic Nicaragua. *Journal of Political Ecology, 23*(1), 223–245.

World Bank. (2006). *Inspection Report No. 35470: Honduras Land Administration Project.* Washington: World Bank. Retrieved from http://documents.worldbank.org/curated/en/510281468034825301/pdf/35470.pdf.

World Watch Institute. (2019, July 11). Finding Sustainable Alternatives to Large Hydropower in Central America. Retrieved from http://www.worldwatch.org/finding-sustainable-alternatives-large-hydropower-central-america-0.

CHAPTER 9

Andean Indigenous Sustainable Development

Indigenous development has been institutionalized in the Andean region more than in any other region in the world (with the possible exception of Bhutan). This is most apparent when we consider the constitutions of Ecuador and Bolivia, in which multiple indigenous concepts of governance and citizenship have been enshrined (Schilling-Vacaflor 2010; Hidalgo-Capitán et al. 2019). Debates over the particularities of these national constitutions notwithstanding, these Andean countries provide an essential case study of indigenous sustainable development. Taken together, the 40 million-plus indigenous citizens of Bolivia and Ecuador represent 20 percent of the entire indigenous population of Latin America (Yashar 1999). This manifests an indigenous majority in Bolivia and large minority in Ecuador. Given the relative size of the indigenous populations in these countries, along with other historical, economic, and political particularities, it should not be surprising that indigeneity has had such force in the region. This chapter will examine the case of Ecuador specifically, as it provides a prescient example of the entanglements (Radcliffe et al. 2002) involved in the mainstreaming indigenous sustainable development.

Indigeneity and Nation-Building in Ecuador

Struggles of indigenous groups within the country have often dovetailed with efforts of international agencies towards ethnodevelopment, helping to produce a uniquely indigenized politics in Ecuador. Classification is an

T. MacNeill, *Indigenous Cultures and Sustainable Development in Latin America*, https://doi.org/10.1007/978-3-030-37023-7_9

issue with defining indigeneity in the country, but it has been estimated that the indigenous population is somewhere between 7% and 40% of the total population. This indigenous population is significantly poorer than the *Mestizo* majority (Radcliffe et al. 2002; Masala and Monni 2017). Since the mid-twentieth century, numerous indigenous groups of the country have organized politically. Initially, this organization was focused on local associations, then more regional affiliations, and, since the mid-1980s, national confederations were formed. As a result of this work, Ecuador has developed one of the strongest national indigenous rights movements in the world (Yashar 1996; Escobar and Alvarez 1992).

Not surprisingly, the most intense indigenous organizing began following externally imposed neoliberal restructuring in the 1980s. Extreme wage repression during the neoliberal period aggravated social conditions to the point that nearly 80% of the population lived in poverty by 1990 (Masala and Monni 2017). These issues were compounded by a fall in the price for oil—the country's main export—and a related crisis of inflation. These crises exacerbated the conditions of the country's poor, by pushing the unemployment rate to 30%, and reducing real incomes drastically (SIISE 2015). The government dollarized the economy in 2000 in an attempt to address the inflation problem. This further increased poverty and inequality, stimulating a high volume of emigration to Canada and the United States (Acosta 2006). Ecuador's colonial history had assured that indigenous people were especially marginalized; therefore, despite a lack of ethnically disaggregated statistics before 2000, we can expect that these crises impacted that group disproportionately. Social exclusion if indigenous peoples due to their geographical distance from power structures, poverty, and continued racism further diminished their status (Masala and Monni 2017).

As was the case throughout the globe, the neoliberal, and later post-neoliberal, periods saw the rise of NGOs and other elements of civil society as the state was retracted. A global indigenous movement became especially forceful in 1992, with the 500-year anniversary of colonialism and the Nobel Prize of Rigoberta Menchu. Ecuadorian indigenous groups both took inspiration, and were integral to, this movement (Radcliffe et al. 2002). Largely in response to pressure from the transnationally linked national indigenous rights movement, Ecuador ratified ILO 169 in May 1998. This changed customary law significantly in the country and also related to a shift in cultural and political power for indigenous people—many of whom were appointed to important development boards or elected to congress (Radcliffe et al. 2002). This indigenous movement was integral to the broader-based Ecuadorian *Revolución Ciudadana*, which began to mobilize around values such as solidarity, equality, and dignity for indigenous peoples (Masala and Monni 2017).

Beginning around 2000, the postneoliberal period saw the injections of the concept of indigenous social capital into economic development theory. Due to perceived inadequacies in neoliberal marker fundamentalism, the idea that social capital could be harnessed as a corrective to market failures became widespread (Fine 2002). To those in the guiding global development institutions, indigenous culture became a marker for social capital. A World Bank working paper, for example, claims that

> indigenous peoples in Ecuador suffer from economic deprivation but are well-endowed with social capital (for example, organization, solidarity patterns, and shared social and cultural values). (van Nieuwkoop and Uquillas 2000)

What has become known as ethnodevelopment encapsulates these ideas. Ancestral knowledge, reciprocity, non-market exchange, collective identity, a capacity to mobilize labour, and close attachment to ancestral lands have now all become key resources for ameliorating market failures according to development economists (Radcliffe et al. 2002). This, according to postneoliberal development economics, contributes to economic growth while lessening the probability of negative environmental consequences. As one World Bank report phrases it, "strengthening cultural identity and promoting sustainable socioeconomic development are mutually reinforcing" (Deruyttere 1997).

As a result of the mainstreaming of social capital and ethnodevelopment, funding and political support for indigenous groups intensified globally (Radcliffe et al. 2002). Ecuadorian indigenous institutions benefitted significantly from this. The World Bank, for example, created a $50 million *Indigenous and Afro-Ecuadorian Peoples' Development Project* that was active from 1998 to 2003. The project specifically sought to facilitate land access and funding for indigenous communities and other groups. Its four goals included strengthening indigenous organizations, securing land and title for indigenous communities, providing investment in community infrastructure and micro-enterprise, and strengthening the National Council of Indigenous and Afro-Ecuadorian Development (World Bank 2019). Similarly, since 1996, multiple mainstream international agencies have funded the Fund for the Development of Indigenous Peoples in Latin America and the Caribbean (Fondo Indigena), from which Ecuadorian groups continually benefit (Fondo Indigena 2019). Fondo Indigena supports capacity building in indigenous civil society organizations as well as investing in community-level projects, cultural revitalization, and indigenous education.

Such programmes have increased the interpolating power of the national indigenous movement and of the *Revolución Ciudadana*. The result was an increased incorporation of the indigenous movement's four main goals into national politics in Ecuador. According to Radcliffe et al. (2002), these goals are "*to strengthen their own cultures, to construct a plurinational state, to gain self-determination as a people with right to land and collective rights; and self-management of their own development*" (p. 5).

Although indigenous movements in Ecuador have gained funding and legitimacy via postneoliberal development policy, it is important to note that the goals of movements such as *Revolución Ciudadana* align only partially with those of development economists and funding agencies. As Radcliffe et al. (2002) put it, "[u]nder social capital models culture is an asset, while for indigenous movements, culture represents a successful politics of anticolonialism" (p. 11). As social capital, indigenous culture is supposed to make markets work better, but new economic models of development have little theoretical space for the radical, communitarian, and often anti-capitalist politics of indigenous movements. Just as with examples from Guatemala and Honduras, this theoretical and practical misalignment provides opportunities for indigenous peoples at the same time as it introduces tensions. These tensions occur as the economic development imperatives of states and multilateral institutions misalign with alternatives to development often advocated by indigenous groups. These tensions become obvious when we consider the politics around the Andean indigenous concept of *Sumak Kawsay* and an associated plan for resource non-extraction in the *Yasuní* region.

Sumak Kawsay and the Ecuadorian Constitution

The Andean indigenous concept of *Sumak Kawsay* has received a good deal of attention recently as it is likely the most systematized, institutionalized, and clearly delineated proposal for an alternative to development that has emerged from Latin America. While the Maya of Guatemala and Garifuna in Honduras can only hope to attain the physical, discursive, and political resources required to systematize indigenous development, Ecuadorians have gone some distance in realizing a true alternative to modernization. This should not be taken to imply that *Sumak Kawsay*, and related policy and politics, has achieved a pure vision that has been systematically implemented. The concept and its use by indigenous communities and the state are embattled and multiply interpreted. Thus, studying the incongruencies associated with *Sumak Kawsay* allows us to understand better the pitfalls and possibilities involved in establishing and institutionalizing indigenous alternatives to development.

Although the concept of *Sumak Kawsay* is deeply rooted in indigenous cosmology, the concept has emerged only recently as welfare or development paradigm. Hidalgo-Capitán et al. (2019) explain that this formalization began with the *Amazanga Plan*, initiated by the *Pastaza Indigenous Peoples' Organization* of Ecuador in the early 1990s. The plan documented, for the first time, what is called the *wisdom of the people of the jungle* (*sacha runa yachai* in Kichwa). This "philosophical framework," according to Hidalgo-Capitán et al. (2019, p. 2), is embedded in three concepts. The first, *Sumac Allpa*, indicates a "land free of evil," the second, *Sumak Kawsay*, implies a "clear and harmonious life," and the third, *Sacha Kawsay Riksina*, evokes the "art of understanding-knowing-convincing-being" (ibid.). Carlos Viteri, a *Kichwa* anthropologist, then "systematized this concept until it became a theoretical proposal for welfare and a proposal for social transformation" (ibid.). Despite previous uses of the term, it is Viteri's ethnography-based synthesis that has been increasingly evoked by the signifier *Sumak Kawsay.*

The concept combines spiritual, ecological, and communitarian elements and rests on indigenous perceptions of multiple, interrelated spheres. The first of these, *Amasanga*, is described by Coq (2017) as "the spirit of the forest," which "acts as an energy that flows through an extended perception of the ecosystem" (p. 169). This extended notion of ecosystem includes animals and insects, humans, water, soil, as well as "spirits of the forest" (ibid.). Thus, *Amasanga* is "essential for understandings interconnections amongst different sets of elements (social, natural, spiritual)" (ibid.). *Nunghui*, according to Coq-Huelva et al. (2018), is the spirit of things that are made, or nurtured, by humans—such as gardens or handicrafts. Vitally, this concept is also associated with equilibrium and stability. The third sphere of *Sunghui*, the source of life, is interrelated with the other two spheres.

Sumak Kawsay is intimately related to these spheres as they interact within a given locality. Thus "people cannot be understood without territory, and territory cannot be understood without people" (ibid.). In turn, "[t]he community not only includes people but also animals, plants, ecosystems, even forces and spirits that supposedly live in the territory" (ibid.). *Sumak Kawsay*, therefore, implies the nurturance of well-being of this community that extends beyond the simple human elements, evoking the importance of balance with nature where human needs cannot predominate the well-being of nature. Consequently, according to Coq (2017), "[c]ommunitarian harmony is not only the product of but also the guarantee of good family living" (ibid.). Therefore, "having a good family and residing in a non-conflictive human community that conserves forests and their associated spirits are essential elements" of indigenous understandings of being (ibid.). This translates into a "preference for self-sufficiency," often articulated in terms of food sovereignty as well as a bio-centrism (ibid.).

Given these characteristics, *Sumak Kawsay* has found many allies in postneoliberal political and economic paradigms. The idea has resonated well with streams of decentralized new socialism that have emerged in twenty-first-century Latin America. Increasingly powerful discourses of sustainability and environmentalism have found a congruence with the concept as well. The global food sovereignty movement too supports, and is supported by, the idea (as well as the Andean indigenous movements that have propagated it). Furthermore, the idea that Andean indigenous peoples have a transcendent understanding and relation with nature fits well with the indigeneity-as-social-capital postulates of post-Washington-Consensus development policy. All of these things have produced a perfect storm for the ascendance of *Sumak Kawsay* in Ecuador. As the idea has gained formality and popularity, however, its essence of localism and bio-centrism may have been ejected. This can be seen clearly with the inclusion of the concept in the Constitution of Ecuador.

Due to the multiple political, economic, and discursive forces outlined above, *Sumak Kawsay* emerged at the forefront of the Ecuadorian political imagination in the period leading up to the institution of a new national constitution in 2008. Although the concept has a complex meaning that is differently interpreted in various locales (Uzendoski 2018; Coq 2017), it came to be translated to *Bien Vivir* (to live well) in Spanish. This was part of a massive undertaking by the leftist government of President Rafael Correa to create a national constitution that would be later touted as the "most radical in the world" (Lalander 2016, p. 623). Although that description may be appropriate, many tensions emerged with *Sumak Kawsay*'s interpretation and institutionalization into the constitution. The most striking of these tensions is between the indigenous concept and attempts of the Correa government to simultaneously institute a new socialism. Following the emergent "red tide" in Latin America, this new socialism focused on decentralization and egalitarianism, funded by resource extraction.

The constitution of 2008 was propelled largely by the *Revolución Ciudadana, which advocates* "policy aimed at abolishing social stratification along ethnic, gender, religious and class lines" (Lalander 2016, p. 629). This abolishment of stratification does not mean the elimination of difference, however, as the Constitution's first article declares the country to be intercultural and plurinational. This recognition of difference in worldview along with a progressive, extractivist, model of development inspired many to label the Constitution as an exercise in "*Sumak Kawsay* Socialism," as opposed to being a definitive expression of indigenous ideals (Ramírez Gallegos 2012, p. 33). Thus, As Lalander (2016) argues, the use of *Sumak Kawsay* in the Ecuadoran Constitution signifies a process through which "ancient indigenous traditions are applied in new contexts to create alternatives to global capitalism" (p. 631) that are not necessarily in opposition to modernizing development. Consequently, recognition of indigenous relations to nature was secured amidst a national effort to intensify development through large-scale mining. Typifying the new commitment to indigenous cosmovision, Article 71 of the Constitution, states that:

> Nature, or Pacha Mama, where life is reproduced and occurs, has the right to integral respect for its existence and for the maintenance and regeneration of its life cycles, structure, functions and evolutionary processes. [Furthermore] All persons, communities, peoples and nations can call upon public authorities to enforce the rights of nature. To enforce and interpret these rights, the principles set forth in the Constitution shall be observed, as appropriate. The State shall give incentives to natural persons and legal entities and to communities to protect nature and to promote respect for all the elements comprising an ecosystem.

Article 72 follows by declaring that nature has a right to be restored if it has incurred damages. Following this, Article 73 delineates measures that the government must take to prevent or restrict damage to the natural environment. Article 57 applies specific protection to peoples who are living in voluntary isolation, and to their environments. The article states that they "are an irreducible and intangible ancestral possession [of their land] and all forms of extractive activities shall be forbidden there." Subsequently, "[t]he State shall adopt measures to guarantee their lives, enforce respect for self-determination and the will to remain in isolation." In accordance, "[t]he violation of these rights shall constitute a crime of *ethnocide*." These articles are all in accordance with the sentiment extended in the preamble, which states:

> We women and men, the sovereign people of Ecuador … hereby decide to build a new form of public coexistence, in diversity and in harmony with nature, to achieve the good way of living, the *Sumak Kawsay*. (República del Ecuador 2008)

Lalander (2016) points out, however, that although the Constitution, and ILO 169, contain language emphasizing the right to free, prior, and informed consultation in the face of planned resource extraction in their territories, the related requirements are ambiguous. As Lalander (2016) suggests, the Constitution makes clear in multiple articles that the state has a responsibility to use natural resources in the interest of social welfare. For example, Article 276 delineates state development responsibilities:

> 1. To improve the quality of life and life expectancy, and enhance the capacities and potential of the population within the framework of the principles and rights provided for by the Constitution. 2. To build a fair, democratic, productive, mutually supportive and sustainable economic system based on the egalitarian distribution of the benefits of development and the means of production, and on the creation of decent, stable employment. (República del Ecuador 2008)

Although territorial and environmental protection remains uncommonly strong in the constitution, there are many such caveats. For example, Article 405 declares:

> Activities for the extraction of nonrenewable natural resources are forbidden in protected areas and in areas declared intangible assets, including forestry production. Exceptionally, these resources can be tapped at the substantiated request of the President of the Republic and after a declaration of

> national interest issued by the National Assembly, which can, if it deems it advisable, convene a referendum. (República del Ecuador 2008)

The Constitution of Ecuador does, in general, stand as an exemplary and revolutionary document in its protections for plurinational indigenous rights and rights accorded to the natural environment. It is, however, an incorporation of some biocentric and indigenous principles into a developmentalist state apparatus that is interested in neo-extractivist new-socialist development. Development remains a form of modernization premised on resource-based economic growth, albeit one that emphasizes protections for nature and cultural alterity. The ambiguities generated by this document, and the cultural political economy in which it is situated, are visible in the politics around the failed Yasuní-ITT initiative.

The *Yasuní* Plan and Its Failure

Yasuní-ITT refers to the protected ecological area of the Yasuní National Park and three untapped oil blocks contained therein—known collectively as Ishpingo–Tambococha–Tiputini. Ecuador's main indigenous organization CONAIE demanded the suspension of exploitation of oil resources in the area in 1995 (Lalander 2016). The Tambococha and Tiputini both lived in voluntary isolation in Yasuní, and CONAIE claimed that their ancestral territories and ways of life were extremely vulnerable to expanded oil exploration (Fierro 2017). In 2007, before the national endorsement of the 2008 Constitution, President Correa and his government initiated a bold plan for the protection of the area, which contained some of the nation's largest oil reserves: the Yasuní-ITT initiative.

Purportedly following the spirit of *Sumak Kawsay*—which had become a guiding principal for both CONAIE and the federal government—the Yasuní-ITT proposed to keep all oil of the area "in the ground." The simple idea was to ask the international community to compensate Ecuador for half the loss of income it would incur due to the non-exploitation of oil. This would protect carbon sink, flora, and fauna in one of the most ecologically diverse areas of the world, and the way of life of the region's indigenous inhabitants, while providing social development funds (Lalandar 2016).

Specifically, as a UNDP document claims, the project would leave 846 million barrels of oil in the ground. This oil would be worth approximately

$90 billion in 2019-adjusted dollars. Since the government of Ecuador would voluntarily forfeit half the opportunity cost of the oil, Correa was seeking international support in gaining $45 billion to establish a Yasuní-ITT trust fund. Touted as a new model for development, this initiative specifically proposed the following:

(a) An innovative option for combatting global warming by avoiding the production of fossil fuels in areas that are highly biologically and culturally sensitive in developing countries.
(b) Protecting the biodiversity of Ecuador and protecting the voluntary isolation of indigenous cultures…
(c) Social development, nature conservation and implementing the use of renewable resources. (Larrea 2009, p. 2)

Capital gained via the fund would be invested in the production of renewable energy via solar, wind, and hydroelectric facilities. These would provide stable investment income thereafter. The profits of which, along with interest from the remainder in the fund, would be used for:

(a) [C]onserving and preventing deforestation … in 43 protected areas, totaling 4.8 million hectares … equaling 18% of Ecuador's territory
(b) Reforestation, forestation, natural regeneration and appropriate management of one million hectares of forest owned by small landholders
(c) Increase national energy efficiency
(d) Promote social development … with programs that include health, education, training, technical assistance and productive job creation in sustainable activities. (Larrea 2009, p. 3)

The massive project would fund a national-scale attempt to diversify the economy away from a model of development based on oil extraction, towards a new strategy based on equity and sustainability. As Lalander (2016) claims, "the Yasuní-ITT initiative turned into the symbol of another possible world and a rejection of extractive capitalism" for progressives around the world (p. 633). The region and project became a "national refrain of Ecuadorians across the nation, around the identification of the environmentalist purposes of the initiative"; "I am Yasuní" (*Yo soy Yasuní*) or "We are all Yasuní" (*Todos somos Yasuní*) became popular national slogans (ibid.).

The project, however, reproduced tensions between the meaning of *Sumak Kawsay* for indigenous people, and its use by the national government and non-indigenous population. At its root, *Sumak Kawsay* is an *alternative to development*. The Yasuní-ITT initiative, however, espoused an *alternative form of development*. The difference is not trivial. One concept rejects modernization and elevates another, ecologically rooted, way of existing. The other concept advocates modernistic national development via a new-socialist and sustainable development model. Although indigenous groups such as CONAEI supported the initiative, this support was tentative, and such groups did not tend to support the Correa government in general (Lalander 2016).

Fierro (2017) explains that this tension also resulted from Ecuador's position as an oil-dependent developing country within a capitalist global political economy. The scale of the project was too large to be internally financed; thus, Correa had to turn to the international community of nations for funding. These donors balked at the framing of the project because it hinged on the non-extraction of resources. Germany, for example, announced that it would not offer finances because "the proposal is dangerous and might be a precedent for other producing countries to demand a similar amount" (AGENCIA AFP 2010). Although Germany supported many elements of the project, it could not "support the idea of paying compensation to a country for renouncing oil exploitation" (ibid.). Much of the international community balked in this same way, ultimately leaving the initiative virtually unfunded.

Ecuador was not in a position to leave the oil in the ground without compensation, however. The country was not only dependent on oil income, which equaled 66% of its total imports, it was also dependent on oil derivatives (refined petroleum, petrochemicals for agriculture, etc.). In all, 74% of the derivatives used in the country were imported (Acosta 2006). The abandonment of modernizationist development could not be supported by the non-indigenous majority (nor likely by many indigenous Ecuadorians). That the country could only premise non-extraction on payment from the international community, makes obvious its dependent position in the global economy. This dependency exists discursively—in the largely imported cultural norm of modernizationist development. It also exists economically—in the lack of funds available to pursue sustainable forms of modernization (Fierro 2017).

Correa cancelled the Yasuní-ITT initiative in August 2013. The Ecuadorian government had promoted the idea for six years, but sufficient funds were never accumulated. In an impassioned press conference, the president explained, "unfortunately we have to say that the world has failed us … I think the initiative was ahead of its time, and those responsible for climate change were unable to understand it, or did not want to." In his mind, not only had the international community of nations let Ecuador down, but also the global environmental movement and associated individual progressives from all over the world also failed to put their finances behind the project.

But many have also pointed out that the failure was also on the Ecuadorian government's hands. They had promoted a green modernizationist development programme and *de facto* continued embedding of the country within an extractives capitalist world system instead of rejecting that system and pledging simply to keep the oil in the ground without financial strings attached. *Sumak Kawsay* was, in fact, never a cohesive part of the programme. It was a plan for modernization via green new-socialist principles. The plan purported to protect indigenous peoples, but did not take their ideas as seriously as it could have.

Conclusion

Sumak Kawsay, as the idea emanates from indigenous Ecuador, is unprecedented as a well-delineated alternative to development. It is biocentric as opposed to anthropocentric. This biocentrism is achieved as indigenous cosmovision extends the idea of community beyond the human domain and into the natural world. Nature is framed as something to be nurtured and maintained, instead of as a resource for development. There is an idea of development contained in *Sumak Kawsay*, however. This involves the complex ideal of the extended community "living well." This does not necessarily require economic growth or modernizationist development.

Sumak Kawsay emerged in a time typified by the forceful emergence of a neo-extractivist, new socialist model of development in Latin America (Villalba-Eguiluz & Etxano 2017). This model aims to use resource extraction to create economic surplus that will be used to fund a decentralized, egalitarian, but modernizationist form of development. Environmental sustainability is not ejected in new-socialist development models, nor is the protection of indigenous peoples, their cultures, and their land. With their emphasis on economic diversification and equity along modernizationist lines, however, they clash with *Sumak Kawsay*, which is more closely aligned with a de-growth perspective that emphasizes well-being and nurturance of the extended community.

Furthermore, the ascendance of both new socialism and indigenous alternatives to development has emerged within a capitalist and extractivist global political economy. This global political economy favours indigeneity only so much as it is a corrective for market failures. Neoliberal multiculturalism assures that this acceptance of alterity stops where it clashes with capital accumulation. As a result, indigenous culture is supported in a superficial way. When Andean indigenous cosmovisions conjure proposals that eschew economic development via resource extraction, that support stops.

Thus, the Ecuadorian constitution simultaneously includes and excludes indigenous ideas of development. This case study, then, evidences not only a lack of resources that dependent nations have to pursue endogenous development priorities, but also shows a lack of empathy and imagination even amongst sympathetic developmentalist governments. As a result, indigenous alternatives to development have yet to be pursued seriously even in the most sympathetic and progressive governments of the world. Indigenous development in Ecuador does have obvious allies in global de-growth and deep-ecology movements, but these movements are not close to being mainstreamed. *Sumak Kawsay*, along with other forms of indigenous sustainable development, therefore, remains to be marginalized and incorporated only piecemeal. This is true whether they are incorporated by new socialist states such as Ecuador, or predatory, clientalist regimes such as those in Honduras or Guatemala.

References

Acosta, A. (2006). *Breve historia económica del Ecuador*. Quito: Corporación Editora Nacional.

AGENCIA AFP. (2010, September 20). Ecuador Anuncia ante Alemania para conseguir apoyo al ITT, *Diaro El Universo*, Monday.

Coq-Huelva, D., Torres-Navarrete, B., & Bueno-Suárez, C. (2018). Indigenous Worldviews and Western Conventions: Sumak Kawsay and Cocoa Production in Ecuadorian Amazonia. *Agriculture and human values, 35*(1), 163–179.

Correa, R. (2013, August 14). Press Conference. *The Announcement of the Cancellation of the Yasuní-ITT Initiative*, Given by President Correa.

Deruyttere, A. (1997). Indigenous Peoples and Sustainable Development: The Role of the Inter-American Development Bank. *IND97-101*, Inter-American Development Bank, Washington, DC.

Escobar, A., & Alvarez, S. (Eds.). (1992). *The Making of Social Movements in Latin America: Identity, Strategy and Democracy*. Boulder, CO: Westview.
Fierro, L. G. (2017). Re-thinking Oil: Compensation for Non-production in Yasuní National Park Challenging *Sumak Kawsay* and Degrowth. *Sustainability Science, 12*, 263–274.
Fine, B. (2002). *Social Capital versus Social Theory*. Routledge.
Fondo Indigena. (2019). *Indian Background: 24 Years of Working with Indigenous Peoples*. Retrieved from http://www.fondoindigena.org/drupal/en/node/513.
Hidalgo-Capitán, A. L., Cubillo-Guevara, A. P., & Masabalín-Caisaguano, F. (2019). The Ecuadorian Indigenist School of Good Living (Sumak Kawsay). *Ethnicities, 1*, 1–26.
Lalander, R. (2016). The Ecuadorian Resource Dilemma: Sumak Kawsay or Development? *Critical Sociology, 42*(4–5), 623–642.
Larrea, C. (2009). *Yasuni-ITT Initiative: A Big Idea from a Small Country*. UNDP.
Masala, R., & Monni, S. (2017). *The Social Inclusion of Indigenous Peoples in Ecuador Before and After the Revolucion Ciudadana*. SEEDS Working Paper, 10/2017. Retrieved from http://www.sustainability-seeds.org/papers/RePec/srt/wpaper/1017.pdf.
Radcliffe, S. A., Laurie, N., & Andolina, R. (2002). *Indigenous People and Political Transnationalism: Globalization from Below Meets Globalization from Above?*. University of Oxford. Transnational Communities Programme.
Ramírez Gallegos, R. (2012) Izquierda y 'buen capitalismo'. Un aporte crítico desde América Latina. *Nueva Sociedad* 237: 32–48. Retrieved May 3, 2013, from http://www.nuso.org/upload/articulos/3818_1.pdf.
Republica del Ecuador. (2008). Constitución de la República del Ecuador. Quito: Tribunal Constitucional del Ecuador. Registro oficial Nro, 449.
Schilling-Vacaflor, A. (2010). Bolivia's New Constitution: Towards Participatory Democracy and Political Pluralism? *European Review of Latin American and Caribbean Studies, 90*, 3–22.
Sistema Integrado de Indicadores Sociales del Ecuador (SIISE). (2015). *Indicadores sociales del Ecuador*. Retrieved September 20, 2015, from http://www.siise.gob.ec/siiseweb/.
Uzendoski, M. A. (2018). Amazonia and the Cultural Politics of Extractivism: Sumak Kawsay and Block 20 of Ecuador. *Cultural Studies, 32*(3), 364–388.
van Nieuwkoop, M., & Uquillas, J. E. (2000). *Defining Ethno-Development in Operational Terms: Lessons from the Ecuador Indigenous and Afro-Ecuadoran Peoples Development Project*. Working Paper No. 6, World Bank, Latin American and Caribbean Regional Office, Environmentally and Socially Sustainable Development SMU, Washington, DC.
Villalba-Eguiluz, C. U., & Etxano, I. (2017). Buen Vivir vs Development (II): The Limits of (Neo-Extractivism). *Ecological Economics, 138*, 1–11.

World Bank. (2019). *Indigenous and Afro-Ecuadorian Peoples' Development Project*. World Bank Projects and Operations. http://projects.worldbank.org/P040086/indigenous-afro-ecuadorian-peoples-development-project?lang=en.

Yashar, D. J. (1996). Indigenous Protest and Democracy in Latin America. In J. Domínguez & A. Lowenthal (Eds.), *Constructing Democratic Governance: Latin America and the Caribbean in the 1990s: Themes and Issues*. Baltimore: The Johns Hopkins University Press.

Yashar, D. J. (1999). Democracy, Indigenous Movements, and Postliberal Challenge in Latin America. *World Politics, 52*(1), 76–104.

CHAPTER 10

Indigenizing Development

Much work has been done in this book so far to describe both indigenous and "non-indigenous" ideas of development. Since the vital element of indigenous development is a recognition of cultural difference, culture was centralized in development ideas. Using a transmodern perspective allowed us to admit that, although marginalized, the influence of indigenous peoples must have exerted some formational pressure on both enlightenment and development thought. We can expect, therefore, that there will be some congruencies between indigenous ideas of sustainable development and other streams of development thinking.

To my knowledge, there has not been any major attempt to search the annals of historical text to show the influence that the peoples marginalized by colonialism had on enlightenment thought. Although I have not begun that work here, my goal is to go some distance towards finishing it. Towards that end, I will examine the extent to which traditional development theories can be incorporated into contemporaneous indigenous thought. I am not attempting to do the opposite—to integrate bits of indigenous knowledge into mainstream theories. I will privilege the indigenous here. If mainstream development theory is incommensurate with indigenous ideas of sustainable development, the former will not be considered useful. In this chapter, I will use "indigenous thought" and "indigenous development" to describe the Andean, Maya, and Garifuna case studies discussed in this book. It is understood that these are just three of many different indigenous groups in Latin America and

T. MacNeill, *Indigenous Cultures and Sustainable Development in Latin America*, https://doi.org/10.1007/978-3-030-37023-7_10

the world. This language is used for descriptive expedience and is not intended to suggest that all indigenous groups share the same cosmology as those treated here.

Classical Political Economy and Neoclassical Economics

The thinking of the classical political economists of late eighteenth-century Europe had striking similarities to current indigenous thought. This assertion holds especially true regarding the work of Adam Smith and J.S. Mill. Importantly, both of these political economists considered human tastes, values, and propensities—including those to engage in self-regarding individualistic market transactions—to be cultural constructions. These tendencies, especially for Smith in his *Theory of Moral Sentiments*, were products of the social institution of capitalism and forced upon human actors by abject poverty and inequality. Out of poverty came a desperate need to attain the primal elements of life. Out of inequality came the need to show status through emulation. Similarly, Andean, Maya, and Garifuna thoughts often contain a fear that the global capitalist system is creating competitive consumers out of indigenous subjects. They also insist that it is in their relationships with others that human subjects gain their tastes and values.

In this sense, a primal compulsion of the human in both traditions is to build a system of beliefs through communication. The prime impulse, in other words, is not narrow personal gain, but communicative world-building and other-regarding behaviour. This is abundantly apparent in the Maya, Andean indigenous, and Garifuna assertion that the division between community and individual is a false one, and repeated descriptions of the ways in which human wants and needs are cultural products. Similarly, Smith makes a clear assertion in *The Wealth of Nations* that the apparently natural self-interested action of humans in a market society is likely the result of being embedded in such a society and not a natural propensity at all. Mill similarly suggests that a time may come that systemic change will lead to more communitarian behaviour in formerly competitive societies. Smith went even further in his *Theory of Moral Sentiments* (1759/1790) to suggest that it was the ethical other-regarding “inhabitant of the breast” that was the final arbiter of human action as opposed to hedonistic greed (III.I.46).

Classical political economists and indigenous thinkers share scepticism about the fairness of a capitalist system of production and distribution as well. This is obvious in the case of the latter. It is often overlooked, however, that classical political economists shared this scepticism due to the inclusion of the labour theory of value in their theoretical framework. Smith's warnings regarding class divisions in capitalist societies were much more extreme than those found in the work of Mill or Ricardo, but an inherent tension between landed, capitalist, and labouring classes is common to all, as are warnings about tendencies of capitalist classes to accumulate disproportionate economic and political power. For Smith, this tendency was enough to threaten the continuance of democracy itself, as the capitalist class may attempt to force its favoured policies through government at the expense of the well-being of society at large.

Important differences do exist between Latin American indigenous thinking and that of the classical political economists, however. First, the scepticism of the capitalist system is much more profound amongst the Maya, Andean indigenous, and Garifuna. This is not to diminish the substantial distrust Smith had of free markets, but the indigenous ideas discussed here treat the free market with fear and occasionally with cautious acceptance—but the acceptance appears only where the institution is to be governed substantially by democratic processes to ensure the market operates in the interest of social and environmental well-being.

A more fundamental difference exists regarding the propensity of the classical political economists to circumscribe the economy for the purpose of analysis. The classical political economists were guilty of the enlightenment habit of separating the knowable world into distinct parts. The most fundamental of these was the distinction of humans and nature. The latter was consistently characterized as a resource by the classical political economists, while nature is conceived as part of community in indigenous thought. The classical habit of demarcating the economy from culture is just as problematic. If there is a fundamental character to Andean indigenous, Maya, and Garifuna thought, it is that all aspects of humanity, nature, and culture constitute a single system and cannot be abstractly separated.

The nature/human/culture distinction is not the only problematic classical demarcation in relation to indigenous thought. Although Smith and Mill, for example, insisted that moral philosophy must be considered in addition to economic analysis—and Smith even believed that the economic analysis of *The Wealth* was to be subordinate to his more encompassing work in *The Theory of Moral Sentiments*—classical political economists tended to hold these spheres separate in their analyses. This led, for example, to *The Wealth* being read at the expense of *Moral Sentiments* by the social scientists that would follow Smith. This, if we are to take Karl Polanyi at his word, contributed very much to the creation of an economic society.

This economic society is very different from the society that is condoned by the Maya, for example—one in which production, consumption, and exchange of goods are integrated into a cultural system typified by *Maya cosmovision*. The most basic premise of *Maya cosmovision* is that nature, culture, and the material world are one. This implies that a sphere of material production, distribution, and consumption cannot be artificially severed from the other aspects of human existence. It also suggests that nature be viewed as more than simply a resource for production. Cultural sustainability is thus tied to environmental sustainability. An economic science that holds human wants as stable and refuses to situate them historically or culturally—let alone one which refuses the reciprocal relation between human and nature—cannot be thought to be consistent with indigenous development.

The neoclassical economics that was born of the marginalist revolution continued the trend of severing the economic from the cultural. In this move, economics was defined only as the study of exchange in markets and was therefore effectively disconnected from the political, the cultural, or the ethical considerations. Humans were considered to be atomistic and stable in their preferences—only interacting with one another through prices. Neoclassical policy implied that the more liberal markets are, the more efficient transactions will be, the more aggregate economic product will be produced. Development was taken to mean increased gross national product, and free markets were the means to achieve this.

It would be difficult to imagine a theory of development that is further from the indigenous—with its insistence on the cultural and natural embeddedness of all action, the centrality of politics, the malleability of preferences, the broad definition of development to include non-economic factors, and scepticism of the efficacy of markets. The Keynesian turn in neoclassical economics reduced the economists' blind faith in the perfect functioning of markets, and even introduced cultural considerations into conversations regarding policy. It did little to address the other issues that are central to indigenous thought, however, and, in Smithian fashion, held cultural considerations largely apart from economic ones.

The circumscription of an economic field of analysis from the social, cultural, and political milieu had another important implication for development thinking that was to follow. Development itself came to be characterized in terms of material and economic gain at the expense of interwoven social, ecological, political, and cultural considerations. This form of economic reductionism in development thought would remain a dominating characteristic in much of the thinking that followed classical political economy—from Marxism, to neoclassical economics, and modernization theory. It would not be until later cultural approaches to development—such as postcolonialism and post-development—emerged that this econocentric approach would be contested.

Marxian Political Economy

The relation between early Marxian political economy and indigenous thought is difficult to establish with perfect clarity. Given the vastness of Marxian interpretation and debate, it is difficult to make any claim regarding Marxian theory without being challenged by varying contradicting exceptions and alternative readings. It is clear, however, that indigenous thought finds it useful to recognize inherent tendencies towards labour exploitation and material inequality in a capitalist system. Those who control the means of production are assumed to be able to benefit unfairly in such a system and may use this power to produce ideology, which can change the values and beliefs of dominated classes and peoples. Furthermore, indigenous thought resembles that of Marxian/Leninist theories of imperialism, which note that wealthy capitalists in industrial nations have the means and incentives to manipulate government in less economically powerful areas of the world. This neocolonialism at the hands of oligopolistic transnational capital is one of the main concerns that has provoked a focus on political decentralization and relative autonomy for the Garifuna, Andean indigenous, and Maya.

We may, however, interpret early Marxian thought (arguably) to be materially reductionist, overly concerned with aggregate economic output at least at early stages of development, teleological in that it presumes society to advance in a number of predetermined steps to an ultimate state of modern development, and addicted to the enlightenment concepts of "real" human propensities that may be obscured by an ideology or a fetish and a natural world that exists only as a resource for production. Where (or rather if) Marxism ebbs towards these tendencies, it distances itself from indigenous thought.

Later iterations of the Marxian tradition are not so easily characterized in these terms, and therefore fall more in line with indigenous ideas and politics. Gramsci presented an early challenge to the Marxian assertion that the nature of ideas, of consciousness, of culture, is determined solely by the economic base. His assertion that the naturalized ideas which uphold an exploitative system can be challenged is similar to the core ideal that indigenous culture can challenge neoliberal development. Certainly, indigenous peoples' work to valorize indigenous thought vis-à-vis Western capitalist hegemony is reminiscent of a Gramscian battle of ideational position.

Gramscian thought, however, maintains the Marxian presumption that consciousness can be somehow "false." Correspondingly, members of a society are presumed to be misled by capitalist-produced propaganda which prevents them from seeing the true nature of their exploitation. The goal of a Gramscian countermovement would be to expose that the relations of production are working in the interest of a capitalist class at the expense of others and to thereby prompt revolutionary change. Indigenous activists, however, are careful to depict consumer culture, for example, not so much as a false belief system, but as a system of beliefs that has been adopted amidst profound material, political, and cultural power imbalances. As much as there is a large distaste for capitalism and consumer culture among Maya activists, for example, the main problem is not seen to be the nature of this cultural form, but the material and discursive inequality out of which it has been constructed.

The goal of indigenous development is more to institute a thorough discursive democracy than to expose the "true nature" of exploitation through challenging ideas. This distinction is actually quite important in that it disallows the imposition of a new "revolutionary" system that has been designed by radical intelligentsia in the "interest" of the common people. Instead, it promotes the creation of a decentralized sphere of politics and discursive production in which the culturally formed "interest" of the people is constantly, and democratically, renegotiated. There is no "true" economic plan, be it capitalist, socialist, or communist, to be designed by left-leaning technocrats and imposed with the goal of ending exploitation. There is only democracy and participation. Any system, plan, or policy devised as a result of such a thoroughly decentralized democratic process would be thought to be good in an ethical sense, not because of its technical, productive, or even redistributive merits, but because of the extent of the democratic processes from which it emerged.

We might carefully infer here a similarity with the work of Habermas (1989) regarding communicative ethics within discursive democracy. Indeed, one Maya field technician at *El Centro* mentioned an affinity with the European theorist's work to me in correspondence. Although Habermasian ideas stem from Marxian political economy, their focus on intersubjectivity and the socially constructed nature of human identity situate them more closely with the tradition of cultural political economy, which will be discussed later in this chapter.

Sociology and Institutional Economics

Just as with the Marxian tradition, indigenous thought can only be precariously aligned with that of the early sociologists. Neoclassical economists tend to assume that humans have a natural need to increase consumption. Marx argued that this need was not natural, but the result of the materiality of the capitalist social relations of production in which the human subject is embedded. The early sociologists (excluding Marx himself) challenged both of these presumptions by questioning if humans are endowed with any pre-social propensities at all, while arguing that wants and values were produced in the cultural realm and that this had force independent of the material.

This brings early sociologists close to indigenous alternative theories in many respects. Even when arguments of indigenous groups verge on an essentialism which claims indigenous peoples to be closer to nature, for example, this depiction is based on cultural traits, not biological ones. This mirrors Durkheim's claims of human nature being formed from "without," and that the fundamental tendency in humans is not to search for personal gain, but to build communicative relationships with other humans in order to order and make sense of the world.

Cultures are presumed to change in both modes of thought. However, Durkheimian cultural change is prompted by increased population density, as humans engage with an ever more successful "struggle against nature" (1893/1997, p. 38). There is an inevitable directionality in Durkheim's cultural change—towards the individualism and division of labour inherent to *organic society*. This type of depiction remained current through Weberian sociology where Western-style development was presumed to represent the highest yet achieved state of human social evolution and individualistic, entrepreneurial, forward-thinking cultural subjects—the necessary constituents of this social system. As opposed to valorizing indigenous culture, this type of thought tended to demean it and even blame it for underdevelopment. Cultural change towards indigenous values, on the other hand, is seen as positive for Andean, Maya, and Garifuna thinkers. Otherwise stated, indigenous "rationality" is a culturally situated characteristic, but one that necessitates the freedom of subjects from being dominated materially or culturally. The imposition of European-style "rational" thought would be seen as one such domination. Therefore, the imposition of development programmes and thought based in modernization theory would be perceived as a form of domination, and not rational from an indigenous perspective, and therefore as the opposite of development.

This is not necessarily the case for the early economic sociology (or old institutional economics) of Veblen, Commons, Duesenberry, and Polanyi. What seemed to economists as an insatiable appetite for goods and services inherent to human life was argued by the institutionalists to be the result of an innate cultural need to demonstrate belonging. The trajectory of this thinking is that in an unequal society, humans will act as if they are insatiable regarding consumption. In a situation of greater equality, however, this seeming natural propensity to consume will wane. If humans have an insatiable desire, it is for belonging, and perhaps status, within a social group. What this suggests is that beyond a minimal level of health and nutrition (and even this is arguable), there is no one state of human existence that can be called "developed" in the sense that total individual utility, or well-being, has transcended a predefined level. Economic growth amidst inequalities may, in fact, reduce aggregate sense of well-being. Economic growth in an environment of generalized equality may be unnecessary and irrelevant.

The similarity between this form of economic sociology and Latin American indigenous thought is notable. In both traditions, the goals of development policy should be a basic level of health and nutrition and generalized equality. This equality is thought to be symbolic and material in nature (since material commodities are taken to be symbolically valued in any case). Culturally, a developed society could take many forms. In both traditions, ideas have the power to shape society. Liberal economic theory, Polanyi (1944/2001) argued, worked to create market society, for example. Similarly, influxes of Western consumer culture, argue indigenous activists, are changing indigenous society fundamentally in Latin America. The (often inequitable) propagation of ideology and culture is linked with material power in both cases. But culture cannot be read directly from the material relations of production in either. In fact, the latter can be challenged by culture and ideas in the conception of indigenous activists. Indigenous sustainable development thought, in this respect, resembles a Marxian–Gramscian tinged form of economic sociology.

The assertion of these similarities must not be taken as a claim that indigenous development thought is an unwitting form of old institutional economics, however. All human desire, it seems, was not thought to be culturally rooted for the institutionalists. Nurkse (1957) suggests that some Western products are "superior" in a non-social sense, for example, and that knowledge of these would provoke want due to a non-ideological evaluation of the merits of the good. Veblen insisted that human wants were, in fact, insatiable, but that competitive symbolic consumption simply amplified these wants. Similarly, Polanyi argues that humans have a natural inclination to protect themselves from the ravages of the market. This implies a pre-social, biologically imbued state of acceptable existence. The indigenous groups studied in this book tend to shy away from such biological depictions of human nature and centralize the cultural.

A more fundamental break exists regarding the relation between humans and nature. Perhaps victims of their times, the early institutional economists never really challenged the modern cultural disposition to depict human existence in terms of a struggle against nature. The incorgporation of indigenous cosmology into development theory, however, lends itself naturally to the challenging of this presumption. There is no reason that such a challenge could not be mounted within an institutionalist framework, however, and Polanyi, for example, notes the environmental destruction that market society tends to cause. The transcendence of the human–nature divide, however, was never as clearly achieved by the institutionalists as it is by indigenous traditions. Thus, indigenous development is necessarily ecologically sustainable development in that it is biocentric, containing an explicit goal to achieve balance within an extended community that includes nature.

Modernization Theory

Unsurprisingly, indigenous thought often stands in direct opposition to post-WWII modernizationist theories of development. The modernizationist assertion that "traditional" cultures are to blame for underdevelopment clashes fundamentally with attempts to valorize indigenous culture. The groups studied in this book all insist that both democracy and development require the continuity of a plurality of cultural forms as opposed to the institution of a singular form. The modernizationist insistence that any cultural form that fails to promote egoism and insatiability is somehow "not rational" is insulting to Maya, Andean, and Garifuna activists who seek to promote respect of indigenous and communitarian cultural forms. The *homo economicus*, that is the cultural goal of modernization theory, does not resonate with most indigenous cosmovisions.

Indigenous leaders tend also to be much more pessimistic about the ability of capitalism to be conducive to development than are modernization theorists. Maya organizers, for example, argue that capitalism requires self-interested consumers in order to exist, and they see this as a direct threat to their culture and well-being. Moreover, they argue, markets bring profound inequality and exploitation. Maya thinkers often hold equality as *the* end of development. Obviously, this makes unfettered markets more of a threat than an institutional necessity. It is important to note, however, that Maya development thinkers do not reject market-based transactions outright, but do advocate more extreme regulation that modernization theorists tend to endorse.

It must not be overlooked that indigenous theories of sustainable development do not reject the concept of development or progress. There is a sense within indigenous thought, as with modernization theory, that history involves continual cultural, technological, political, and social change. The difference lies in the fact that modernization posited an end point to such change—generally a stage of high mass consumption which is to occur within an institutional structure of Western liberal democracy and capitalism. Indigenous thought implies something quite different, however. It implies, *first*, that there is no predetermined economic, social, political, or cultural endpoint to the development process and, *second*, that historical change can only truly be labeled "development" where it occurs in an environment of material and discursive equality.

Critical Political Economy

The indigenous development ideas studied in this book share much with the critical political economy. With the early structuralists of this tradition, members of indigenous movements share a profound mistrust of free markets. In both traditions, unfettered markets are seen to work in the interest of the industrially powerful nations which can use their capital and established market power to benefit inordinately from trade, resulting in the exploitation of labour of peripheral people and natural resources in peripheral areas for the benefit of consumers and capitalists in industrialized ones. But similarities end at this point. Many of the structuralists, particularly Myrdal (1968), shared with modernizationists the condemnation of traditional culture. Furthermore, the policy recommendation that emerged from structuralist theory was to centralize power in the hands of a strong developmentalist state which would design top-down programmes based in import substitution industrialization. Development is defined as a technical exercise in central management that has the ultimate goal of industrial economic growth and increasingly effective exploitation of natural and human resources. This is entirely incongruent with indigenous assertions, that there is more to development than industrial output, that nature is centrally important, and that political and economic decentralization are both means and ends of development processes.

Dependency theory provides a partial corrective for some of the shortcomings of structuralist vis-à-vis indigenous thought. The most important advancement in this regard was the dependency assertion that the persistent poverty of ethnic minorities was not the result of cultural pathologies but of structural marginalization and racism. The recognition that elites *within* less developed countries tended to benefit disproportionately from economic development and that they often monopolize political control is congruent with indigenous thought as well. There is a divergence as dependency theorists characterize underdevelopment as exclusion from the benefits of industrial modernity and economic growth, while environmental issues are rarely addressed.

Cultural analysis is relatively impoverished in dependency and world-systems approaches when compared with indigenous thought. First, alternative conceptions of the ends and means of development are not considered. And second, alternative cultural identities and practices tend to be simply read off of economic structures in dependency and world-systems theory—thought of as cultural responses to economic marginalization. To begin analysis from a position that is embedded in indigenous cosmovision would be illogical in the often materially reductionist tradition of dependency theory. Indigenous and dependency/world-systems theory do share a lamentation of loss of cultural diversity due to the homogenization that is wrought by Western consumer culture. It is not so much that cultural difference is valued in and of itself for dependency theorists, but rather that homogenization represents a forced incorporation into a consumer culture that impoverished peoples lack resources to participate in properly—it is an invitation to exclusion. This dynamic is noted in indigenous thought as well, but the loss of cultural identity itself is accorded as more severe. According to indigenous ideas of development, a transformation to consumer culture is not simply a fetish that obscures the true nature of capitalist exploitation, but it represents a real loss in and of itself, and one that threatens environmental sustainability as well. Furthermore, to challenge this system of domination is largely thought to be a material process according to dependency theory and much world-systems theory, but indigenous theory contends that cultural alterity and resistance are at least of equal importance in this regard.

There is also a break between critical political economy approaches and indigenous thought regarding the materiality of culture. Much is presumed in dependency theory, for example, regarding the hard reality of material needs and the corresponding necessity of industrial production for development. Indigenous ideas of development, however, tend to privilege the cultural embeddedness of wants, values, and necessities. Beyond a minimal level of health, food, and shelter provided by material production, Maya, Andean, and Garifuna development thought questions that well-being is increased by economic output. This is especially true where increased material production may have adverse environmental or cultural impacts. Related to this, indigenous thought proceeds from an assumption that the separation of material and cultural realms is a false abstraction. Accordingly, the penchant in critical political economy to favour the material in analysis sits rather uncomfortably with indigenous thinkers.

Postcolonialism and Post-development

It is difficult to deny the similarities between indigenous thought and that of early postcolonial theorists such as Fanon and Freire. Both traditions contain a presumption that human wants, values, and understandings about the world (cosmovisions) are produced communicatively via language. Culture, for both, creates what is to be defined as the "good life" as well as the means for attaining it. Modernity and Westernization are seen as forms of imperialism for indigenous activists and post-development thinkers alike. Both traditions note an associated culture of racism and ethnocentrism that underwrites discourses of development. This racism and cultural devaluation is not thought simply to be an ill because it limits opportunity, but because this symbolic violence is harmful in its own right.

The programmatic response at of Maya and Andean organizers has been similar to a Frierean pedagogy of liberation in that culture and ideas are accorded emancipatory power. Participatory learning is undertaken in which indigenous Guatemalans or Ecuadorians become aware of the legal support that exists to help them realize the promise of equality. Indigenous culture and institutions are valorized as well—in order to combat racism and to also disrupt the hegemony which holds Western lifestyle as the endpoint of human social development. Much of this work involves examination of indigenous cosmovision as it relates to nature in a way that is posed as superior to the way it is conceived in the Western tradition. This is undertaken with the purposeful intent of diminishing the superiority attributed to Western culture.

Cultural Political Economy

To the extent that post-structural thought in its postcolonial and post-development varieties tends to privilege cultural difference to the point of succumbing to a relativist trap, indigenous ideas often differ from these traditions. Indigenous thought also recognizes the centrality of the material world to a greater degree than does much post-structural theory. Maya activists' assertions that a development plan that is formulated from *Maya cosmovision* is not possible at this time due to extreme material depravation is telling in this regard. Garifuna leaders have made similar observations, and the politics around the *Yasuní*-ITT initiative underline the importance of economic resources to indigenous initiatives. One cannot imagine away malnutrition and hunger, and one will have little chance of formulating an alternative development imaginary while stricken by disease. Furthermore, access to land, capital, and resources is important to indigenous development not only because of the cultural relation to the land that is inherent indigenous cosmovision, but because it is a productive resource that provides for material sustenance and political power.

These considerations place indigenous thought within the ambit of cultural political economy (CPE). In both formulations, social subjects are formed through discourse, and the social and material world is only made intelligible through such discourse. This implies that human desires, cosmovisions, and related utility functions are cultural constructs. This does not imply, however, that a re-imagination of all things is possible at any time. Discourses, ideas, understandings, and desires have histories, and other discourses, ideas, understandings, and desires are built around these histories. This understanding inserts a theory of cultural path-dependency into indigenous thought and CPE which serves to avoid the whimsical nature of more fickle forms of postmodern thought.

Cultures are not depicted as being stagnant or insular either in indigenous thought or in CPE, however. The groups studied in this book make no claims that indigenous culture today is identical to its pre-Columbian form. In the case of the Garifuna, there was no pre-Columbian form. Nor do they make an attempt to conceptually amputate indigeneity cleanly from modernity. Indigenous sustainable development ideals incorporate the concepts such as human rights, democracy, and development—ideas which more radical early post-development or anti-development theorists would have rejected as modernizationist imperialism. This is congruent with Dussel's (1980) understanding of "transmodernity" which suggests that such concepts were developed not only in European ivory towers but also with input from postcolonial struggles including indigenous movements. The fact that indigenous leaders were involved in the negotiation and design of international human rights instruments bolsters this claim, as does the continued work of Garifuna, Andean, and Maya leaders who utilize and attempt to reinforce the power of national and international human rights instruments.

There is some tension between CPE and indigenous thought regarding their respective understandings of the relationship between the material and the cultural. Dussel and Escobar, for example, imply that there is a material world which exists but that this is only made intelligible through culture. This maintains a nature–culture divide which does not resonate perfectly with indigenous cosmovision.

New Classical Economics

Just as was the case with the neoclassical forbearers of new classical economics, a more substantial divergence from indigenous thought would be difficult to imagine. Where new classical economists equate the free market with freedom and efficiency, indigenous development thinkers view it as an instrument of exploitation and domination as well as material and cultural imperialism. New classicalists believe markets to work for aggregate well-being, whereas indigenous ideas argue that markets tend only to benefit the wealthy at the expense of the poor and the environment.

In both indigenous thought and new classical economics, however, we do see a profound distrust of large-scale government bureaucracy and central planning. In the case of Maya sustainable development, this mistrust comes from structuralist and dependency analyses that characterize central governments as being compromised by internal and external economic and political power. New classical economists tend to share this fear of co-option but tend to root it a generalized animosity towards any system that seeks to interfere with the freedom of market transactions. As a result, respective solutions to this problem diverge significantly. Informed by involvement in the global indigenous rights movement and in congruence with CPE approaches, indigenous Maya, Andean, and Garifuna leaders prescribe radical decentralized pluricultural democracy which would direct economic activity—largely displacing central government control. New classical economists, however, tend to shun any non-market control of economic activity, favouring the complete institution of free and unfettered markets.

On a more basic level, the difference between indigenous thought and new classical economics is ontological. As a form of neoclassical economics, the new classical school begins analysis with *homo economicus*—a naturalized asocial economic actor with stable and insatiable wants, which is inhibited in its consumption only by resource-based constraints. In the indigenous thought addressed in this book, however, these wants are considered to be largely mutable and communicatively produced. Human beings, that is to say, are social beings, not atomistic individuals. This presumption renders the entirety of neoclassical analysis and related market advocacy illogical. To use a quantitative example, if people truly seek to increase their sense of social belonging and ability to manoeuvre in a socially constructed world, it is their relative income compared to other social actors that would determine individual well-being in terms of utility gains. This is the case, since social beings, as is argued by old institutional economists, tend to evaluate their own well-being in relative terms. Inequality could be therefore inefficient, despite generalized gains in material output. To the extent that markets produce inequality, then, they could be inefficient in the production of generalized social welfare. The culturally situated actors that are central to indigenous cosmology violate market principles because choices become based on non-price communication—people actually see and compare themselves with others, encouraging values to change.

A more qualitative example can be provided through a paraphrasing of cultural homogenization fears articulated by Maya members of *El Centro*. In a society that increasingly values Western clothing due to the simple fact that it is increasingly normalized as a result of more common use, it does not matter to your individual well-being how many indigenous garments you can afford to purchase or produce. The increased adoption of Western clothing leads to the increased normalization of such practices, and, in turn, tastes change from indigenous clothing to Western clothing. Such taste changes occur, it should be noticed, because the good that is desired is not simply clothing, but social inclusion as well. Where Western garments are more expensive, a welfare loss will be felt due to indigenous inability to afford socially desirable garments. Indigenous peoples, in this scenario, would also feel a welfare loss due to the devaluation of their own path-dependent identities—which cannot be changed "from night until morning." A programme that seeks to revalorize indigenous practices and counter Western cultural imperialism would be welfare increasing in this case. Such a programme of taste-changing does not make sense in a strict new classical framework.

New Institutional Economics

Although the examples given earlier were meant as interpretations of the logic being used by Maya members of *El Centro*, they are obviously closely aligned to old institutional economics. It is also possible that the new institutional economics (NIE) that has emerged out of the neoclassical school is resonant with indigenous thought. NIE does, after all, incorporate concepts such as market failure and social interaction into analysis. It seems, then, that there could be a resonance between indigenous thought and NIE in that they are both sceptical about markets and that they both base their theories, at least in part, on social, non-price, interactions between humans. NEI is a tricky beast to understand, however, and with a closer look, a significant rift appears between the two modes of thinking about development.

Gary Becker's (1976) four premises of economic method provide a good starting point for questioning the relationship between indigenous development thought and NIE. The first premise is that human agents always engage in utility maximizing behaviour. To a proponent of indigenous thought, this may be problematic first because of language which seems to describe human nature as inherently selfish. Exception might also be taken to this premise on the grounds that according to much indigenous cosmovision, humans only exist as part of a universal whole which transcends the physical, cultural, and spiritual. This would make the separation of a "human" with an "interest" from the rest of the quotidian nonsensical.

However, this first premise translates roughly into *humans always do what they want to do unless otherwise coerced*. This may well be tautological, but without any delineation of wants or constraints, it seems a fairly benign, albeit liberal-tinged conceptual tool. Other than the noted invention of the individual as a physically separate entity, there is no necessary reason that this premise must clash with indigenous thought or old institutional economics for that matter. Furthermore, despite the basic indigenous belief that all things come from, and remain part of, an unnamable incomprehensible something, it is repeatedly asserted by indigenous leaders that the resultant human subjects have a degree of agency. The human agents described in this NIE premise, I believe, are therefore incorporable within an indigenous theoretical framework.

The second premise of NIE is that human agents are rational in that they choose one action over another by calculating, consciously or subconsciously, costs of each option and weighing them against benefits. In reality, this is not all that different from the first premise. It again implies that humans do what they would prefer to do within given economic constraints. It does not necessarily suggest that humans know for sure which actions will make them feel better, or that they understand all associated material or immaterial costs. Again, this premise does not address the question of where costs or constraints come from. There is no reason to assume that all of these could not be culturally generated. There is no necessary reason that this premise clashes with indigenous development theory.

The third premise of NIE is that markets are ubiquitous in all facets of human life. This is provocative in that it may be interpreted as a move to extend neoliberal hegemony by naturalizing the concept of markets. This alone would be enough to put an ill-taste in the mouths of many social scientists and likely members of indigenous movements as well. Even if we agree, however, that the discourse employed here may be problematic and then move to a closer analysis of the concept, we can see that this premise is again nothing more than a reassertion of the previous two. A market, after all, is nothing more than a metaphor used to characterize an act of exchange in which an agent seeks to get what it wants to get in the face of constraints. NEI asserts that people do what they want, but that every action has its costs. Markets are little more than the conceptual space in which this occurs.

Economists, to be sure, tend to depict markets as something real. But they are fundamentally nothing more than a way of describing price-based interactions between humans, other humans, and their environment. For example, if I choose to pick you a flower, I am fulfilling my desire to do something nice for you in order to gain your appreciation. There are costs involved in this, however. I must exert energy in order to find a flower, pick it, and bring it to you. I have engaged in a cost–benefit analysis and engaged in a transaction in the market for your love. Costs are changed for others as well since I have just simultaneously increased demand for flowers and for your love in a market in which supplies might be presumed to be fixed. But really there is no market—markets are simply abstractions that are used to describe human behaviour and relationships in NIE. And the type of behaviour that is presumed is one in which people do the things that they would like to do, given economic constraints. Premises one, two, and three of NIE are conceptually identical.

The fourth and final premise of NIE is a claim that all human agents have a stable set of tastes (preferences), which are, in Becker's (1976) words, "assumed not to change substantially over time, nor to be very different between wealthy and poor persons, or even between persons in different societies and cultures" (p. 5). This premise is not the same as the first three. And this premise, it would seem, is also entirely incommensurate with indigenous thought which presumes tastes beyond minimal needs for physical nutrients (or maybe for all needs) to be mutable cultural constructs.

Premise four is not necessarily incommensurable with indigenous thought, however. Its agreement depends, I would suggest, on the contents of the utility function—the set of unchangeable core wants that human agents prefer. To evaluate this commensurability, we are compelled to question if the indigenous thought examined in this book contains a presumption that there is a stable set of natural wants that are the same in every human. We see evidence in the testimony of Maya organizers of presumed wants for televisions, stereos, and a close-felt relationship with the natural environment, for example. But these things are also claimed to change—for better or for worse. We might think that a minimal level of health and nutrients would be desired universally. Indeed, it is suggested by some Maya thinkers at *El Centro* that for development to be actualized in accordance with indigenous culture, a minimal level of health and education is required.

But these same indigenous thinkers also lamented occasions when they noted that people were buying "equipment for their houses" such as televisions and stereos at times when they did not have enough to provide for their basic health. It seems, then, that there is an observation that even health can be a mutable want, the satiation of which can be undermined by a desire for consumer durables, at least to a degree. Also related to this is the common assertion in literature about indigenous cosmovisions, that any division of material elements such as human bodies and natural resources from the cultural and spiritual leads to a false distinction. This again would make any claim that there exists a universal set of basic pre-cultural needs highly questionable, and the arbitrary designation of such needs correspondingly problematic.

We enter into a tricky area here in indigenous development theory, but tensions between claims of false distinction between cultural and material, and those that imply basic human needs to satiate things such as hunger and thirst, must be reconciled theoretically if we are to explore the commensurability of indigenous thought to the neoclassical method. There is a distinct danger of interpretive colonialism in the theorizing and exploration of this area of thought, however. Any attempt to understand and represent this tension must be undertaken with a degree of careful humility.

It would be prudent to start with the core claim of the indigenous cosmovision. If Heart of Heaven (in Maya cosmovision) is an unconceivable something out of which everything is constructed, then human consciousness, bodies, culture, and desires—physical and otherwise—are therefore part of this construction. There is no prefigured reason why this construction—our social and physical reality—must be of any particular form. This would imply that there is no reason why humans need to experience hunger. Or at least this may imply that our perception of health, hunger, and nutrition is relative to social experience.

We may be able to make the jump to insist that since human actors are part of the construction that emerges out of Heart of Heaven and that they presumably have a small bit of agency in its construction—just as they do with the construction of culture. This is congruent with claims of indigenous thinkers that humans have agency, to varying degrees, in the production of cultural schemata. We can then make a larger jump to suggest that physical human need such as hunger may be in some way at least partially imagined into existence by human belief systems and human consciousness. This makes sense when we remember to incorporate the assertion that culture and material existence are part of a single unitary thing. We would inhabit a perfect post-structuralist thought paradise here if we didn't have to admit a final claim that human consciousness is path-dependent—that we become addicted to our beliefs, that we expect to experience the world as we have experienced it in the past, and so therefore we do. This is an admittedly indulgent interpretation of indigenous cosmovision. But it does serve to illustrate the commonly held refrain that human/nature/culture is one while allowing a space in which hunger, illness, and thirst can exist as well. Such phenomena are simply the physical manifestations of entrenched belief systems.

Put differently, this logic helps us to understand that while hunger, thirst, and ill-health are facts in Guatemala, Ecuador, and Honduras, whether they are physical or cultural facts is not important. When members of *El Centro* claim that most people in indigenous communities do not have enough food, water, health, or basic education to be able to assert their own development at this point, they are suggesting that a certain degree of materiality is required universally. When we incorporate this with the ideas of *Maya cosmovision*, however, we are forced to draw the conclusion that this materiality is, in fact, cultural. But indigenous thinkers argue that cultural belief systems are extremely resilient. We might interpret this as a result of self-reinforcing path-dependence of belief. The more a particular element of a cosmovision—a way of understanding the world—is used, the more real it becomes. The idea that humans are organic material beings which require food and water to survive may be interpreted as a physical fact, or as the oldest cultural assumption. If we conceive of cultural belief systems as path-dependent and if we agree with proponents of Maya cosmovision that any division between the cultural and material is only abstraction, then hunger, thirst, and ill-health are facts. What we conceive as hunger or thirst is both cultural and material because the categories of cultural and material seem functionally identical at this extremity of path-dependency.

A metaphysical excursion such as the one mentioned leads us into uncomfortable territory—especially for those such as I whose conceptual schemes are rooted in Western scientism. It is a necessary excursion for those who wish to explore deeply, and hopefully contribute to, a cultural political economy of international development that gives due respect to indigenous cosmovision. It is also necessary if such scholars and policy analysts are to enter into meaningful conversation with neoclassically trained economists regarding culture and its relation to development theory and policy. How do we begin this conversation? First, by mentioning parenthetically that the depiction of the relationship between the cultural and the material that resulted from an interpretation of indigenous cosmovision is commensurable with some of the most recent advancements in both physical and social-scientific theory. I speak here of quantum physics and the complexity sciences. Second, we could begin this conversation by suggesting a way in which such ideas may be incorporated into neoclassical theory.

I would suggest beginning with Gary Becker's (1976) assertion that there is a universal set of human wants which exist across cultures and time—proposition number four of NIE as stated earlier. In light of the exploration earlier, we would be forced to deduce that the content of this universal preference set would be *cosmovision* according to indigenous development theory. At root, human beings need a way in which they can symbolically order their world in order to make that world comprehendible. This cosmovision is established through non-price communication. Such an assertion suggests a substantial transformation of neoclassical economics. It implies that the base impulse of human nature is to share information with other humans through non-price communication. New institutional economists tend to assume that non-price-based communication only occurs when markets fail, however. The aforementioned assertion turns this presumption on its head by implying that non-price communication is the prerequisite for the existence of markets in that it is how values, preferences, and the presumed natural order of things come into existence. This theoretical incorporation would transform new institutional economists essentially into old institutional economics, since values, beliefs, wants, desires, and ordering systems become socially established.

This need not imply that a cartoonish version of infinitely fickle post-modernity be integrated into economic analysis, however, since the concept of path-dependency must also be included (as, I would suggest, it is with any responsible theorization of post-modernity). This concept of path-dependency, as was discussed in Chap. 3, has two related variants in NIE. First, a human institution such as a cultural belief, law, or social norm may become more resilient with use, thus continuing to mediate human behaviour even at a time when that institution has become inefficient—in that it does not prescribe the most economically efficient behaviour possible. Second, a path-dependency may exist in tastes. The consumption of a good may provide information about it that makes consumption of the same good easier the next time. These two variants of path-dependency collude to suggest that we may rationally develop addictions to institutions and also to consuming certain goods.

The dual assumptions of cultural constructivism of wants and of path-dependency complicate the economic theory of human behaviour substantially. If we allow that the primal human want is for a cultural ordering system with which we may understand the world, it becomes evident that the satiation of this want must necessarily generate a secondary order of wants. Once the idea that humans are organic beings that need food to survive has been established, for example, the need for food would appear as a second-order want. A third order of wants might then appear regarding what objects are preferred as food. Normal Beckerian-style analysis might well be incorporated at this point in order to establish the reasons associated with particular third-order choices.

Due to path-dependency, the more these wants are expressed through markets or otherwise, the more permanent—the more real—they become. There is a feedback loop—or an endogeneity problem in econometric terms—in that the satiation of a want changes the intensity of that want in the future. If second- and third-order wants are based on first-order want, then the satiation of a third-order want could also be presumed to reinforce the stability of the wants that preceded it.

The implications of this for economic theory, empirical research, and policy would obviously be substantial. First, as noted earlier, the relationship between the desires that inhabit the utility function and the satiation of these wants would be presumed to be nonlinear. That is to say there would be feedback loops as the satiation impacts future desire in complex ways. Second, due to path-dependency, some wants may be perceived as more stable than others. Need for food and water would be, as discussed, the most stable of these wants. However, wants for the maintenance of a particular cultural heritage or of a particular type of relationship with the natural world may also be quite intense. One might find that a third order of wants is generated from these second-order ones—perhaps for particular clothing, political institutions, musical expressions, or foods. As we move away from the first order of want for cosmovision, the related desire might be presumed to diminish in its stability. Probabilities may even be attached to such propensities if they can be realistically approximated.

It is not the place of this current work to designate such a theory in its completeness. Such work should be done, I would suggest, through collaboration with new institutional economists, complexity theorists, and communication theorists. It should be noted, however, that extensive empirical work would be required in order to map the nebulous structure of wants and associated stabilities, as well as costs and constraints. The evolving nature of such wants would suggest a repeated engagement with empirical work amidst constant analysis and policy output on the part of economists. At the very least, this would require a meaningful engagement between anthropologists, sociologists, and economists who are doing empirical work.

Given the volume of ever-changing information required for modeling, analysis, and policy design in such a scenario, it is likely that such levels of data collection and planning would become unwieldy, however. The new classical fallback point would be to not interfere with markets. But new institutional economics—the mainstream of current development economics—presumes that markets at least occasionally fail, resultantly requiring intervention. Furthermore, while indigenous thought suggests that non-price communication is fundamental to human existence, non-price communication is indicative of market failure to new institutional economists, as is path-dependency.

The theoretical implication of this in NIE terms is that markets always fail, although we may be able to assume the existence of a workable approximation of markets at times where utility function seems reasonably stable. This implies that a web of measurements must be made and policy interventions devised in order for an economist to steer the social world to a point at which resources are efficiently utilized in the satiation of wants, or even to discern if it is reasonable to consider utility functions to be fixed for the sake of analyzing the problem at hand. This is indicative of a high degree of central planning and technocratic control.

The extent of design and technocratic intervention that would be implied for an economist to direct development processes under assumptions commensurate with indigenous thought would not be received well in more than one camp. Neoclassical economists of the more liberal persuasion could easily revisit Hayek's (1944) warnings about extreme levels of centralized planning leading society down a "road to serfdom." Most cultural political economists could be expected to be similarly uncomfortable with such top-down management of development processes by Western trained technocrats.

A method of escape from such a quagmire is suggested from within indigenous development theory itself, however. A radical decentralization and democratization of policy and planning processes may ensure that decision-making power rests in the hands of those with most recent and pertinent information regarding their goals and constraints. The incorporation of indigenous cosmovision into new institutional economics, then, is possible, but it would imply a programmatic response involving either a high—perhaps impossible—degree of central planning, *or* a thorough democratization of planning and political processes similar to that which is advocated by indigenous rights movements. I would suspect that most liberal-minded economists as well as cultural political economists would prefer the latter.

Such a commitment is already emerging from the murky waters of the capability approach. As was discussed in Chap. 3, much of the ambiguity of the approach is due to that fact that the conversation in that sphere is being undertaken as older ideas (ironically associated with new institutional economics) are being confronted by new ideas (ironically associated with old institutional economics). Much of the debate in this expansive field is between those such as Nussbaum (2007) and the older incarnation of Sen (1977), who presume the existence of a stable set of universal core functionings, and those such as Sen (1999, 2004), who don't. This distinction is fundamental since the former implies that development is a technocratic problem of devising plans to achieve predetermined needs, and the latter implies that development is a form of democracy in which both ends and means are continually negotiated. Sen seems to have resigned himself to the latter, and perhaps his prominence can act as a motivator for a move in the capabilities approach from NIE techniques to those that more closely resemble a neoclassical theory of development that is encapsulated within indigenous thought.

Conclusion

In this chapter, resonances and discords between indigenous thought on sustainable development and numerous other theoretical traditions of development were discussed. Interesting congruencies with classical political economy, Marxian political economy, neoclassical economics, institutionalist economics (economic sociology), modernization theory, critical political economy, new classical economics, postcolonialism, and post-development were discussed. Profound differences between each of these schools and indigenous thought were also located. When the relationship between indigenous thought and cultural political economy was discussed, however, similarities seemed far more evident.

An attempt was then made to explore the possibility of incorporating indigenous cosmovision into new institutional economics—that is, into the newest variant of neoclassical economic approaches to development.

This was done by pushing each approach to its logical extremity and searching for areas of possible commensurability. The most realistic answer to the commensurability question in this case would be that the two theoretical frameworks are incompatible. To morph indigenous thinking to a degree that it becomes compatible with NIE would require the abandonment of the fundamental belief system that undergirds indigenous thought. That is, it would require the abandonment of the assertion that human institutions, desires, even costs and benefits are culturally constructed. It would also require the abandonment of a *Maya cosmovision*, which denies the separability of nature and culture, human and resource, actor and constraint. To bend NIE economics to suit indigenous cosmovision, on the other hand, would require the discipline's transformation into a nonlinear social science which ejects the presumption that life begins with markets. Where policy is concerned, such a theoretical incorporation would require either an extreme level of technocratic monitoring of society, or a substantial decentralization of political and economic power. The former would be distasteful to any neoclassical economist. The latter would be less so, I would guess, however, it may involve local decisions to embrace non-capitalist forms of collective economics. This may not sit well with many development economists. Such a conceptual bending of NIE seems unlikely. However, it should be noted that such terrain seems to be explored diligently by neoclassically trained economists who have embraced the capability approach, and also by heterodox behavioural and experimental economists.

References

Becker, G. (1976). *The Economic Approach to Human Behavior*. Chicago: University of Chicago Press.

Durkheim, E. (1893/1997). The Division of Labour in Society. Trans. W. D. Halls, intro. Lewis A. Coser. New York: Free Press, 1997, pp. 39, 60, 108.

Dussel, E. D. (1980). *La pedagógica latinoamericana*. Bogotá: Nueva América.

Habermas, J. (1989). The Public Sphere: An Encyclopedia Article. In S. Bronner (Ed.), *Critical Theory and Society: A Reader* (pp. 136–145). New York: Routledge.

Hayek, F. A. (1944). *The Road to Serfdom*. Dymock's Book Arcade.

Myrdal, G. (1968). *Asian Drama: An Inquiry into the Poverty of Nations*. Harmondsworth: Penguin.

Nurkse, R. (1957). *Problems of Capital Formation in Underdeveloped Countries*. Oxford: Blackwell.

Nussbaum, M. (2007). *Human rights and human capabilities.* Harv. Hum. Rts. J., 20, 21.

Polanyi, K. (1944/2001). *The Great Transformation: The Political and Economic Origins of our Time.* Boston: Beacon Press.

Sen, A. (1999). *Development as Freedom.* New York: Anchor.

Sen, A. (2004). How Does Culture Matter? In V. Rao & M. Walton (Eds.), *Culture and Public Action* (pp. 37–58). Stanford: Stanford University Press.

Sen, A. K. (1977). Rational Fools: A Critique of the Behavioural Foundations of Economic Theory. *Philosophy and Public Affairs, 6*(4), 317–344.

Smith, A. (1759/1790). *The Theory of Moral Sentiments.* London: A. Millar.

CHAPTER 11

Indigenous Sustainable Development

This book was designed to address some specific questions that would aid understanding of indigenous concepts of sustainable development. This has involved some empirical and theoretical inquiries into the tricky concepts of culture, development, and sustainability. Since the goal was to update our understandings of development theory by interacting those with indigenous perspectives, the first large task was to understand the place of culture in the history of development thought. The next task was to update theories of development and culture by synthesizing them with indigenous thought.

This began with an assumption that to understand indigenous concepts of sustainable development, these must be politically, economically, and historically situated. Case studies of Maya, Andean, and Garifuna development ideas were undertaken towards this goal. Each of these case studies was embedded in a specific local political economy, but they did share a common attribute: a history of economic, political, and cultural marginalization. The ways that these local histories interacted with colonial domination, as well as more current global material and cultural flows, produced each of the ideas. That is, indigenous ideas of sustainable development were produced as deep cultural histories interacted with rights and environmental movements at both local and global levels. Indigenous ideas of sustainable development, of course, continue to change with such interactions.

T. MacNeill, *Indigenous Cultures and Sustainable Development in Latin America*, https://doi.org/10.1007/978-3-030-37023-7_11

In the last chapter, interacting indigenous ideas with "Western" ideas of development led to some interesting tensions and insights. The relation between indigenous thought and sustainability was not overtly addressed, however. In this chapter, we will explore this relation specifically. A preliminary description would be something like this: *indigenous cosmovision does not create a separation between the natural world and a human one. Therefore, equity in material and non-material forms, insomuch as it reduces the marginality of indigenous peoples, will bend economy, politics, and culture towards ecological sustainability.* Once indigenous perspectives are given their appropriate weight, related ideas such as deep ecology, biocentrism, or de-growth take a less radical, more pragmatic, aura.

To understand the implications of indigenous ideas to sustainable development, it is important to avoid two countervailing tendencies. One of these ebbs towards discounting indigenous thought as being "not real" or an "invented tradition." The other tendency reifies, freezes, or essentializes indigenous ideas—framing them as immutable, time-transcendent, and unrelated to other modes of thought, such as modernity, that may corrupt them. In truth, indigenous tradition, just like any tradition, is at once rooted and mutable. This becomes most apparent when we consider the origins in indigenous sustainable development, address issues of essentialism, and then explore indigenous sustainable development and its possible implementation.

Where Does Indigenous Sustainable Development Come From?

A central concern of this book was to locate the cultural, political, and economic origins of indigenous sustainable development. Discerning this required the interpretation of "grassroots," "bottom-up," largely inductively devised indigenous theories of development. Although indigenous development has become popularized in recent decades, it is obviously not a new idea. Rather, ideas of indigenous development have materialized through deep histories of thought and experience. The ideas of progress, development, and human rights that are so often associated with "Western" or "enlightenment" thought are present in this history. So too are the remnants of historical experience of Spanish conquest and association with an "indigenous" identity that was created as an "other" to the Spanish.

More recent histories of civil war, dispossession, marginalization, genocide, racism, and persecution are also included in this history.

Contact with Marxist and postcolonial thought as well as the anticolonial pedagogies and assertions of Friere and Fanon are traceable in the discourse and practice of Maya and Andean development programmes especially. Current discursive structures such as International Human Rights, and Indigenous Rights law, as well as interaction with indigenous and environmental movements, were cited as key factors that assisted the historical emergence of Maya, Garifuna, and Andean ideas of development. These ideas were equally born of involvement with local, community-level interactions with and oppositions to the impositions of externally devised development projects, whether they be from international companies, development organizations, or national governments. Indigenous sustainable development, then, is best described as an iteration of existing ideas from varying sources as they interact with the historical and current every-day experience of indigenous communities.

Indigenous sustainable development, this implies, is not a new idea in the sense that it has emerged in a pristine form that is unrelated to other modes of thought. It has an expansive history of engagement with ideas that stem from modernity and coloniality. It is a transmodern idea of development—that is, an idea that is not modern or traditional, but both. A look at the origins of the idea makes obvious the fictitiousness of an assumed binary that separates the modern from the traditional. Indigenous sustainable development represents an interpretation of development that is informed by indigenous culture and historical experience. It is not a pure idea of development that has emerged from some pristine "other" of modernity, however. It has been forged by a continual relationship between coloniality and modernity, as the colonized mind is articulated by the modern, which is, in turn, articulated by the colonized. They are not separate, but constituent parts of a transmodern cultural, political, and economic reality. Indigenous ideas of sustainable development emerge from this transmodern reality, but unlike the majority of such ideas, they favour the perspectives and knowledges of the historically marginalized.

Substantial critiques may be raised regarding Maya, Andean, Garifuna, and indigenous movements in general regarding a tendency towards the essentialism and romanticization of indigenous culture. If Maya culture is as egalitarian and as rooted in a deep integration with nature as members of *El Centro* tend to argue, it might be asked, then, why do indigenous people so regularly throw plastic, paper, and metal refuse out of the windows of cars and public buses? Why do tourists learn upon visiting the ancient Maya ruins at Copan that that civilization disappeared due to the severe environmental degradation it wrought on its local natural environment? Why does culture in Maya villages seem so patriarchal, and why are women severely underrepresented in communal mayorships? Maya culture does not reveal itself to the outside observer to revolve around the types of ideals that are encapsulated in the so-called Maya cosmovision. The same could be said of Garifuna and Andean traditions.

Certainly, it seems fair to say that all indigenous people do not display nature-centric, communal, and egalitarian tendencies. A responsible development practitioner or policymaker would be wise to think about this before funding or designing any development intervention. The carte blanche support of an indigenous group that makes such claims may not lead to intended consequences. If this cultural characterization is dishonest, an indigenous-run grassroots project that is intended to promote gender equality and environmental sustainability may fail to achieve its goals. Blind trust in the egalitarian and naturalistic tendencies of indigenous culture could lead to bad programmes and misplaced development assistance funds.

When confronting indigenous leaders regarding this issue, the answer one receives is as simple as it is uncontestable: indigenous people who diverge from ideals of environmentalism and egalitarianism, it is explained, have/had lost their way. They have/had lost touch with their culture and the wisdom of their ancestors. Patriarchy and disrespect for the natural environment, it is argued, are largely Spanish colonial imports, and pre-Columbian divergences from nature and equality were temporary departures from ingrained cultural traits. Such answers are inscrutable due to their tautology. But the asking of them might just miss the point of movements for indigenous sustainable development in general.

It should be clear from the account given in this book that claims that the people have "lost their way" are a way of saying that indigenous culture has been transformed in a climate of severe discursive inequality—that cosmovision has been dominated, and that this is not democratic, nor does it represent development. This cultural domination (along with its economic and political counterparts) is contested by indigenous movements as they attempt to move towards an ideal of pluralistic democracy. Such a democracy, in its ideal form, would ensure that all cultural knowledges, understandings, and identities carry the same persuasive force. The valorization of indigenous cosmovisions in Guatemala, Honduras, and Ecuador is a political project designed to counter cultural domination that maintains discursive and material inequities. It is not intended to maintain an "indigenous" culture in a pre-assumed frozen state.

These indigenous democratizing projects were born at an intersection. One of the metaphorical roads in this meeting brings a deep historical past which includes an egalitarian, nature-centric ethic, as well as divergences from this. It also includes a history of colonial marginalization. This road carries the past. The other road brings current thinking on topics such as the environment, indigeneity, human rights, and development. It also carries the material and cultural realities of conflict with international mining, extraction, or tourism interests, and various laws and/or development projects. This road carries the present.

Many of these concepts of the past and present have resonance at the crossroads at which indigenous development thought works, and the items which resonate exude the pitch of a local-centric, nature-centric, egalitarian, indigenous, and endogenous political project. *It is the strength and depth of this resonance which is the item to be judged for its "authenticity"—not its relation to historical "fact."* The essentialist question oversimplifies the claims and the project connected with indigenous politics in Latin America and elsewhere. It may be functional as a limited academic trope, but is of limited functional interest where policy choices, development projects, and political assertions are concerned.

The sustainable development projects described in this book are not so much concerned with the revival of indigenous culture. They are concerned with building new manifestations of indigenous culture as remnants of the past mix with ideas of the present. These new manifestations place emphasis on equity and respect for the natural environment. Practitioners and policymakers that wish to engage similar culture-based, indigenous-run organizations in the interest of collaborative development would benefit from considering such things. An indigenous organization that simply references the assertion of culture as its policy goal is different from one that also has programmes enacted that seek to promote environmental sustainability and gender equality. These types of markers are important when considering development assistance or political solidarity.

What Is Indigenous Sustainable Development?

But what, in the end, is the relation between indigenous culture and sustainable development? To answer this, it must first be understood that indigenous ideas of development resonate strongly with the group of ideas that were labelled *cultural political economy* (CPE) in this book—this includes more recent and less relativistic variants of post-development theory. At the very root of indigenous development theory is the depiction of humans as social subjects that are formed through discourse—which also serves to make the social and material world intelligible. Such discourses also shape the materiality of the physical world as humans enact their cultural relation with their environment. The material environment simultaneously formats the range of possibility available to society and culture. Fundamental to indigenous sustainable development, then, is the inseparability of the material and the cultural—these are part of the same substance. Separation of them can occur for descriptive and analytical purposes, but this split should not be reified in the process. In indigenous thought, nature and culture are one. Indigenous thought posits a similar relationship between the individual subject and larger community. Individual subjects, with their range of beliefs, tastes, and values, are produced socially and communicatively. One may be able to pull the individual apart from the social temporarily for descriptive or analytical purposes, but the fact that they belong to one substance should not be left aside. The individual and its social world are continually iterating one another. The connections between these two typological categories are so substantial that, in practice, they cease to be separable entities.

With this, an image is created of a circular, mutually constituting relationship between subject, society, culture, and nature. It would be more accurate, in fact, to describe these interrelated spheres as one substance. This substance is described in terms of the *Heart of Heaven/Heart of Earth* relationship in Maya cosmovision. Similar unities are implied in Andean and Garifuna insistences that the people cannot be conceived of separately from the land, and that development should be culturally defined. In the interest of generalizability, and in recognition that many indigenous cosmologies around the globe contain a similar concept, the term *naturacultura* will be used hereon to refer to this.

The world that is assumed at the base of indigenous sustainable development is one in which the *naturacultura* is continually shifting. One could easily misinterpret this as a suggestion of an unstable postmodern world, the structure of which can shift at any moment at the whimsy of social imagination. This would be a misrepresentation, however. *Naturacultura* is always embedded in a history that structures the possibility of its form. It is highly path-dependent. Any change in it must be iterative—built onto the past, not in denial of it. Policies that are devised to direct this iteration can only be imagined in relation to it, and they must resonate with it to have impact.

Andean, Garifuna, and Maya thinkers and practitioners are vitally aware of power in this relationship, however. Being a constructivist theory at its root, the vision of power contained in indigenous sustainable development is generative and productive. It works to create conceptions of the world and—due to the fact of *naturacultura*—it shapes that world itself. This idea of power, it should be noted, is not dissimilar to those concepts generally associated with the French theorist Michele Foucault. And, as was Foucault, indigenous thinkers are aware that economic, political, and cultural power tends to congeal—that it is not equally distributed. The structural form of *naturacultura* has very much been determined by the power relations suggestive of a colonial and neocolonial history, by racism, patriarchy, and physical and symbolic variants of violence. Given this, the degree of environmental degradation and indigenous marginalization that exists in Latin America should not come as a surprise.

In practice, indigenous sustainable development involves attempts to build multiple physical, political, and cultural capacities in a culturally applicable way. This requires direct support for indigenous institutions such as the indigenous mayorship of Maya communities. In Ecuador, it involves the rewriting of the constitution to contain elements of *Sumak Kawsay*. In the predatory state of Honduras, this involves struggles for Garifuna autonomy and food sovereignty. Official integration of such institutions into more mainstream regional, national, and international governance and legal frameworks is vitally important to this goal. This can be achieved through articulation with both legal instruments and social movements on these various levels. In other words—the goal is to build *social capital* by facilitating the networking of indigenous institutions with a myriad of other entities such as national governance structures, political parties, media, international NGOs, and social movements on all levels.

Indigenous development movements do not just seek to increase awareness and visibility of indigenous institutions, however. Beyond this, they seek to increase the recognition and sense of legitimacy attached to these institutions—in both the eyes of external actors and members of their own communities. This might be framed as a project to build what Pierre Bourdieu (2005) has called *cultural capital*, or what Taylor (1995) called the *terms of recognition*. It involves a valorization, or an increase of the respect attached to indigenous culture, institutions, and practices. This recognition is vital in increasing what Appadurai (2004) has called the *capacity to aspire*. Recognition means that indigenous institutions can function more effectively in asserting claims. It also means that these claims can be asserted in a way that is culturally relevant to the communities involved. This, so the argument goes, would lead to a sense of empowerment where members of the local community gain the ability to credibly imagine and enact the steps that are necessary to improve their conditions.

Increases in both social and cultural forms of capital, however, are not thought to be sufficient in the pursuit of culturally sustainable development. Andean, Garifuna, and Maya leaders all insist via alternative wordings that social capital and cultural capital cannot be built independently of physical capital—especially in the form of land and related natural resources. It is not reasonable to expect poor Garifuna or Kechwa who work most of their waking hours in handicrafts production, as farm labour, or in other facets of the informal economy, to also invest serious energy in local governance and in participating in community groups.

The sustainability of such groups in the face of material constraints was the largest single problem voiced by the Maya organizers of *El Centro* as well. Put simply, the time expended on work necessarily undertaken by community members in the interest of survival on the most basic of levels often makes the building and maintenance of social and cultural capital almost impossible. Access to land as well as proceeds from (and control over) natural resources such as gold deposits are necessary if any meaningful pursuit of culturally sustainable development is to be undertaken. Like *naturacultura* itself, the elements of social, cultural, and physical capital are mutually reinforcing.

As anthropologist Charles Hale (2004) has suggested, the hegemonic neoliberal global political economy does not conceptually blend physical resources with social and cultural ones, as Maya, Garifuna, or Kechwa activists do. Neoliberal multiculturalism has an ability to tolerate rights to cultural expression and political voice, and to prevent discrimination. When indigenous peoples make appeals to rights to physical resources, however, neoliberal multiculturalism reaches its limits of tolerance. For the indigenous leaders, intellectuals, activists, and rights educators, these limits of neoliberal multiculturalism can have stark implications. *El Centro Pluricultural para la Democracia*, the focal point of the Maya case in this book, was placed on a national list of terrorist organizations, its funding was subsequently revoked, and it was eventually dismantled. Indigenous rights education programmes of *El Centro* came to be seen by foreign capital and the Guatemalan business elite as a threat to profits. Garifuna rights and environmental activists continue to be targets of state suppression in Honduras. Finally, as the *Yasuní*-ITT initiative illustrated, indigenous rights cannot insulate lands from extractive exploitation even in a country with one of the world's most progressive constitutions.

Practicing Indigenous Sustainable Development

Building social, cultural, and physical capital is the core of indigenous sustainable development. This capital formation can be pursued through education programmes and the establishment of community working groups. Indigenous sustainable development should be utilized by development practitioners, sympathetic academics, or active citizens only under certain circumstances, however. First of all, a cultural revivalist movement must preexist in a particular community—it cannot be conjured as the romanticization of a well-meaning outsider. As in the Maya case, this movement must have evolved to solve current problems and not simply for the valorization of antiquated culture. Indigenous sustainable development is only possible where things like environmental sustainability and gender equality are held as primary components of development.

This is often the case with indigenous movements. As with the Maya, Kechwa, and Garifuna, many of these search for traces of environmentalism and gender equality in their own cultural histories. They then centralize these cultural traits in the iteration of a new indigenous cultural form. New ideas attach themselves to old cultural traits within these movements to create something newer still. But, just as with the cases in this book, these programmes are rarely simply cultural—they are material as well. Physical resources are linked to cultural realities. Access to land is especially important in most indigenous movements and should be an essential component of any indigenous sustainable development programme as well.

In assisting such movements, practitioners, citizens, or sympathetic academics could do a number of things. First, since the provision of material resources is essential in such projects, development assistance funding should be pursued. So too should access to land for nutritional, economic, and cultural subsistence. Further on this point, assistance in the prevention of degradation of communal lands by outside agents such as mining or tourism companies is in the spirit of indigenous sustainable development—since the degradation of the land is also thought to degrade the culture, not to mention the health of the community. Working with groups to ensure that cultural revivalism projects include components that centralize equality, environmental protection, and access to land is paramount.

If these things are all in place, practitioners and policymakers must then take a hands-off, supportive approach. Indigenous sustainable development projects must be self-driven. The idea is for development to be pursued via cultural systems of understanding that exist in the community. The well-intentioned assertion of a romanticized ideal of indigenous culture or attempts to impart purified modern rationality on indigenous communities will not work. The content of an indigenous sustainable development programme must be internally sourced—it must find its fuel in the transmodern reality of local culture.

This should not present itself as a foreign idea to university-trained academics, policy analysts, or development practitioners. There are many components in that culture too that could be centralized in the interest of pursuing and understanding indigenous sustainable development. It was argued in this book that the most innovative current trends of thought in development thinking already do this. These trends were typified as cultural political economy approaches to development. The goal in such approaches is building the capacities of communities and individuals to assert their will and ideas in a more equitable environment, and thus reinforcing the *capacity to aspire* (Appadurai 2004) of such entities through programmatic attempts to create an *equality of agency* (Rao & Walton 2004).

Analysts whose intellectual tradition comes more from economics than the other social sciences might find a resonance with indigenous sustainable development in newer nonlinear theories such as those of the complexity sciences (Urry 2005; Colander 2000; Bowles 1998) and cultural theory (Williams 1977; Kaufman 2004). They might also look to the "old" institutional economics of Veblen (1899/1994), Dusenberry (1949), and the foundational work of Adam Smith (1759/1790).

The policy implications of indigenous sustainable development could be dramatic in some ways, particularly to development economists. Arguments that free markets be embraced as the most efficient means of ensuring material development would become nonsensical, since the fundamental theoretical premise on which such ideas stand—a stable and sovereign *homo economicus*—would have to be abandoned. The old habit of measuring development in absolute quantitative terms such as GNP per capita would cease to make sense since well-being would need to be measured relatively and qualitatively. Importantly, a shift should take place from defining development in terms of output to defining it in terms of equality. That is to say that indigenous sustainable development projects would seek to ensure that the *naturacultura* is used and recreated in a democratic way by the humans that both compose and are composed of it. This would ensure the most efficient allocation of resources given that equality in the composition and maintenance of *naturacultura* is the goal instead of crude aggregated economic output.

I have been speaking of this point about the implications of indigenous sustainable development to issues in what is often called the developing world, the Third World, or the Global South. A suggestion was made in the introduction of this book, however, that the idea might have value to a larger society that needs to think its way out of substantial large-scale social, economic, and environmental predicaments. Certainly, conflict that is rooted in reified nationalisms and essentialized ethnicities remains commonplace throughout the globe—whether we are referring to well-publicized (an often reified) tensions between Islam and the West, or ethnic and nationalistic conflicts in places such as Sudan, Kashmir, Somalia, and Yemen. Perhaps the non-essentialized view of culture used by indigenous thinkers might contain a fragment of thought that could help inform attempts to solve such serious and persistent conflicts.

The constant threatening global economic crises that have been indicative of life in the twenty-first century may also be addressed somewhat by these ideas. If economic instability has stemmed from increased debt levels in the advanced economies, and if this increased debt is the tangible result of competitive consumer cultures that have become unmoored from the natural environment to which all consumption is ultimately tied (Schor 2005), then indigenous cosmovision may be of some help. The ideals of both discursive and material equality that are embedded in indigenous ideas, along with the rejection of overly powerful Western media, could reduce the need for competitive consumption in general, if we allow, as Veblen (1899/1994) and Frank (1985) suggest that consumption is fuelled by drives towards *relative* wealth and its display as opposed to absolute measures.

Considering the Latin American indigenous development programmes discussed in this book leads to an important, and obvious, conclusion: to speak of indigenous development is to speak of sustainable development. Garifuna, Maya, and Andean groups do not conceptually separate nature from the human community. They also utilize a holistic concept of development. To improve the welfare of the community, from these perspectives, is to improve the health of the natural environment. Development that disrupts, or fails to repair, harmony between the human community and environment, cannot be defined as development from such perspectives.

This creates an imperfect fit between indigenous development and the United Nation's Sustainable Development Goals (SDGs)—the most notable mainstream development programme that considers both environment and development. Listing the 17 SDGs separately, or choosing one or two to focus on, is common practice amongst researchers, practitioners, and policymakers who prioritize mainstream sustainable development. The separation, or singling out, of any SDG, however, is in conflict with the indigenous, holistic vision of development. All must be considered at once to resonate properly with indigenous concepts.

A further issue is that two SDGs do not make sense within indigenous cosmology. SDG 8 *Decent Work and Economic Growth*, lists in its title two elements that are not necessary for indigenous sustainable development. Indigenous perspectives have a close resonance with de-growth or no-growth development and often see economic growth as harmful to healthy communities and environments. Work in formal labour markets sits equally uncomfortably, although work redefined to mean activity taken to benefit the family, environment, or community may resonate with indigenous thought.

Equally problematic is SDG 9 *Industry and Infrastructure*. To resonate with indigenous sustainable development ideas, both of these elements would have to be defined in ways that prioritize community and environmental wellness as opposed to economic growth. Oil extraction attempts in the *Yasuní* National Park, gold mining in Maya territory, and tourism infrastructure projects in Garifuna lands have all failed local indigenous communities and their natural environments. Unless directed by indigenous communities themselves, and subsumed in their own cosmovisions, industry and infrastructure projects are likely to diminish community and environmental well-being. Thus SDG 9 can often make little functional sense from an indigenous perspective.

Indigenous ideas could be used to guide SDG implementation and global economic policy towards more holistically sustainable outcomes, however. The concept that nature and culture are inseparable implies a reinstated cultural connection to the natural environment and its preservation. Greater discursive and material equality may encourage the easing of competitive consumption. This could go a long way in easing the impact of human behaviour on the natural world. The incorporation of such ideas into mainstream models, policies, and proposals could be effective in ushering the globe in the direction of a truly sustainable human and ecological future.

References

Appadurai, A. (2004). The Capacity to Aspire: Culture and the Terms of Recognition. In V. Rao & M. Walton (Eds.), *Culture and Public Action* (pp. 59–84). Stanford: Stanford University Press.

Bourdieu, P. (2005). Principles of an Economic Anthropology. In *The Social Structures of the Economy* (pp. 193–222). Cambridge: Polity.

Bowles, S. (1998). Endogenous Preferences: The Cultural Consequences of Markets and Other Economic Institutions. *Journal of Economic Literature, 36*(1), 75–111.

Colander, D. (2000). *Complexity and the History of Economic Thought*. London: Routledge.

Dusenberry, J. S. (1949). *Income, Saving and the Theory of Consumer Behavior*. Cambridge, MA: Harvard University Press.

Frank, R. H. (1985). *Choosing the right pond: Human behavior and the quest for status*. Oxford University Press.

Hale, C. (2004). Rethinking Indigenous Politics in the Era of the "Indio Permitido". *NACLA Report on the Americas, 38*(2), 16–22.

Kaufman, J. (2004). *Convergence Culture*. New York: New York University Press.

Rao, V., & Walton, M. (2004). Culture and Public Action: Relationality, Equality of Agency, and Development. In V. Rao & W. Walton (Eds.), *Culture and Public Action* (pp. 3–36). Stanford: Stanford University Press.

Schor, J. B. (2005). Sustainable consumption and worktime reduction. *Journal of Industrial Ecology, 9*(1–2), 37–50.

Smith, A. (1759/1790). *The Theory of Moral Sentiments*. London: A. Millar.

Taylor, C. (1995). The Politics of Recognition. In *Philosophical Arguments*. Cambridge, MA: Harvard University Press.

Urry, J. (2005). The Complexity Turn. *Theory, Culture and Society, 22*(5), 1–14.

Veblen, T. (1899/1994). *The Theory of the Leisure Class*. New York: Dover Publications.

Williams, R. (1977). *Marxism and Literature*. Oxford and New York: Oxford University Press.

Index[1]

[1] Note: Page numbers followed by 'n' refer to notes.

T. MacNeill, *Indigenous Cultures and Sustainable Development in Latin America*, https://doi.org/10.1007/978-3-030-37023-7

The manufacturer's authorised representative in the EU is Springer Nature Customer Service Centre GmbH, Europaplatz 3, 69115 Heidelberg, Germany. If you have any concerns regarding our products, please contact ProductSafety@springernature.com

Printed and bound by CPI Group (UK) Ltd, Croydon, CR0 4YY
30/09/2026
02225453-0005